ED MARCINIAK'S
CITY AND CHURCH

ED MARCINIAK'S CITY AND CHURCH

A Voice of Conscience

CHARLES SHANABRUCH

ED MARCINIAK'S CITY AND CHURCH
A Voice of Conscience

Charles Shanabruch

Edited by Gregory F. Augustine Pierce
Designed and typeset by Andrea Reider
Cover art: "Chicago from Blue Island Avenue," where Ed Marciniak and
other Catholic Workers founded St. Joseph's House of Hospitality in the
1930s, by Steve Shanabruch. Used with permission. All rights reserved.

Published by ACTA Publications, Niles, Illinois,
www.actapublications.com, 800-397-2282

Publisher's Note: Ed Marciniak spent his entire life working for gender
equality. He used to say that "a liberal is a conservative whose daughter has
just been denied her first job or promotion because of her gender." Early
on in his life, Ed and others often used "man" to mean "men and women" or
"all people," as was the practice at the time, but in no way does this reflect
Marciniak's well-known conviction that men and women are equal, and
his life testifies to that. Therefore, this book follows a style guide from
the University of Wisconsin, which ACTA Publications has adopted as
its house style, to change "man" when the speaker clearly meant "men and
women" or "all people." These changes are made in the text with brackets
to alert readers that this change has been made from the source material
quoted by the author, with the author's permission.

Library of Congress Catalog number: 2023939446
ISBN: 978-0-87946-727-2
Printed in the United States of America by Total Printing Systems
Year 30 29 28 27 26 25 24 23
Printing 10 9 8 7 6 5 4 3 2 First
Text printed on 30%-post-consumer-recycled paper

Contents

Dedicated to the People of Chicago
Past, Present, Future

Prologue

On a warm September evening in 1990 the throng of well-wishers who attended the "All City Salute to Ed Marciniak" to raise money for a scholarship fund for disadvantaged youth were glad for the air conditioning in the crowded Bismarck Hotel Ballroom. As they expectantly waited for the program to begin, they exchanged greetings with friends and collaborators. Rev. Daniel Cantwell, the slight, bespectacled godfather of Chicago Catholic action, was the first to take the podium. He began by asking how many of the 600 guests considered themselves "close to Ed." To no one's surprise, a sea of waving hands shot up. Next, Cantwell asked how many found it easy to work with Ed; that drew only a few hands but a room full of laughter.

Msgr. John Egan recounted that John McCarron, the Pulitzer Prize-winning urban affairs editor of the *Chicago Tribune* said of Ed: "That guy is no 'voice of conscience'— he is just a big pain in the butt for the city." John McDermott, who had headed the Chicago's Catholic Interracial

Council in the 1960s explained why the guest of honor was difficult at times: "Ed never answers a question but responds with another of his own, until gradually he takes over the conversation." McDermott then became serious, calling Marciniak "one of the most important and innovative Catholic lay leaders in the U.S." He went on to address an issue that many wondered about, which was Marciniak's working for Richard J. Daley in the 1960s. McDermott, who had on occasion disagreed with Ed on strategies, did not question his friend's commitment to justice and emphasized that Marciniak was "neither left nor right wing."[1]

~

Not all the words of recognition came from the podium. Amid the hundred or more letters about Marciniak delivered that night (which now fill a file in the Archives of the Archdiocese of Chicago), three stand out.

Msgr. John M. Hayes, whose copy of Dorothy Day's *Catholic Worker* had landed in Marciniak's hands at Quigley Seminary decades before, wrote about Ed: "I saw people suffering, as you did. You took off and gave your life to the underdog, employing your God-given intelligence effectively and persistently."[2]

The second was from Lutheran minister Rev. Martin E. Marty, a distinguished University of Chicago Divinity School professor, who cogently put Marciniak in historical context:

While writing a book on the mid-century decades in American religion, I am impressed to see how often your name comes up in these decades-ago documents. They confirm my own impression: that you are among the durables, the evergreens.

When America and Catholicism go sillily right, you appear to be leftish; when it goes erratically left, you appear to be on the right. But that does not make you a dull centrist. It means that you have picked a path, formed by pragmatism, a democratic vision, a Catholic sensibility, and the stamina to stay with them.[3]

The third letter was from Marvin E. Aspen, Judge of the U.S. District Court, who reflected on their meeting in the early 1960s in city government. Judge Aspen thanked Ed for helping start him on his judicial career and recalled his "commitment to and compassion for using the resources of government not for political aggrandizement or enrichment, but for the betterment of urban life for all segments of our multi-racial and multi-ethnic city." Judge Aspen was particularly grateful for Ed's assistance in the "Gautreaux case" by getting the plaintiffs and CHA and HUD "on the same wavelength and making sure that scattered site housing [was] implemented expeditiously and fairly."[4]

＿

When it was Marciniak's turn to speak that night, he dismissed the plaudits, thanked his family and many friends, and got down to business. He spoke bluntly of the failure of municipal bureaucracies to perform the functions for which they were created: "to help move the poor, immigrants and refugees into the urban mainstream." He regretted that they were doing a miserable job of moving people up the "educational and income ladders." His impatience rose as he called for "a new urban agenda" which focused on the education of children. He told his audience that there were good people working in the municipal bureaucracies, but they were "swallowed up by the system" that demoralized good people and did not reward excellence but tolerated slovenly and absent workers because "accountability is missing." He added, "Soon everything slides to the lowest common denominator. These systems need challenging, total overhaul. Alternatives need to be provided."

The scholarship fund, Ed said, "was but one way to help tomorrow's children…not be worse off educationally, economically, or morally than their parents today." He concluded: "It can be done. That is my urban agenda for the 1990s. To confront the municipal establishment. Will you join me?"[5] Characteristically, he not only asked the last question but added a promise to his guests, that "if enough of you do, we can turn our urban agenda into a people's crusade."[6]

NOTES

1 Jim Bowman, "Honoring Ed Marciniak, Champion of Lay Catholics and the Poor," October 5, 1990, Religious News Service release. Marciniak Papers, Shelf 8, Position 2. The box also contains the addresses of Monsignors Cantwell and John Egan.

2 September 17, 1990, Marciniak Papers, Shelf 8, Position 2.

3 September 24, 1990, Marciniak Papers, Shelf 8, Position 2.

4 Aspen to Marciniak, September 27, 1990. Marciniak Papers, Shelf 1, Position 1.

5 Draft of Marciniak's speech at the Bismarck Hotel, September 27, 1990, Marciniak Papers, Shelf 8, Position 3. See also, "Fund Drive to Help the Poor," The New World, October 5, 1990.

6 Marciniak, "All Chicago Salute to Ed Marciniak," September 27, 1990., Marciniak Papers, Shelf 1, Position 1; and draft of Marciniak's speech at the Bismarck Hotel, September 27, 1990, Marciniak Papers, Shelf 8, Position 3. See also, "Fund Drive to Help the Poor," The New World, October 5, 1990.

Introduction

For more than five decades Edward Marciniak was a leader in Catholic social action, worker's rights, civil rights, affordable housing, and vital neighborhoods. This is a story of his life and ideas, boundless energy, and enterprising work and how he affected the city and church that he loved. His voice stands out for its clarity and consistency among many Catholic social activists, as does the range of his commitments and impact.

Marciniak's life—who he was—prompts several questions. Among them are how did a boy born of poor Polish immigrant parents grow up to be "a voice of conscience" for his city and his church? What inspired him? What sustained him in founding and leading impactful organizations, editing three newspapers, and writing five books and hundreds of articles for various magazines and journals? How did this unlikely person become one of the most prominent Catholic social activists in the middle decades of the Twentieth Century? What can members of new generations learn from Marciniak in their quest to improve race relations, protect the environment, and humanize work-places today? This biography is an account of who Ed was, his motivations, and how he accomplished all that he did.

Marciniak's vocation to a life of fighting for justice began by spying a discarded copy of a "radical" Catholic paper in a high school classroom. From that adolescent encounter with *The Catholic Worker* and subsequent contact with Dorothy Day and other Catholic social justice advocates, he intentionally seized opportunities to improve and build a better world. A dominating theme in his life is choosing action over passivity, hope over despondency. Marciniak's religious motivation put him at the heart of the Catholic social justice movement just before the 1962-1965 Vatican Council encouraged more widespread activism. He believed, as he often said, "To wait and do nothing is to be nothing." By a combination of initiative, intelligence, persistence, and force of person-ality, Marciniak made himself "someone" of consequence.

Marciniak began his life as a Catholic activist by co-founding St Joseph's House of Hospitality to feed and shelter victims of the Depression. He was twenty years old. That was only the start. By the time he was thirty, Ed was one of the Chicago's foremost Catholic activists. He marched the picket lines and taught his beloved parlia-mentary procedure and principles of labor action to the numerous organizations that he had joined or cofounded.[1]

One story, maybe apocryphal, told of a prominent sociologist walking down the corridor of a convention hotel when he heard Marciniak's distinctive, carrying voice in an adjacent room addressing a sub-meeting and alerted his fellow sociologist: "Good heavens, Marciniak is in there alone, and he's starting another organization. Send someone in fast to stop it in time."[2] Marciniak founded practical, effective organizations to promote social justice as well as being an active participant in many more. He believed passionately in the importance of acting in concert to effect change in society.

His union activities began on the picket lines in support of striking Hearst journalists and Armour and Company meatpackers and eventually led him to become International Vice-president the American Newspaper Guild. Marciniak's work for racial justice eventually led to his appointments as Director of the Chicago Commission of Human Relations. His commitment to community planning and development paved the way to his nearly twenty years as President of the Institute of Urban Life at Loyola University of Chicago. He would become an advisor to union officials, mayors, senators, congresspeople, judges, and cardinals, bringing the Catholic social justice tradition into policy-making counsels.

✎

Marciniak's ideas and advocacy produced thoughtful discussions that improved institutions and policies and nitty-gritty change on specific blocks in Chicago, including advocacy for the demolition of high-rise public housing. Ed's students, formal and informal, still pursue justice in their work in journalism, education, banking, community and nonprofit housing development and government. They are his living legacy.

His ideas still have cogency for citizens of this nation as they reflect on racism, economic disparity, homelessness, climate change, and the proper role of government and special interests in setting the agenda for the common good. He used fundamental principles of the Beatitudes when addressing social problems, knowing that solutions change as they are often unique to a time or generation and shaped by events and circumstances.

Marciniak was a challenger whose probing made comfortable people uncomfortable, or as some associates thought, "difficult." He asked questions to get to the heart of matters, to find the underlying suppositions that provide a way to reach common ground. He valued compromise, knowing that advancement toward audacious goals is often a series of small steps. Incrementalism was not to be scorned. He scorned intolerance because it impeded progress. Of equal importance, he respected the dignity of every person and believed in their capacity for good when empowered with the tools of education and a sound moral compass. He had faith that decent people would support each other in their mutual quest for a better world for all people.

The achievements brought about by his work in and through government, businesses, and nonprofits groups are a testament to his intense convictions. Sometimes his achievements were bridges to a more decent life in vibrant neighborhoods, and sometimes the contributions were the dismantling of barriers to the vitality of those same communities, such as his own Edgewater community in Chicago. Ever the pragmatist, when Ed looked to the past it was to find solutions to make positive change, not to impede it. He never wavered in his belief that what he called "insiders" in business, government, churches, and community, should take the initiative for social justice.

Ed Marciniak's life and words still challenge those of us who wish for a brighter future in our neighborhoods, cities, nation, and church.

NOTES

1   *Today.* "Young Man with a Cause."
2   *Ibid.* The paper listed twelve organizations to which he belonged at the time. Several of these he had founded or helped to launch.

Chapter 1

Becoming a Catholic
Social-Action Leader

I am not accustomed to sitting in the bleachers;
my forte is the playing field.

Edward Marciniak[1]

A high school student sat alone in a seminary classroom of the large Gothic structure more reminiscent
of Paris than its location in Chicago. He did this often as
the solitude in the quiet space gave him the opportunity to
teach himself moves to improve his chess game and study.
One day the student, Edward Marciniak, looked around
and came upon a copy of a newspaper, *The Catholic Worker,*
which a student from the prior class had accidentally left
behind. He picked it and began to read. He was amazed at
its content. This accidental encounter began an intellectual
and spiritual rebirth, one entirely unexpected and one that
would change the course of his life and positively affect the
lives of many others in Chicago and beyond.

per was the publication of the Catholic Worker movement, founded by Dorothy Day and Peter Maurin in 1933. Day's Catholic Worker movement not only published a monthly paper but opened a house of hospitality on Mott Street in New York's Bowery district to care for the needy and marginalized victims of the Depression. The paper spread the message that work was noble and that all humans were endowed with dignity and rights because they were children of God. It preached the Gospel beatitudes and, significantly, the house of hospitality bore witness to the message. For young Americans who were seeking employment and meaning during the horrible economic times marked by a near twenty-five per cent unemployment rate and even higher underemployment, the message was attractive. It challenged materialism and questioned the efficacy of the capitalist system, but it did not go as far as the American Communists in calling for socialization of means of production and property. The hallmarks of the Catholic Worker movement were voluntary poverty, houses of hospitality, personal accountability, and reformation.[2]

For Marciniak, who was but a teenager just beginning his journey toward the priesthood, all these ideas were new. He had never heard of the ideas and course of action advocated in the *Catholic Worker*. "It was a revelation," he recalled. "I had never known anything like this." He marveled, "It tied faith and works—faith and life—together in a way no one had been able to do previously. That's what excited me and exhilarated me."[3] The paper was a call to reflection and action that soon formed the basis of his religious trajectory. He not only read *The Catholic Worker* avidly but soon subscribed, buying four copies each month and leaving the extras on elevated trains or giving them to friends.[4] The youthful enthusiasm was now engaged and given direction.

Marciniak took the lessons of Dorothy Day's movement and adapted them to fit the immediate needs he would encounter in his city. He would fully incorporate them into his life as a social actionist and Catholic layman when he left the seminary in 1936. His ability to integrate ideas of Catholic social justice and put them into action marked his life as a Chicagoan and a Catholic lay leader. Marciniak began his post-seminary life as a twenty-year-old Catholic activist by co-founding St. Joseph's House of Hospitality to feed and shelter victims of the Depression. He continued to organize and lead religious, labor, and civic associations to fight economic injustice and racism throughout his life.

Among the entities Ed helped to found and lead were the Catholic Labor Alliance, the Catholic Interracial Council, the National Center for the Laity, as well as the Neighborhood Housing Services and the Community Investment Corporation, which helped provide affordable and low-income housing. His union activities on the picket lines of a strike eventually led him to become Executive Vice-President of the Chicago Newspaper Guild and International Vice-President the American Newspaper Guild. Marciniak's lifelong work for racial justice eventually led to his appointments as Director of the Chicago Commission of Human Relations and Deputy Commissioner of the Chicago Department of Planning and Chairman of the National Center for Urban Affairs.

In addition, Marciniak became a well-known teacher and writer on social, economic, and religious issues. He believed in the critical role of the press and helped launch the *Chicago Catholic Worker* as an expression of Dorothy Day's movement, and then he started *Work*, which influenced both Catholic and secular unionists and brought his theory of economic democracy to a national audience. Even when he left editorship of *Work* to take up public service, he helped found and contribute to a successor publication, *New City*, which addressed broad matters of urban affairs and social justice. Until his final days, Ed sustained his writing in both academic and general interest journals such as *Commonweal, New Republic, National Catholic Reporter*—as well as insightful *op-eds* for Chicago's secular newspapers—and authored five books on religion and public policy.

Marciniak's lay vocation to a life of fighting for justice seemingly began by chance in spying a discarded copy of a radical Catholic paper; however, chance cannot explain the constancy of his path and the substantial consequences of his life of service to others. From that encounter with *The Catholic Worker* and subsequent contact with Dorothy Day and like-minded Catholic social justice advocates, he intentionally seized opportunities to improve and build a better world. Like all people, he made mistakes and failed at times. Marciniak's religious motivation put him at the heart of the Catholic social justice movement before the Vatican Council encouraged more widespread activism by the laity. He believed, as he often said, "To wait and do nothing is to be nothing."

EARLY YEARS

Ed Marciniak's youthful endeavors were critical in shaping his awareness of the issues and opportunities that would come his way. Born on December 21, 1917, Edward Allen Marciniak—known by everyone as "Ed"—was delivered by a midwife in his grandfather's apartment and was the first of three children born to Walter and Jadwiga (Hattie) Marciniak, members of Chicago's large Polish immigrant community.[5] His father was raised on a farm in the vicinity of Warsaw and in 1913 emigrated to Chicago to avoid conscription. Hattie was born in Chicago of parents who had immigrated from the Austrian section of Poland. Hattie's father, Albert Kleszcz, worked as an elevator operator in Chicago, while her mother cared for their five children. When Hattie finished basic schooling, she worked as a seamstress at Hart, Schaffner, and Marx, a clothier in the garment district west of the Loop. The Kleszcz' took Walter in as a boarder and he eventually asked for Hattie's hand in marriage.[6]

By 1920, twenty-three-year-old Walter had become a supervisor at a Chicago ironworks, while twenty-one-year-old Hattie cared for Ed and his infant brother, Henry. The four of them resided with Hattie's parents and her four siblings in a crowded apartment at 2417 S. Spaulding in the South Lawndale neighborhood, a few blocks from Cook County Jail. It was a bustling area that was home to the gigantic McCormick Reaper Works on the east and the Western Electric's Hawthorne Works on the west, with the Sears and Roebuck Company headquarters a mile to the north. Numerous machine shops and commercial businesses dotted the landscape. There were plenty of Poles like the Kleszcz family, but Czech (Bohemian) peoples predominated in this polyglot neighborhood that was so typical of Chicago, which was home to Mayor Anton Cermak, who became leader of Chicago's Democratic party and served until he was killed in an assassination attempt on President-elect Franklin Roosevelt in 1933. The Kleszcz family owned the sturdy three story, brick apartment building and rented the other two units to Bohemian immigrants.[7]

While living with in-laws certainly helped advance financial stability for the young Marciniak family, it was not always easy for ten people to share such tight quarters. In 1921, Bernice Marciniak, a third child was born, and shortly thereafter the family moved often seeking better accommodations. Ed later boasted that he attended eight different grammar schools in four years: Farragut, Hammond, and Everett public schools and St. Casmir's, St. Blaise's, St. Barbara's, St. Mauritius,' and finally Five Holy Martyrs' parochial schools—all of them except St. Blaise on Chicago's southwest side.[8] In 1927, the family put down roots at 4607 S. Whipple Street, just two miles from Ed's first home. Walter traded in his steel-making tools for a remunerative butcher's cutlery and apron and opened a grocery store. The family's new stability enabled Ed to complete his final four years of elementary school in one place. Five Holy Martyrs was founded in 1910 for the fast-growing Polish immigrant population that was spreading southwesterly along Archer Avenue.

The Marciniak's grocery store and home on Whipple Street was a solid two-story brick building that covered almost the entire surface of the 25-by-125-foot lot typical of Chicago's working-class neighborhoods. Their home was within smelling distance of the giant Union Stockyards and less than a block from the 47th Street streetcar that carried workers to the huge stock pens and slaughterhouses a mile and a half to the east. When the family moved into their home in Brighton Park, the neighborhood was nearing its industrial employment and population peak. Its 1930 population reached 46,552 and the neighborhood, which had been Anglo-Saxon Protestant in its early days was predominated by Polish immigrants who comprised 37% of the population by 1930. Here many languages were spoken, and customs maintained in the numerous churches that sprouted up. Besides the Five Holy Martyrs, there was another Polish parish, St. Pancratius, as well as a parish of the Polish National Catholic Church—a hyper-nationalist group that broke away from the American Roman Catholic Church in 1907. Brighton Park's working-class economic bustle and ethnic diversity, as well as the pervasive culture of devout Polish Catholicism, were powerful shaping forces in young Ed Marciniak's life and education.[9] He would reside here for two decades.

The first floor of Walter Marciniak's building contained his grocery and butcher shop in the front and the family apartment in the rear. The red-orange glazed-brick façade was accented with limestone squares above and below the windows on the second floor, which contained two apartments rented to two families of Polish descent. Walter had taken out a mortgage to purchase the building and relied on the income from both customers and tenants to pay the mortgage and support the family.[10] The chores of butchering meats, making sausage, plucking chickens, and stocking shelves kept all the family members busy from early in the morning until late in the day. His father's store, more than any elementary school, provided Ed with enduring lessons in economics, justice, charity, and community relations. It was a practical classroom that would shape Ed's deeply ingrained sense of justice and appreciation for diversity.

Working in the store enhanced Marciniak's fluency in Polish as he conversed with customers unable to speak English. His mother spoke English to her children, as she believed they should speak it as much as possible, but the Polish language was ever present. An early account of Marciniak's life noted that the bi-lingual environment could be heard in his speech even many years later. "On a lecture platform before a group of college professors," the writer noted, "(Marciniak) is still likely to slip into an occasional 'dese' and 'dose' under the pressure of a stimulating environment."

While the young boy had devoted numerous hours to the family store, he loved education and reading. He read adventure and mystery novels as well as books that had a factual bent. He was described as a walking 'Information Please' service "due to his single-minded application to the *Daily News Almanac*," a digest that published thousands of current statistical data that seemed to intrigue him.[11] This interest in data and its application would never wane. Reflecting on his childhood, Marciniak once told a group that as a teenager he had headed up the Brighton Park Literary Club and noted it was devoted to baseball, billiards, and blackjack instead of books. He reminisced:

> Upon my retirement, as the first and last president, the members presented me with a token of their esteem and teen-age shrewdness. It was a book, a

biography of Voltaire, the eighteenth-century French philosopher; its author, Alfred Noyes. Why would a non-literary club have presented me with a book? The catch was that it was on the Index of Forbidden Books and the club's wily members assumed that I would not read it, thus keep the club's non-literary tradition unblemished.[12]

At an early age Marciniak became especially acquainted with the economic challenges facing most workers. The family's grocery was one of those neighborhood institutions that extended credit based upon a personal relationship between the proprietor and the customers, who often fall short on funds. Seasonal layoffs at the nearby plants were reflected in the growing piles of credit slips kept by a store. Marciniak recalled that the credit slips that piled high in his father's store after the crash of 1929 taught him early about "the narrow line that divides subsistence from want."[13] Besides extending de facto credit to its working-class customers, the Marciniak's grocery store also performed as a currency exchange, cashing payroll checks for those unable to access banks. These functions taught firsthand lesson about economic disparity. In a much later article on the role of unions, Marciniak told of his experience behind the grocery counter:

> When cashing checks, I noticed that the railroad men and machinists brought in pay checks that were on average $15-$25 a week higher than those brought in by workers from the stockyards and steel mills. I asked my father the reason for the difference. He explained very simply: "The men with the bigger pay

checks belong to a union." (This was, of course, in the days when unionization had not yet come to the steel and packing industries.)[14]

Reflecting on his childhood, Ed said, "I came from a working-class family" that struggled through the Depression, as did all the people who lived in the immigrant neighborhood. "We were conscious of the economic limitations of the family," he recalled. "That family background was especially important." He noted his uncles and aunts on my mother's side were most supportive in tough times.[15]

SEMINARY DAYS

The deep religious faith of his parents, the neighborhood's regard for the clergy, and the impact of the Catholic faith in the immigrant community certainly affected young Ed Marciniak. Upon graduation from elementary school, he decided to attend the archdiocesan preparatory seminary for high school as the first step toward becoming a priest. Although there is no recorded account of Ed's sense of the priestly vocation, it was a common path for bright young men of his community. Quigley Seminary was named for Chicago Archbishop James E. Quigley, who oversaw rapid growth of churches and schools during his tenure between 1902 and 1916. Quigley was recognized for his pastoral care and support for sustaining the ethnic-pluralism approach of his episcopal predecessors who had sought to uphold a unity of Catholic faith in the sprawling, multiethnic Chicago diocese. He did not force a unitary approach to religious practice. Ethnic parishes and multiple languages (despite the universal Latin of the Mass) were pervasive in early twentieth-century Chicago.

When Marciniak entered Quigley in 1931, the archdiocese had continued its spectacular growth, but its ethnic character, while it still persisted, had become less pronounced. Immigration declined dramatically during World War I and nearly ceased with the passage of restrictive immigration legislation passed by nativist senators and congressmen and signed by President Calvin Coolidge in 1924.[16] Archbishop George Mundelein, who succeeded Quigley in 1917, began a centralization of administrative functions and launched a clerical education program to gradually "Americanize" his highly pluralistic flock.

Mundelein replaced the former high-school seminary with truly grand buildings that would stand out as one of Chicago's architectural gems. Completed in 1920, the huge complex of Gothic style buildings in Chicago's Loop was anchored by St. James Chapel on the Near North Side modeled after Sainte-Chapelle in Paris. Here young Marciniak began his preparation for ordination under the direction of priests personally selected by Mundelein to expose budding young scholars to new ideas and the richness of Chicago's ethnic diversity. Cardinal Mundelein left little to chance, as he also sought to put his stamp on the young men who entered the major seminary. No longer would the seminarians prepare for service in seminaries focusing on specific ethnic traditions; they would attend St. Mary of the Lakes Seminary, a collection of Georgian architectural buildings in a distant suburb that would reflect the nation's colonial origins and the cardinal's Americanization agenda.[17]

Seminarian Marciniak's days began early. He regularly rose at 5:15 a.m. and walked into the adjoining store and stocked shelves and butchered meat for his father's grocery before taking public transportation downtown. Now, he left the comfortable confines of his parish and neighborhood and rubbed shoulders with people of different ages, ethnic groups, and economic classes. The 1936 Quigley yearbook photo shows a serious young man with a round face and full head of slicked-down hair, and it records that he was President of the Latin Academy, a Senior Lifeguard, and a member of the Gregorian Choir. For unrecorded reasons, he earned the nickname *"Pluto;"* and the Quigley high school yearbook of the time noted: "Pluto studies diligently and as a result was awarded with good marks and an abundance of knowledge. When he wasn't studying, he probed the causes of present circumstances of the European crisis."[18]

While pervasively Catholic, Quigley was a melting pot and here Marciniak met other young men who shared a common religious belief but came from a variety of economic and ethnic backgrounds. Some of these men would become Ed's lifelong friends and partners in making the Catholic faith a real force in the world. Among them were Daniel Cantwell, president of the Quigley class of 1933, and Jim O'Gara, who was in Ed's class and would soon join with Marciniak in numerous undertakings. The experiences at Quigley exposed Marciniak to new ideas beyond his parochial neighborhood and prepared him for the careers he would later assume. His five years at Quigley (the training included a fifth year with first-year college credits) prepared him how to approach difficult problems and take on challenges with confidence.

Most important for Marciniak, it was at Quigley he found that copy of the *Catholic Worker* and met men such as Msgr. John Hayes, a Catholic social activist priest already involved with the budding Catholic Worker movement and labor union organizing in Chicago. From the *Catholic Worker* (CW) and Hayes, Marciniak learned "a more concrete presentation of a Catholic personalist approach" than the traditional pious fare promoted by Catholic magazines like the popular *Messenger of the Sacred Heart*.[19] The message of Dorothy Day and Peter Maurin was eye-opening to Marciniak, as he recalled more than 50 years latter:

> For me at that point, the CW brought into focus the liturgy, the church's interest in the labor movement, and that personal responsibility—the initiative of lay people. We were to be self-starters, not merely followers.[20]

The seminarian was strongly attracted by the Catholic Worker movement's message and especially by the possibilities of being actively engaged in ministry as a lay person rather than as a priest. While it had supporters among Catholic priests and sisters, the Catholic Worker was an entirely lay endeavor. When Marciniak completed his fifth year of classes at Quigley, he was slated to go to the major seminary to continue his studies. He came to realize, however, that his calling to serve and renew the world in the spirit of the Gospel could be done as a layperson. His contribution need not be as a priest who ascended the pulpit and celebrated Mass, but as a person of faith in the world who could identify social needs, offer solutions, and help organize people and entities to create positive change with Catholic social teaching.

Marciniak explained to a friend that he did pass through a "vertigo of indecision" before becoming "certain that my job as an instrument of God's will was to be accomplished in the world" rather than the institutional Church.[21] His decision caused some "turbulence" when he did not arrive at the major seminary. He later recalled that there was a good deal of surprise, especially by his former Quigley classmate, Paul Marcinkus, who had the room next door to the one assigned to him. Marciniak noted that Marcinkus, who later became a prominent archbishop and President of the Vatican Bank (1971-1989), said he "always wanted to know where the hell Marciniak was."[22]

BECOMING A LEADER

In the fall of 1936, Ed Marciniak enrolled as a sophomore at Loyola University, Chicago's Jesuit university, and spent three years earning a degree in sociology. He honed his writing skills as a reporter on the student newspaper and sustained his love of facts and ideas and skills on the debate team. As a member of the debate team, he was appreciated for his research talents and ability to fashion strong arguments. As a debater he was not diplomatic. His sometimes direct and forthright style would infuriate audiences and judges. Because of his mastery of debate topics, he was often assigned to the role of debate-team resource person. His teachers remembered him with sometimes mixed emotions. One professor recalled: "'I felt like strangling him in class. He kept asking [me] when I thought we were getting somewhere. It was like Socrates, always making me examine my assumptions."[23] On one occasion Marciniak's defense of a specific union strike, with greater ardor than tact, caused his professor to eject him from the class. When Marciniak was gone, the professor told the other students that he would not tolerate "Communists" in his class.[24]

While at Loyola. Marciniak also devoted himself to organizations that focused on religious service. He became an officer of the Sodality of Mary a national organization then under the charismatic direction of Rev. Daniel Lord, S.J., a native Chicagoan based in St. Louis, who was a prolific writer, playwright, and songwriter as well a widely known Catholic apologist. Lord made Marciniak much more aware of the social dimension of Catholic tradition as set forth in the doctrine of the Mystical Body of Christ, which was being strongly emphasized at the time in contemporary movements of Catholic renewal.

This doctrine, based upon the New Testament and writings of Fathers of the Church, stressed that all members of the Church, not just the clergy and hierarchy, are charged with continuing Christ's work to renew the earth. The analogy to a human—yet mystical—body called to mind an image of the constituent members of the church united for a common effect. The doctrine teaches that the moral unity of the Mystical Body members is guided by Christ, the head of the body. Each member is regarded as having special gifts and contributions to make and each person is deserving of dignity and respect as an essential part of the whole.[25] This doctrine strongly influenced Catholic social activists in the United States and elsewhere in the interwar years and was formally promulgated by Pope Pius XII in

1943 his encyclical, *Mystici Corporis Christi* (*The Mystical Body of Christ*).

In an undated outline for a speech Marciniak was to give, entitled, "Mystical Body of Christ and Economic Life," he quotes an uncited article from a Chicago monthly newspaper of the time published by John Cogley, who later went on to become an editor at *Commonweal*: "As Christ became man to bring mankind into a more intimate union with God, so Christ's mystical body must clothe itself with the flesh and blood of the twentieth century to make our life divine and fully human." Marciniak added: "Love is...to realize that when one part of the body suffers, I suffer."[26] Marciniak's growing commitment to this belief guided his decisions and was integral to his selfless actions in future endeavors.

Marciniak also joined Chicago Inter-Student Catholic Action (CISCA), a dynamic organization that brought together high school and college students to learn and practice Catholic social action. It emphasized a process of "observation, judgment, and action" in living out the gospel in the world. In 1938-39, Ed became president of the city-wide young person's organization. CISCA's priest adviser, Rev. Martin Carrabine, S.J., emphasized the role that lay people should have in the Catholic Church and gave Marciniak confidence in his decision to leave the seminary.[27] Carrabine was unusual for the time because he strongly encouraged Catholic high school and college students to advocate and work for racial equality, labors' right to organize, and other "radical ideas." Marciniak praised his mentor as a "perfect match" and recalled "[Carrabine] wanted young people to think for themselves, to be self-starters, to take risks, to put on the mantle of personal responsibility standing up for the right and resisting the wrong. With all his heart and soul, he believed that young people could do great things if they were encouraged, inspirited rather than being corralled or fenced in."[28] Carrabine's mentorship and trust enabled Marciniak to develop leadership skills that would be essential throughout his career.

The Loyola years were the most formative for the young man and shaped his entire life. The Catholic Worker movement and its message of personal reform and social justice especially attracted him. In 1936, Marciniak attended his first Catholic Worker meeting in the library of St. Ignatius High School in order to hear a series of lectures by Peter Maurin, the eccentric French layman who had convinced Dorothy Day to create the *Catholic Worker* to broadcast the message of "personalism and accountability and intentional poverty.[29] From the these sessions with Maurin, a core group developed and formed the first Catholic Worker organization in Chicago, meeting initially in the basement of Old St. Patrick's Church. The leader of the group was Dr. Arthur Falls, a Black physician, active member of the Urban League, and prominent Catholic advocate for racial justice. Marciniak joined Falls, Hayes, and others in their regular Sunday afternoon meetings at St. Patrick's Church to hear lectures and discuss the ideas presented. The fervent Catholic activists hosted lectures by Jacques Maritain, the French neo-Thomist philosopher, then on the faculty of the University of Chicago, and other notable speakers who discussed current issues in the light of Catholic theology and philosophy. They always went home late and "tremendously stimulated."[30] In November 1936, Falls rented an abandoned building at 1841 W. Taylor Street and opened a

Catholic Worker house. It had a community library, meeting space, a neighborhood childcare center, and later a credit union. Unlike Day's New York House of Hospitality and other similar houses springing up around the country, Falls' enterprise did not provide food and shelter but dedicated itself to ideas and education in the hope of providing tools to enable the downtrodden overcome social and economic problems.[31]

That same year, Marciniak learned that Dorothy Day would be speaking at St. Ita's Catholic Church in the Edgewater neighborhood, a short distance from the Loyola University lakeside campus. The crowd, including some of Ed's friends from Saint Patrick's, was so large that Day's presentation was relocated from the school hall to the church proper. The experience remained memorable for Marciniak even more than thirty years later as he noted in his first book, *Tomorrow's Christian*. He wrote that Day mounted the magnificent white, stone pulpit of the large Gothic church and spoke of the "need for peace, for racial equality and voluntary poverty.... She shared her abundance with others, as Jesus did on the mount when he broke bread and distributed it to the hungry gathered around." Remembering the power of the laywoman's words from the place of ecclesial authority, he added, "The pulpit is an ideal platform for prophets, though not always hospitable to them."[32]

STARTING OUT AS AN ACTIVIST

Soon Ed Marciniak was not satisfied with only discussing issues, he wanted to do something to make real the ideas that he and others had been considering. Early in 1938, the twenty-year-old Marciniak and Alex Reser, a Catholic Worker activist who had been involved with German Catholic social action in Chicago's Central Verein organization, decided to do something concrete. They raised $15.13 between them and proceeded to rent a small, vacant bakery factory. Reser had negotiated a fifty per cent reduction in rent to $15.00 a month plus two months free for cleaning the filthy two-story building at 868 S. Blue Island Avenue. It was in a neighborhood of overcrowded tenements occupied by disparate ethnic groups, just blocks from Hull House, which Jane Addams had founded decades before. The two passionate young Catholic activists borrowed furniture, begged food from neighborhood grocers, and began to feed the unemployed and homeless.[33]

Chicago's second Catholic Worker House thus opened on Good Friday, 1938, and they named it Saint Joseph the Worker House of Hospitality. On the first floor they built a kitchen, and on the second floor they created the primary sleeping area for the homeless left destitute from the Depression. Reser and another friend slept at St. Joseph's House, and occasionally now collegian Marciniak did as well. However, he spent most nights at his parents' home, where he could study and be up early for his still-urgent duties butchering meat and stocking shelves for the grocery each morning.

Ed became deeply involved at the house of hospitality by recruiting volunteers to help with the enterprise through his role as CISCA president and delivering donations of bread from his father's store. On Saturday mornings, he led nearly 400 students in weekly seminars to discuss issues of social justice, Catholic social teaching, and the implications of the Beatitudes. He was also able to engage several of them in joining the work of serving the needy and securing food and supplies. In addition, they were joined by students from the St. Mary of the Lake Seminary and nuns from various orders who brought supplies and even furniture.[34]

John Cogley, a Chicago native and Loyola graduate who had served a brief stint at the Day's Mott Street House of Hospitality in New York, joined the other young Catholic Workers on Blue Island Avenue soon after St. Joseph's House opened, and he later vividly told of life at St. Joseph House: "The stench of unwashed bodies, and filthy clothing ...eerie nightmares, and shouts of troubled sleep...a frightening scene of human tragedy and degradation at night." And during the day, he noted, the office was "constant bedlam."[35] In June 1940, he wrote in the *Chicago Catholic Worker*:

> Dorothy's visits are always a tonic for the work. She has the knack of presenting all over again the vision that we should have always before us. It is impossible to live at a high pitch, and discouragement and dryness often overwhelms us. The same old thing day in, day out. The breadlines outside our door twice a day all year, just as ragged, just as hopeless, just as hungry. This serving the long lines of tired, silent men passing through every day is in itself discouraging. You feel helpless, so ashamed of the little you offer. There is generally a death like silence among them and their faces are the stony, sad faces of the dead walking the earth again. We offer very little to them and it is even a struggle to get that.

This constant association with misery and
extreme shadows every day. If ever we lose the vision,
we are through. Today things look bleaker than ever.
It is hard for any of us to have hope, to keep the vision
of a new world before us. Down here where we daily
see the scars of unemployment and social injustice it
is especially difficult. And yet if we cease to hope and
to struggle...Dorothy reminds us to pray violently.
Unless we pray and use every supernatural means we
have at hand, she says we have no right to preach to
others against violence.

Marciniak wholeheartedly embraced the vision of service that Day imparted, and it would remain his animating
force. But the pressures of the times were severe. In 1940,
Cogley was called to a retreat with the heads of Catholic
Worker houses to discuss the divisive issue of pacifism as
the prospects for the United States participation in World
War II increased. Marciniak had hoped to attend but stayed
behind to take care of the St. Joseph House and attend
classes. When Cogley returned, he found the twenty-one-
year-old Marciniak overwhelmed and wrote Day:"Ed Marciniak decided that it is too much of a strain on him to keep
up with his work at Loyola and stay at the House too—and
he is right. It was a terrific strain and a terrific drain, too,
even those few weeks I was in N.Y. He lost 14 lbs. just in
that time."[36]

Within two months the founding of St. Joseph
House, Cogley spear-headed the effort to launch a monthly
newspaper that was modeled on Day's successful New
York publication. Because of his experience on Loyola's

newspaper, Marciniak became Managing Editor. The paper, *The Chicago Catholic Worker*, intended to make Chicagoans aware of the work done at St. Joseph House, gather support for its mission, and educate readers on issues of economic and social justice. Day fired their enthusiasm with her brief telegram of support: "Go ahead and God bless you."[37]

In the first issue of the new publication, John Cogley explained the moral imperative animating the paper writing, "If at the same time we are engaged in binding the wounds of the casualties, we ignore the evils of our society we would not be fulfilling our duty to justice.... Silence in the face of the manifold abuses that make the breadlines possible and even a necessity would be a betrayal of trust."[38]

The *Chicago Catholic Worker* especially focused on labor news, connecting the labor cause to issues of social and economic justice, and the vocation of all to live out the Gospel message. Begun as a two-page broadsheet, the *Chicago Catholic Worker* grew to an eight-page monthly with a circulation of 5,000. The paper was sold on street corners and handed out to striking workers at factory gates and used by study clubs at Catholic high schools and colleges. It was even circulated among the sick at Cook County Hospital and prisoners in Illinois state penitentiaries.[39]

For the Managing Editor, the paper was also a vehicle to educate industrial workers, call them to action, and support those engaged in the struggle for better conditions. In the first issue of the paper, Marciniak reported on the creation of a Catholic Union of Unemployed to enlist the victims of the Depression, especially the thousands of unskilled, jobless railroad workers. Its first action was to protest cuts in relief for the unemployed homeless who were forced to live on the street.[40] Once the immediate crisis of renewing funds in Chicago's City Council had been dealt with, the *Chicago Catholic Worker* pursued a larger role for workers and urged them to join the Association of Catholic Trade Unions "to actively play a role in the future of this great labor movement." Marciniak asked readers: "Will they sit on the *outside* and watch the Communists sabotage it, or will they be on the *inside* fighting with the rest of the workers for a stronger and better labor movement?" [original emphasis][41] This was the first of many challenges by Ed to motivate his audience of Catholic activists to become institutional "insiders" rather than remain "outsiders."

These were heady days for Marciniak, running from classes to meetings at the university, to the house of hospitality to presentations and lectures, and then to late-night union meetings, not to mention still working hours at the family store. He was always on the move, with a bulging briefcase full of articles to read and submissions to edit. The experience of working on the run became habitual. Even in later years he preferred taking a train rather than flying so he could catch up on the contents of his briefcase.[42]

When Marciniak graduated with his bachelor's degree in 1939, he immediately began work on a master's degree in Social Administration, which he received 1942. With seemingly unlimited energy, he worked toward his advanced degree while he continued his responsibilities for the family business and at St. Joseph the Worker House of Hospitality. He also began his teaching career as an instructor in sociology at Loyola University. Studying sociology gave him a chance to blend his interest in economic and social justice with his Catholic social commitments and his love of data.

From his experience as a Catholic Worker and his friendship with Dr. Arthur Falls, whose advocacy and activism on race issues strongly influenced him, Marciniak was made acutely aware of the prejudices in society. As part of his Catholic social activism, he early on began working to end racial and religious intolerance. As a sociology graduate student and then as adjunct faculty member at Loyola University, he focused his research on racial issues at a time when few white scholars were attending to race. In 1940, Ed created and conducted a course in interracial problems, which he called, "the first such course in Chicago metropolitan area at any university," and wrote his master's thesis on the attitudes of Chicago Catholic college students towards Blacks.[43] Based upon his survey of eight Chicago-area Catholic colleges, he concluded that education supported by genuine interaction of the races was necessary to break the cycle of prejudice in society.[44] Not only did he study prejudice, but along with Rev. Daniel Cantwell he worked to establish the Catholic Interracial Council (CIC) in 1943 to address racism in the city. The aim of the CIC was to increase awareness of racial injustice in education, housing, and employment and to build bridges between the races.[45]

Marciniak also joined efforts to combat anti-Semitic prejudices which had grown stronger in America during the Depression, including among some Catholics. Rev. Charles Coughlin of Detroit initially supported many of the President Franklin D. Roosevelt's New Deal policies, but the priest became a severe critic of the president for being too lenient on bankers and monetary policy and used his national radio platform to stoke anti-Semitism and fostered sympathies for fascism. The priest's toxic message, which found its greatest support on the East Coast, was challenged by Dorothy Day's *Catholic Worker*. In Chicago there was less overt anti-Semitism. However, the *Chicago Catholic Worker* was a strong and consistent critic of the Detroit radio priest as well. In an open letter to Coughlin, the Chicago paper declared that the priest had the responsibility to set his followers straight because "anti-Semitism among Catholics is due to [your] inept, untimely, stupidly misconstrued study of Judaism."[46] Chicago's Catholic Workers helped to create the Committee of Catholics to Fight Anti-Semitism, forming a speaker's bureau that enlisted the support of professors from Notre Dame and the University of Chicago to address local parish and school groups on Judaism and anti-Semitism. Marciniak became the permanent chair of the group, coordinating appearances, writing articles, and planning radio broadcasts on its behalf. [47] Often involved with Jewish social justice advocates, Marciniak continued his work for interfaith understanding and harmony throughout his life, often traveling across the Midwest speaking on religious toleration and cooperation.

Marciniak's work to promote racial and religious understanding was central to his life mission and a ready extension of a strong religious conviction he shared with other Catholic Workers. The Gospel of Matthew (25:31-46), describes the final judgment calling on Christians to feed the hungry, give drink to the thirsty, welcome the lonely, cloth the naked, and visit the imprisoned—all of whom are, Jesus says, none other than himself. These admonitions were central to Marciniak and in alignment with his belief in the Mystical Body of Christ.

Late on a rainy night in the 1940s, as Ed waited for his train to depart St. Louis for Chicago after participating in a roundtable of the National Conference of Christians and Jews, Marciniak reflected on his life and goals and later shared these thoughts with a mentor."[48] He wrote:

> The first serious outlines of my desires and aspirations for my manhood came to me during my early days with the CW. Prior to this I was merely a bundle of habits without any well-defined form to direct them. These desires of mine, these hopes for a life hungering and thirsting for justice, for a future to doing God's designs for me, received strengthening during my regime as president of CISCA. For during that year—fortunately for me—the CISCA meetings centered around the eight beatitudes.[49]

As part of this reflection, Marciniak recalled the "fires" the Catholic Worker had enkindled were made stronger and brighter by the CISCA experience and Father Carrabine. Yet, he lacked "a solid unifying principle, a balancing sense of direction" to assimilate and nourish his CW and CISCA experience. "Once the decision to be a crusader was definite—I like the word *agitator* better—I had to make a decision as to whether I had a vocation to the religious or priestly state, or to the lay life," he continued. He noted that he passed through a period of indecisiveness about his vocation before becoming "certain that my job as an instrument of God's will was to be accomplished in the world." His decision to dedicate himself to a life of activism was solidified. It became final when he took counsel with others who gave him the confidence that he could serve God in the world. Confidently, he noted:

I was going to be a lay agitator—God willing. I wanted to give my body, my mind, my heart to whatever cause Christ's revolution demanded. I made no definite plans for the future. How could I? My job was to do whatever came along.[50]

THE WAR YEARS

Ed Marciniak's convictions and character were to be tested as the Depression came to an end. When the factories geared up for war preparations, the bread lines at St. Joseph House thinned out. The Chicago Catholic Workers were aligned with Dorothy Day on non-violence and the ugliness of war. The newspaper made clear its opposition to war, but it focused most of its editorial attention on economic and racial justice issues. In 1940, the St. Joseph House's staff stated its opposition to war, but focused on building up a "moral defense against totalitarianism by ensuring the millions of the unemployed were put back to work." As the drumbeat for war increased and Congress debated conscription legislation, *The Chicago Catholic Worker* confirmed Day's position and argued that the military draft "is the serious beginning of a totalitarian form of government."[51] But when the atrocities of Hitler's regime were disclosed, the question of absolute pacifism became controversial and several of the Chicago Catholic Workers, according to Francis Sicius, "viewed the evil of Nazism as far greater than war."[52]

Dorothy Day was adamant in her opposition to war and called for pacifism in a 1940 issue of the *Catholic Worker*. She pressed all the Catholic Worker houses throughout the United States to declare for pacifism. Such an action would put her movement in opposition to the patriotism that swept the nation and, most especially, the nation's Catholic bishops, who were still trying to prove Catholics were as American as the nation's Anglo-Protestant majority.

When the United States declared war against Japan and Germany after the bombing of Pearl Harbor on December 7, 1941, the members of the Catholic Worker house of hospitality on Blue Island Avenue had to decide what course to take. Some Catholic Worker houses refused to distribute Day's New York *Catholic Worker* with its adamant pacifist stand, and others simply shut down as the young men who ran the houses signed up for the military out of a sense of patriotism or hostility to fascism.[53] Cogley and several others in Ed's circle, including his high-school seminary friend Jim O'Gara, enlisted in the armed services; and St. Joseph House of Hospitality became another casualty of the war.

Edward Marciniak's approach to these urgent issues was ever thoughtful and thorough. His decision about participation in World War II testified to his characteristic deep reflection, followed by decisiveness. A year before Pearl Harbor, Marciniak and Paul Kalinauskas had co-authored a lengthy article titled, "The Case for Conscientious Objection." In it, they defended conscientious objection as a morally correct response to war. The issue was not a theoretical question of conscience but a "practical moral judgment." They believed that people must admit that they can make a judgment on the morality or immorality of a particular war, in fact they were compelled to do so by Catholic just-war teaching. To have a "doubtful conscience" and go along to war without reflection was morally wrong. The article then logically outlined the six moral principles to be met in declaring a just war that were agreed upon by Catholic theologians. There were six conditions: 1) war must defend a strict right; 2) follow only when all means of settlement have been tried; 3) entail a responsible hope of victory; 4) intend only to right a wrong not gain an advantage or vanquish; 5) use means in accord with truth, justice, and love; and 6) ensure that the evils caused by war not be greater than the good which results. They emphasized that not all elements need be present; rather, the objector must verify only the absence of one element.[54]

The essence of the argument for conscientious objection was that if a government passes a law that does not meet these six criteria, it is a "perversion of God's law" and conscience requires that "we not participate directly." While the nation may present the case of the common good, the state's claim holds no moral imperative if it is lesser than a "higher good." An individual's obligation, they believed, is to God and the "true good of all men, not just the common good defined by the state." The authors concluded with a quote by Jacques Maritain that called on all to strive against the "monstrosity which is modern war and the crime which lies in desiring war, in poisoning millions of men with lies and hatred so that finally they destroy one another—millions of men of their own account would want peace."[55]

Marciniak had formulated his own position on modern warfare and shared it with Dorothy Day in a letter on the Feast of St. Philip Benizi on August 24, 1940. Ed often used feast days rather than calendar dates in his writing.[56] Marciniak said he did not agree with the war effort and when he was called to register for the draft the following year, he chose to be a conscientious objector and sought 4E status. He was not opposed to all wars but was very much opposed to fighting in World War II. He made clear that he was a conscientious objector rather than a pacifist.[57]

Marciniak's letter to Draft Board No.20, on August 30, 1941, requested conscientious objector status. His request contained a series of responses that explained his signing a statement of opposition to participation in war. His response was grounded in his religious convictions: "It is my sincere, reasoned, prayerful conviction that modern warfare fails to fulfill these conditions laid down by the moral theologians of the Roman Catholic Church, and consequently I am bound in conscience not to take part in modern military conflict." He explained the formation of his conscience in his home, in parochial schools, Quigley Preparatory Seminary and Loyola University as well as five years engaged with the Catholic Worker and CISCA. Finally, he referenced his own studies on the subject that made him aware of "the responsibilities a Christian has as a member of society to be a peacemaker." Attached to his letter was a five-page document that quotes and summarizes moral opinions from Pope Innocent III, St. Augustine, St. Thomas Aquinas, papal pastoral letters, and contemporary theological articles on morality. The final page contained Ed's "supplementary statement":

> In an addition to the previous statements I would like to explain my opposition to non-combatant service under military direction. It seems to me that any kind of service under military direction would be aid either material or formal towards the continuation of the war. It would be foolish and insincere on my part to object to modern warfare on the basis of conscience and then turn right around to aid the promotion of

BECOMING A CATHOLIC SOCIAL-ACTION LEADER

the very same war which I believe to be unjust. There are many other ways, I feel, in which I can be of service to my country without placing myself under military direction.

In conclusion, I would like to insist that my refusal to participate in war is not to be interpreted as any sterile or selfish contribution towards the common good. I realize the serious responsibilities I have shouldered as a conscientious objector, and I know that I will try with all capabilities that God gave me to make positive contributions toward the welfare and well-being of society. The existence of racial prejudice, discrimination, economic oppression, and destitution among millions of Americans affords the opportunity for concrete contributions to President Roosevelt's "four freedoms." Furthermore, the dissolution of [the] modern family and the absence of fundamental, absolute value in social life indicate the need of change in human thought and action. In these fields I feel that I have something to contribute to the world.[58]

In November the draft board notified Marciniak of his 4E classification. He was grateful but made one more request. He asked that he not be sent away for the next few months for alternate civilian service so that he could complete his thesis while his survey data was current, and he offered to "drop in at the board whenever convenient for you."[59] This request was also granted.

Marciniak was convinced that people could be brought together to settle arguments rather than resort to violence. Even as he acknowledged the evil character of Nazi

37

leadership, he could not endorse war. He believed that the tactics used by Hitler, such as concentration camps and indiscriminate bombing, were immoral, but they were just as immoral, whether used by fascists or democratic nations.[60] In an interview more than forty years later, he appeared to struggle with details of the draft saying, "I recollect…how can you recollect all of the emotion of that period?" He again emphasized that he was a "conscientious objector, not a pacifist," He noted that his objector status and his of deferment alternate service seemed to have been granted "so they would not have to deal with me."[61]

This was a challenging time for Marciniak as his close friends had signed up for military duty and his brother served in the Navy. In August 1943, while the United States was waging war against Japan in the Solomon Islands and pushing the German and Italian armies out of Sicily, Marciniak wrote to John Cogley that his stand against the war was "a seeming handicap which I possess in communicating with my fellow brothers in Christ." He also maintained contact with those Catholic Workers who were pacifist, some of whom had been recognized as conscientious objectors and assigned to alternate service at Chicago's Alexian Brothers Hospital. They reestablished the St. Joseph's House of Hospitality at a site a block from the hospital but lacked the time and means and volunteers to serve the community as the original one had. They were too busy attending the needs of patients and taking classes to become nurses. These Catholic Workers did, however, invite speakers and develop a study program designed to aid in what they saw as the process of postwar social reconstruction. Marciniak frequently visited the new St. Joseph's House of Hospitality and gave lectures.[62]

Lacking the fellowship of those in alternate service projects, however, Marciniak struggled. Writing to Cogley, who was in the service behind a desk stateside during the war, he shared his mood: "It isn't easy, I assure you John, to sit home while the rest of the people you know and love are in the thick of battle, shouldering a gun or riding a plane. Physical isolation is bad enough, but to be isolated from the spiritual mind and mandate of the community in which you live is a thousand times worse...."[63]

Marciniak continued to agonize for two years before coming to terms with his position. To Cogley he wrote:

I've been confronted with a personal, moral dilemma which brings home to me, on the one hand the diabolical nature of Nazism—the horrendous menace of the Axis powers to our way of life; but on the other hand, I find that the only way in which a society I live in can remove these evils is to create a situation of means and principles, and results to which I cannot give my allegiance. Morally, I must refuse my cooperation. The dilemma becomes even more excruciating for me when I realize that perhaps the only way to stem the tide of Hitlerian nihilism is to utilize the methods which makes my conscience squirm. Really John, I cannot conceive of a modern war to which I could subscribe my heart and mind, I don't think that the kind of war I would conceive could be used today against Hitler, & Co.[64]

In conclusion he told Cogley that he might be wrong in his moral judgement but added, "I am certain that I am not." However, his beliefs made him confront the challenge of what he should do as a Christian during the crisis "to restore all things in Christ." Marciniak had wrestled with the best way to serve his Creator and live so that those who died on the field of battle would not have died in vain.[65] In fact, he seriously considered joining the medical corps as a conscientious objector after getting his 4E status, but then reconsidered and withdrew the request he had made to his draft board explaining that he realized "even medical service under military direction would aid toward the continuation of the war." He explained that he sought as a conscientious objector "to try with all my capabilities that God gave me to make a positive contribution to the welfare of society."[66] Even months before his death, more than sixty years later, Marciniak said that he felt the same way about modern warfare. While viewing, *Saving Private Ryan*, a movie about WW II, Marciniak told a friend who had taken him to see the movie: "That's what I was against; the brutality."[67]

SOCIAL WORK, ACADEMIA, AND LABOR

Through the trial of his isolated stance during the war, Ed Marciniak developed a sense of urgency to dedicate himself to renew the world. While others fought the war to win the peace, Marciniak told his friend that there was much fighting to do "along the familial-socio-economic-juridic, moral front."[68] Having completed his master's degree in Social Administration at Loyola in 1942, he continued to teach the course titled "Principles of Social Action," an analysis of the papal social encyclicals. He began graduate work at the University of Chicago and undertook a new initiative to deal with economic and racial inequities.

From 1943 through 1945, Marciniak did graduate work with the Committee on Social Thought, taking classes with and personally getting to know leading scholars and intellectuals of the day. Among them were Robert Maynard Hutchins, the innovative president of the University of Chicago; Mortimer Adler, philosopher, noted author, and driving force behind the Great Books Program; Robert Redfield, the Dean of Social Sciences and renowned anthropologist; John U. Nef, historian and Director of the Committee on Social Thought and historian; Wilbur Katz, the Dean of the Law School; and Daniel Boorstin, American historian and later Librarian of the United States Congress.[69]

Chicago's Committee on Social Thought had been founded on the belief that the serious study of any academic topic or philosophical or literary work benefited from a "deep acquaintance" with fundamental issues presupposed in all studies, rather than through narrow departmental or disciplinary lenses. Further it was believed that students should learn by a knowledge of certain ancient and modern texts in an "interdisciplinary atmosphere."[70]

What is clear from a paper on corporate farming that Marciniak submitted for a course in economic history as well as from his correspondence with faculty,[71] he was indeed dealing with the presupposed fundamental issues from his own distinctly Catholic point of view. He questioned the premise of corporate farming as an effort to industrialize farming that failed to recognize farming's role in the culture of Americans and its stabilizing impact on democracy.

Ed seemed to find the University of Chicago environment exciting and made a pronounced impression on the
faculty. He was asked to teach the Great Books curriculum
and was paired with Wilbur Katz. Preparing to teach in
the program with the Dean of the Law School deepened
Marciniak's knowledge of the classics in literature, philosophy, government, and economics. Though he never finished
his dissertation at the University of Chicago, he became a
lifelong member of the Great Books Foundation's Board of
Directors.[72]

Simultaneously, he built on his Catholic Worker experience and relationships as he developed plans to make real
what he had learned and taught while pursuing his doctoral studies. He wanted to sustain the goals of the Catholic Worker movement; however, he saw a need to deal more
directly with social and economic structures than Dorothy
Day's personalist approach. Dorothy Day and Peter Maurin
believed in the prophetic value of witness in feeding the poor
and opposing the war to communicate Christian ideals. Marciniak was more intent on effectiveness; he sought to remove
barriers to justice for all and advocate the creation of policies
and programs to secure that justice. He was assisted by his
contacts and the mailing list of the *Chicago Catholic Worker*,
he soon secured three thousand dollars for the start of a new
entity to be called the Catholic Labor Alliance (CLA) and
to create an associated monthly newspaper, *Work*. With the
assistance of a cadre of Catholic lay people and clergy who
believed that even as the war progressed it was time to lay the
ground for a healthy social and economic order.[73]

While the organization was founded and led by Catholics, it hoped to win the active collaboration of all regardless

of religion who "will support the common democratic objective of working out in America a socio-economic order according to the principles laid down as universally right and applicable in the encyclical letters *On the Condition of Labor* and *The Reconstruction of the Social Order.*" Further, it sought to engage business owners and managers and professionals who saw the benefits of collective bargaining. In the first edition, *Work* stated the organization had no political aspirations nor alignments with existing unions but sought to cooperate with all honest union leaders. It would be aligned with the interests and problems of workers. It would provide the kind of coverage absent from the popular press and would analyze the news that impacted social issues of labor, housing, farming, race, and more. The best interest of capital and labor, it contended, result from mutual respect. CLA posited that "the work of establishing a just society cannot be kept on a strictly partisan level. It is impossible for a minority group alone to ever establish justice." Marciniak did promise that the principles guiding CLA would be "the norms of economic morality" outlined by the Pope.[74] Using the journalistic and editorial skills honed at Loyola and the *Chicago Catholic Worker*, Marciniak assumed the role of editor and retained a guiding hand in the journal for more than fifteen years.

CLA also formed a "Labor School" to educate workers to be active and articulate members of their unions—a widespread goal of Catholic Labor activists of the time that Catholic labor schools advanced. By training workers to make their own case as well as understanding their employer's case, they would be able to contribute to effective collective bargaining. This was a "pressing" issue, as Marciniak noted, "Outside of Communists circles it practically does not exist in Chicago."[75] Classes in the curriculum included social science and philosophy as well as practical topics such as negotiating strategies and parliamentary procedures. The goal was to prepare workers to become confident in their dealings with their union and company management as well as with the Communists who dominated some of the major unions in Chicago and elsewhere at the time.

Marciniak soon became one of the Chicago's foremost Catholic activists as he pursued his mission. He spoke about papal encyclicals wherever "he could find three people assembled." He marched the picket lines and taught his beloved parliamentary procedure and principle of labor action to the numerous organizations that he had joined or cofounded.[76] Marciniak was more than a provocateur. He founded practical, effective organizations to promote social justice, as well as being an active participant in many more. He believed passionately in the importance of acting in concert to effect change in society. Through his organizational connections he spread his message. Further, he met and mobilized people who could and would become his allies in future engagements for change.

While directing the work of the Catholic Labor Alliance, Marciniak engaged with business, union, and political leaders who would become part of a network of supporters and advisers as he pursued his mission. He became convinced that advancing democracy was the responsibility of all citizens. Shortly after the Allies' victory in Germany but before the war ended in Japan, Marciniak succinctly enunciated his vision for the nation in a commencement address he gave at Wells High School. The Chicago public school served an ethnically diverse, lower-middle class student body at the edge of an industrial area that was the home to newer immigrants, much like the one into which Marciniak had been born twenty-seven years earlier.[77] He urged the graduates to complete the work their parents had just fought for in defeating Hitler:

> I'd like to say that your parents and mine have not finished the job of building a free America. And this is where your job comes in, as long as there are people who can't own their own homes, who don't have enough money to send their children thru college, who don't have a decent place to live in, as long as there are people whose wages aren't high enough to provide a living with all of the good things of life, who don't get good medication, as long as there are people who fail to recognize the debt they owe God, as long as men hate each other, as long as there are slums in Chicago, as long as there is injustice, you and I have work to do.[78]

Marciniak's experiences and initiatives in the 1940s prepared him for his next decades of trying to "finish" the work of building an America in which all would be free from discrimination and hunger with access to a good education and decent housing.

PERSONAL LIFE

While Marciniak found fulfillment in his organizing enterprises, he also knew that his life was incomplete. While his feverish schedule was not "cupid-designed," he made clear to his friends that he was not averse to marriage.[79] In fact, he hoped to marry and have a partner to share his work. In the previously cited letter to his mentor, D.A, in which he explained his decision to leave the seminary to become "a lay agitator," he also made clear that being married was an essential part of his plan. He explained that he was a *"weak guy"* who needed someone to share his troubles, help carry his burdens, advise and encourage him, share his ideals and ambitions. Further he needed "someone to work, plan, and pray with…someone for whom I could do the same that she would be doing for me." He was willing to wait to find a wife "whose ideals were mine and for whom my ideals would be hers."[80]

Ed went on to explain, in accordance with Catholic doctrine, that marriage was especially important to him because of his belief in its "mystic, supernatural, *sacramental* significance" of marriage "making sacred each loving action of husband and wife." He then dealt with what he considered his "negative" reasons for his wanting to marry. "One, I would like to show a lot of scoffers that people can *try* to live saintly lives in the married state; that the call to perfection is not confined to the cloister; that mediocrity is not only not a necessary part of married life, but that it is possible to live a married life without mediocrity." Further, he wanted to disprove the "satanic notion" that married life was "sterile" and routine. "To this pious misrepresentation of a sacrament, I would say 'baloney' by showing otherwise in my own life as a husband and in the life of my co-partner in Christ, my wife." It was nearly a decade later that Marciniak found the person who would fulfill his hopes and dreams. Her name was Virginia Cecilia Volini. Virginia was born in 1930, the daughter of Dr. Italo Frederick Volini, a surgeon and the medical director of Loyola University Hospital, and Marcella Ringwald Volini. One of ten children, she grew up in a rambling Victorian home in Oak Park, a leafy Chicago suburb made famous by Frank Lloyd Wright's architectural studio and the many noteworthy structures he built there.

During World War II, the Volini family moved to a farm near Mundelein and then to 1511 North Dearborn Street on Chicago's Near North side. "Ginny," as she was called by her family, graduated from Immaculata School for Girls and then pursued a degree in French at Mundelein College in Chicago. Virginia had secured a position working at Nina Polcyn's St. Benet Book Store, a locus for Catholic intellectuals and social actionists in Chicago. Before coming to Chicago, Nina Polcyn had worked with Dorothy Day in New York, had founded a Catholic Worker house in Milwaukee, and become a friend of Marciniak. Apparently on a visit to the bookstore, Marciniak was taken by the attractive, gracious, and bright Volini. According to the family history, Virginia left the city to pursue a master's degree in philosophy and theology in Toronto, but Marciniak "ever the prolific writer, wooed her back to Chicago after an intensive love letter exchange." The correspondence is tender and playful with hand-made valentines and poetry written by Virginia and Ed's newsy letters exhibiting his smitten state and hopes for their future together. They also exhibited their deep religious faith and strong shared interest in theology, philosophy, and service.[81]

Years later, a friend who volunteered at the CLA office reminisced with Marciniak: "You asked me to send a Catholic Labor Alliance application blank to Miss Volini at St. Benet Bookshop, as I recall. The next thing I knew was that you two were engaged."[82] In April 1953, Marciniak and his young bride were married in a solemn high mass ceremony at Holy Name Cathedral in Chicago, followed by a simple reception in the cathedral courtyard with guests served cake and coffee. The newlyweds honeymooned at a Smokey Mount resort.[83]

Afterwards they lived in an apartment near the CLA office and began to raise a family as Ed sustained his incredible pace of engagement. In one concession to relieving that frantic schedule, Marciniak resigned his part-time position as a union organizer for the Chicago Newspaper Guild, a position that he had held since 1943. For the first time he committed himself to one job rather than juggling several part-time endeavors.[84] For several years, Virginia assisted with *Work*, but the responsibility of raising four daughters assumed priority. Catherine Vianney, Christina Maria, Francesca Louise, and Claudia Noel were each born two years apart and brought a special joy and pride to both parents. A 1962 magazine photo shows the Marciniak's living room with a grand piano, a smiling Virginia seated on its bench with the youngest daughter on her knees and another at her side, and her laughing husband seated on the floor with one daughter on his shoulders and another splayed at his feet. The caption read: "Marciniak's business friends can't imagine this side of the man."[85]

As the children grew up, Virginia pursued her artistic talents as a writer, poet, and accomplished soprano becoming a soloist in the Chicago Chamber Orchestra as well as other musical groups and a free-lance writer for Chicago magazines and newspapers.[86] Virginia was an essential support and partner in all that her spouse did, including providing editorial critiques of his work and sartorial advice. She accepted the many evenings when Marciniak was absent attending to numerous other endeavors and committee service (since he did not resign these as he had the Newspaper Guild). He seemed always to be on the move and working, but his close friends and family saw the other side of the man. His devotion to Virginia and his daughters was fierce and he tried to shield them from many of the trials he faced in his work.

In 1955, as their family expanded, the Marciniaks joined with Ed's sister, Bernice, and her husband, Russ Barta, to purchase a two-flat apartment at 4932 North Francisco. The building was red face-brick with limestone accents and three corbels to support flower boxes below the living room windows of the Barta family's first-floor apartment. Each unit had three bedrooms and a bright airy living room surrounded by a bay of eight windows.[87] Its location near the greenway along the North Branch of the Chicago River and River Park a block to the north was a perfect setting for the Marciniak and Barta children. The Francisco housing arrangement lasted for seven years until the Marciniaks moved to a larger home in the Edgewater neighborhood and the Bartas to nearby Evanston.

The friendship of Ed Marciniak and Russ Barta was lasting and led to numerous collaborations between the brothers-in-laws. Barta was a couple years younger than Marciniak but shared common experiences and interests. Russ was born in Chicago of working-class Czech parents, grew up in Berwyn, attended Chicago's seminaries, and like Marciniak left before ordination. He went on to earn his doctorate in sociology at the University of Notre Dame and taught at Nazareth College in Michigan. He returned to Chicago and between 1955 and 1963 directed the Archdiocese of Chicago's Adult Education centers, establishing programs in many neighborhoods. Marciniak and Barta shared congruent convictions on the nobility of work and the vision of Christians working to secure justice and peace.[88]

Thus was the scene set for the next great chapter in Ed Marciniak's remarkable life.

NOTES

1   Edward Marciniak to Ralph McIneray [sic], August 20, 1986, Marciniak Papers, Archdiocese of Chicago Archives, Shelf 1, Position 1. The collection consists of letters, reports, newspaper and magazine clippings and photos that are contained in 27 boxes that have not yet been catalogued. For this reason, reference to these papers herein is by shelf and position of the box for the referenced item.

2   A great deal has been written about the Catholic Worker Movement and Dorothy Day. Day's own memoir, *The Long Loneliness*, and Peter Maurin's *Green Revolution*, provide personal accounts of the movement and its religious grounding. For a broader look at the Catholic Worker Movement and Day see Mel Piehl, *Breaking Bread: The Catholic Worker and the Origin of Catholic Radicalism*, (Temple University Press, Philadelphia, Pennsylvania, 1982) and William D. Miller, *Dorothy Day: A Biography*, (Harper and Row, San Francisco, California, 1982).

3   Rosalie Riegle interview with Edward Marciniak, January 6, 1988. The interview transcript is in the Interview Files of the Archdiocese of Chicago Archives, p. 1.

4   *Today*, "Young Man with a Cause, Edward Marciniak," May 1946, p. 10; and Kimball Baker, *"Go to the Worker": America's Labor Apostles*, (Marquette University Press, Milwaukee, Wisconsin, 2010), pp. 117-118.

5   William Droel, "Chronology of Marciniak's Life." Droel, a longtime associate and close friend of Marciniak prepared the document.

6   Damian Barta, interview by author, January 29, 2021.

7   US. Census 1920. The census report indicates Hattie was born in Illinois, however, her naturalization papers dated September 27, 1929 (Petition 74879) document her former nationality as Polish. At the time of her marriage, U.S legislation required women who married aliens to renounce their citizenship. After Walter became a citizen, she applied for the citizenship she had been forced to renounce. Marciniak Papers, Shelf 5, Position 5,

and Meg Hacker, "When Saying I Do Meant Giving Up U.S. Citizenship," *Genealogy Note*. Retrieved July 13, 2021, https://www.archives.gov/files/publications/prologue/2014/spring/citizenship.pdf.

8   "Young Man with a Cause," Walter Marciniak "bought and sold buildings in a small way" causing the family to move often, according to an Illinois General Assembly House Resolution honoring Marciniak, House Resolution 1043, 2004.

9   Charles W. Stockwell, "Brighton Park," *The Encyclopedia of Chicago*, (University of Chicago Press, Chicago, Illinois, 2004), p. 94.

10   U.S. Census, 1930.

11   "Young Man with a Cause."

12   Marciniak Address at the All Chicago Salute to Ed Marciniak, September 27, 1990, Marciniak Papers, Shelf 1, Position 1. Although now likely unknown by many, the *Index of Forbidden Books* (*Index Librorum Prohibitorum*) was a list of books forbidden by Catholic Church authority as dangerous to faith and morals.

13   "Young Man with a Cause."

14   Marciniak, "Americans United: The Place of the Labor Union in the Democratic Scheme," a draft. Marciniak Papers, Shelf 2, Position 3.

15   Riegle Interview, p. 16. However, each child assumed personal responsibility for his or her education. His brother, Henry, realized his family could not send him to college so he, on his own, secured an appointment to the Naval Academy. His sister, Bernice, finished Saint Xavier College in three years because she knew her father could not afford a fourth year of school.

16   The legislation restricted immigration in absolute numbers and gave preference to the immigrants based upon the origin of citizens in the United States in 1890, before dramatically increased immigration from southern- and-eastern-European nations that had arrived in the United States in later waves.

17   Charles Shanabruch, *Chicago's Catholics: The Evolution of an Americanization Identity*, (University of Notre Dame Press, No-

tre Dame, Indiana,1981) and Edward Kantowicz, *Corporation Soul: Cardinal Mundelein and Chicago Catholicism* (University of Notre Dame Press, Notre Dame Indiana, 1983).

18 Quigley Yearbook, 1936, Marciniak Papers, Shelf 1, Position 2.

19 "Young Man with a Cause," and Kimball Baker, "*Go to the Worker*," pp. 117-118.

20 Riegle Interview with Marciniak, p.1.

21 Marciniak to D.A., n.d. (the author's handwritten notation at the top of the carbon copy is: "1940s." Marciniak Papers, Shelf 1, Position 2. "D.A" likely was Daniel A. Lord, S.J., a well know peace writer who also served as the national president of the Sodality when Marciniak served as president of its chapter at Loyola University. In the letter he notes that he had just read "Queens Work," one of Lord's publications. See: See Stephen Werner, "Daniel A. Lord, S.J.: A Forgotten Dynamo of the Early Twentieth Century," *American Catholic Studies* (Summer, 2018), pp. 39-57.

22 Riegle interview with Marciniak, p. 17.

23 Strubbe, Rita and Charles, *Saint Anthony Messenger*, "Target: Human Dignity," June 1963, p. 25.

24 "Young Man with a Cause," p. 11.

25 "Mystical Body of Christ." *New Catholic Encyclopedia,* Encyclopedia.com. (July 31, 2019). https://www.encyclopedia.com/religion/encyclopedias-almanacs-transcripts-and-maps/mystical-body-christ.

26 Marciniak Papers, Shelf 3, Position 2.

27 "Young Man with a Cause," p. 11; Baker, p. 118.

28 Marciniak Address at the All-Chicago Salute to Ed Marciniak, September 27, 1990, Marciniak Papers, Shelf 1, Position 1.

29 For an account of Maurin's life and selected writings, See: Dorothy Day with Francis J. Sicius, *Peter Maurin: Apostle to the World*, (Orbis Books, Ossining, New York, 2004).

30 Marciniak quoted in "Young Man with a Cause."

31 Sicius, pp. 57-78.

32 Pp. 87-88.

33 Herr, Dan, *The Sign*, "The Chicago Dynamo," September 1962, p. 12.

34 Sicius, pp. 89-90.

35 Cogley, *Storefront Catholicism*, p. 447, cited in Sicius, p. 96. Cogley was a member of Dr. Falls' Catholic Worker group and then, at Dorothy Day's urging, opened a second Catholic Worker house to serve Blacks in Chicago's Black communities. That enterprise was abandoned because St. Elizabeth Catholic Church's pastor more than adequately served the needs of the people in those communities and had their allegiance. Eventually, Cogley went to work with Day in New York, but he returned to Chicago and became a mainstay of the second Catholic Worker House there. He finally returned to New York to become one of the editors of *Commonweal* magazine.

36 Marciniak to Dorothy Day, August 23, 1940, and Cogley to Dorothy Day, September 26, 1940, correspondence in Marquette University Dorothy Day Collection.

37 *Chicago Catholic Worker*, June 1938.

38 Ibid.

39 Why a Paper?" *Chicago Catholic Worker*, August 1941.

40 "Chicago C.U.U. Underway," June 1938.

41 *Chicago Catholic Worker*, July 1938.

42 "Young Man with a Cause," and Strubbe, p. 24. Ed's first flight was in 1952 and he marveled at seeing Chicago spread out below him as the plane approached Midway airport.

43 Marciniak, Resume c 1983, Marciniak Papers, Shelf 5, Position 3.

44 Edward Marciniak, "The Racial Attitudes of Students in in the Colleges of the Chicago Area," (master's thesis, 1942, Loyola University) pp. 98-101. While preparing his own survey, Marciniak consulted with Rev. John LaFarge, S.J., who founded the Catholic Interracial Council of New York and, in 1937, authored *Interracial Justice: A Study of the Catholic Doctrine of Race Relations*.

45 Karen Johnson https://indigo.uic.edu/bitstream/handle/10027/9929/Johnson_Karen.pdf?sequence=1, January 24, 2019.

46 May 1939.

47 Sicius, pp. 125-127.

48 Marciniak to D.A., n.d., Marciniak Papers, Shelf 1, Position 2. Marciniak wrote at the top of the carbon copy "1940s." He ended his letter with the close: "Devilishly yours, your most persistent pupil."

49 Ibid.

50 Ibid.

51 September 1940.

52 Sicius, pp. 189-190.

53 Sicius, pp. 146-186; Miller, William D., *A Harsh and Dreadful Love*, (Image Books, New York, New York, 1974) p. 169; Piehl, pp. 155-159.

54 *Chicago Catholic Worker*, December 1940.

55 Cited in Ibid.

56 Marciniak to Day, Marquette University Achieves.

57 On an index card with his other notes on conscientious objection he had scrawled: "It takes heroism to be labelled unpatriotic, cowardly, etc. It takes heroism to exhibit the heroism of the cross in fighting off in exhibiting the spirit of love in the struggle for truth, fight for social justice, for a new order." He elaborated that those individuals "prone to raise moral and ethical doubts about pacifism are the last ones to raise the same doubts about militarism." Marciniak notes, Marciniak Papers, Shelf 1, Position 3.

58 Marciniak statement to draft board, August 30, 1941, Marciniak Papers, Shelf 1, Position 3.

59 Marciniak to Thomas A. Shanahan, Chicago Local Board 20. November 27, 1942, Marciniak Papers, Shelf 1, Position 3.

60 Ibid.

61 Riegle interview with Marciniak, p. 11. See also: Sicius interview with Marciniak, footnote #41, p. 191.

62 Sicius p.213. See Sicius for a detailed account of the Chicago Catholic Workers who did not enlist, pp. 201-235.

63 August 30, 1943, Marciniak Papers, Shelf 1, Position 3.

64 Ibid.

65 Ibid.

66 Marciniak to Thomas A Shanahan, Chicago Local Board No.20, June 21, 1942, Marciniak Papers, Shelf 1, Position 3.

67 William Droel to the author, February 28, 2019.

68 Marciniak to Cogley, August 30, 1943, Marciniak Papers, Shelf 1, Position1..

69 Marciniak Papers, Shelf 1, Position 1.

70 "About the Committee," U of C web site, https://socialthought. uchicago.edu/page/about-committee. January 11, 2019.

71 Untitled paper, Marciniak Papers, Shelf 1, Position 1 that Marciniak wrote in 1942-43 with the course title. See correspondence from Daniel Boorstin to Marciniak, Dec 13, 1944; John U. Nef to Students and Associates of the Committee on Social Thought, March 2, 1945: "Addendum" by Marciniak, n.d; Marciniak Papers, Shelf 1, Position 1.

72 Cyril O. Houle to Great Books Instructors in the University College, April 3, 1945; and Wilbur Katz to Marciniak, October 1, 1945. Marciniak Papers, Shelf 1, Position 1. The first year reading list for the students, many who were older adults, included three works by Plato, and portions of works by Thucydides, Aristophanes, Aristotle, Plutarch, St. Augustine, St. Thomas Aquinas, Machiavelli, Montaigne, Shakespeare, Locke, Rousseau, Smith, Marx and the Declaration of Independence, the U.S. Constitution, and nearly twenty of the Federalist papers. All the readings as well as his sociology and theological training, prepared Marciniak for his new enterprise. See also: *Volini Family History*, p. 133.

73 Thomas Gavagan, "Five Years of *Work*, 1948," CCWL File, Chicago Historical Museum Archives.

74 July 1943.

75 Ibid.

76 "Young Man with a Cause."

77 Ibid. The paper listed twelve organizations to which he belonged at the time. Several of these he had founded or helped to launch.

78 Hand-edited draft of speech given at Wells High School, [no date- but after German surrender and before Japan's] Marciniak Papers, Shelf 1, Position 1.

79 "Young Man with a Cause."

80 August 30, 1943.

81 P. 121. This author is grateful to the Marciniak daughters for sharing a copy of the *Volini Family History* and making their parents' courtship correspondence available.

82 Joan Kerns Ciavarella to Marciniak, September 27, 1990, Marciniak Papers, Shelf 1, Position 1.

83 *Chicago Tribune*, April 26, 1953, and Ibid.

84 Marciniak to Fletcher Wilson, January 23, 1952. In his resignation he wrote:"This letter is born of more than a month's labor. It isn't an easy letter to write because the decision which prompts it was not a simple one.... With my impending marriage and the fresh obligation that this new vocation imposes, I must finally resolve that exists when a man tries to hold down two jobs—even part-time ones such as these are. Marciniak Papers, Shelf 1, Position 1.

85 Herr, p.11.

86 *Chicago Tribune*, "Obituary," October 23,1990, https://www.newspapers.com/clip/56655723/obituary-for-virginia-volini-marciniak/.

87 Herr, p. 11.

88 Damian Barta interview and *Chicago Tribune*, "Obituary," September 23, 1997, https://www.chicagotribune.com/news/ct-xpm-1997-09-23-9709230164-story.html.

Chapter 2

Insisting on Worker Rights

We don't believe that profits have priority over wages.

Edward Marciniak[1]

As World War II ended, some Americans looked with satisfaction at the large profits and enhanced balanced sheets of major corporations. One such person was the financial editor of the Chicago *Herald American*, John H. Vanderpoel, who was buoyed by a report that large corporations had amassed $47 billion dollars in savings and were well-positioned for the future. The journalist's crowing jarred Marciniak's sense of fairness and prompted a retort in *Work* that America had "failed to make the nation's wealth work for the good of all." He decried the "miserable" failure of the system which enabled corporations to stockpile billions by not paying more than ten million workers a wage adequate to meet basic needs. The *Herald American's* Vanderpoel, rejoined that Marciniak had not told the "whole truth...just a part of it." He charged that *Work's* editor omitted the fact that millions of American workers had received the highest wages ever and that they had been able to save billions of dollars, giving them the greatest financial strength that they had ever known.[2]

Vanderpoel's chiding rankled Marciniak and prompted a strong and direct retort in *Work* that was characteristic of his blunt and unvarnished collegiate debating style. He minced no words. He characterized the *Herald American* financial editor's effort to present both sides as "the refuge of fence straddlers" and labeled the feigned neutrality "irresponsible" when the nation's workers were not treated fairly. This disparity between corporate reserves and wages was, he argued, akin to an economic disease that threatened the social body and called for a realistic diagnosis. Marciniak wrote that America's "basic economic disease is one of distribution and we don't pull any punches in saying so." He continued: "Our fundamental economic evil today is that tens of millions of Americans can't earn a decent living in our economic system. Small groups of men receive a lion's share of our wealth each year, while millions of hard working men and women receive a pittance for their toil. **There are no two sides to this problem.**" [boldface original][3]

Work emphasized that 60 percent of American workers received less than one dollar an hour in the prosperity boom of 1945. Marciniak's paper did admit that millions of workers received the highest wages they had ever received, and some were able to salt away funds. This did not mean they were overpaid, however. The reality was lopsided as Marciniak pointed out. Data from the War Finance Division of the Treasury Department supported Marciniak's view. It reported that in 1944 of the $160 billion held in reserve purchasing power 60 per cent was held by ten percent of the population and 90 percent of the population had only 40 percent. Marciniak especially disagreed with Vanderpoel's opinion that labor was asking for **"wages not justified by production."** [boldface original] That view assumed that it was industry's prerogative to operate at a profit even when workers received less than a living wage. "This loss is never written into our national profit and loss statements," Marciniak counselled the financial editor.

Marciniak's last rebuff to Vanderpoel was an augment for distributive justice for workers:

> We don't believe that profits have priority over wages. Business enterprise is not entitled to any profits until everyone who works for the business enterprise (superintendents, maintenance men, executive officers, laborers, office employees, etc.) gets a decent return on his labor. Certainly, the wage rate should take into consideration the condition of a business but working people in a plant have first call on the fruits of production. When the demands of justice are satisfied, then the coupon clippers can pull out their scissors and get to work.[4]

This exchange between Vanderpoel and Marciniak illustrates the central issue in the post-WWII debate over of workers' rights to just compensation for producing wealth. Under Marciniak's editorship *Work* would defend worker interests and make sure that readers had the facts that they deserved to dispel flawed corporate reasoning and advance labor's interests.

To fight inequality required workers to organize and develop solidarity to thereby advance their legitimate striving for a decent life for themselves and their families, Marciniak said. He was pragmatic and knew that there was no silver bullet to end inequality. The process would be slow and require workers to unite and do the unremunerated work of attending meetings, forming committees, drafting resolutions, staying informed, and striking when necessary. He believed that unions that embodied principles of participation were the best force to counter unregulated capitalism and workers' best hope to achieve economic justice. Were he alive today, Marciniak, undoubtedly would champion increased minimum wages for essential workers and support gig workers, whether free lancers or temporary workers, who seek rights and benefits due them for their contributions to an economic enterprise.

Youthful idealism is characterized by impatience, expecting goodness and catchy phrases to win the day. Marciniak developed a mature idealism, a long-haul idealism. He learned that mastering details whether of economic data, voting patterns, sociological and industrial trends, zoning and building codes and fine points of Roberts Rules of Order needed to be combined with the patience and tedium of sub-committee meetings and report writing. He reflected on opposing positions, accepted criticism all the while staying true to the calling. His idealism was characterized by tenacious, arduous work in the trenches focused on collective actions that made lasting change.

CATHOLIC SOCIAL TEACHING

Marciniak was hardly the only one to make a mark as an advocate for workers' rights. Yet constancy, drive, and initiative and blend of religious idealism and practicality set him apart. What initially had been a personal response to the needs of individuals during the Depression soon evolved into a commitment to address systemic problems created by economic injustice. Marciniak's message blended both Catholic social justice theory and an American democratic perspective in the struggle to protect workers' rights to organize and to secure just compensation and safe working conditions. Papal encyclicals and the 1919 American bishops' program for social reconstruction provided a rationale and direction. Helping to solve the problems of economic justice required, then and today, people in the trenches like Marciniak who lived among and rubbed shoulders daily with the employed and unemployed.

The encyclicals of Popes Leo XIII and Pius XI were the primary documents that laid the foundation for Catholic social action in the United States as they did in Europe. In 1891 Pope Leo XIII's penned the encyclical *Rerum Novarum*. This letter, known in English as *On the Condition of Labor*, addressed the relationship and duties of capital and labor which moved the church away from its old-world philosophy of *noblesse oblige* to one that called for just wages rather than charity. It became the foundational document in Catholic social thought by articulating the duties of both capital and labor as well as government. Leo XIII sought to better the conditions of the urban poor oppressed by industrialization. The pope advocated for the rights of labor to create unions and bargain collectively. Further, he rejected the ideologies of socialism and communism. One of its most radical points was to define a fair wage, *a living wage*, as one that permitted a worker to support his family and with a little saving left over to allow him to improve his condition. Leo XIII did not create new principles but tried to apply traditional Catholic teaching on justice to the situation of the industrial age and to promote harmony and calm class conflict. As socialist ideas were gaining traction in Europe, he proclaimed that individuals had the right to private property. Leo XIII's, support of property rights, however, broke from the philosophy of unrestricted capitalism noting that property comes with a social obligation and that both owners and labor had duties to the common good.[5]

In 1931, the fortieth anniversary of *Rerum Novarum*, Pope Pius XI elaborated on Leo XIII's message in *Quadragesimo Anno*, known by its English title *On the Reconstruction of the Social Order*. Pius XI sought to reduce tension in Europe between capitalism and socialism by proposing cooperation along functional and occupational groups. The encyclical's most important contribution was to introduce the idea of "social justice" to describe the need to ensure the "common good." Pius XI wrote that the law of "social justice" forbids one class from excluding others, that all must share in some way the benefits of economic development. He stated that the right order of things was for the fair distribution of created goods, "which as every discerning person knows, is laboring today under the gravest evils due to the huge disparity between a few exceedingly rich and the unnumbered propertyless, must be effectively called back to and brought into conformity with the norms of the common good, that is social justice."[6] His emphasis was on the common good not individual good. *Quadragesimo Anno* made clear that Catholics not only *ought* to form associations as a matter of self-interest, but they *must* form associations, noting that labor unions should function according to Christian principles.

Chicago had been the locus of numerous labor disputes and the center of labor agitation for workplace justice years before *Rerum Novarum*. Struggles for the eight-hour day and the Haymarket affair in 1886, the American Railway strike of 1894, and the Memorial Day Massacre of 1937 all demonstrated the ruthless power of management supported by police power, to protect a *status quo* in which workers' rights were virtually nonexistent. For decades, these violent engagements between workers and the interests of capital forced civic, religious, and political leaders to take sides in the effort to seek fair solutions to reduce unrest that destabilized cities and the nation.

In the United States the Catholic Church was a predominantly immigrant institution in the nineteenth and early twentieth centuries. Similarly, most of the workers in the large industries were immigrants. It was natural, then, that it sided with workers in most of their struggles. In Chicago, its consistent position on unions and economic justice was to support the workers' right to organize for better conditions and wages; however, the primary thrust of its efforts was to care for the poor through orphanages, asylums, hospitals, and settlement houses.[7] This focus changed during the Depression years into the 1950s when the priests and laity became much more active in their advocacy of economic and social justice.

In that period, Chicago became the center for progressive action and policy to secure justice in the workplace according to Catholic ideals. In the 1930s, George Cardinal Mundelein nurtured and vocally supported workers' rights as did his auxiliary bishop, Rt. Rev. Bernard Sheil, and his seminary rector, Msgr. Reynold Hillenbrand. Cardinal Mundelein contended that Catholics had too often allied themselves with the wrong side because they were flattered into believing the Catholic Church was respected for being a great conservative force at the same time it was asked by the corporations to be a police force over workers who were paid a pittance.[8] In an address to Catholic men Mundelein stated the Church's position: "Our place is beside the poor, behind the working man."[9]

Cardinals Samuel Stritch and Albert Meyer continued their support of workers' rights through funds for education and support of unions in the 1940s and 1950s.[10] Contributing to the intensity of the movement for workers' rights were lay activists who joined the picket lines, dispensed aid to the unemployed, and challenged the *status quo* in public and private forums. Marciniak was one of the most ardent of these.[11]

Marciniak's initial perspective was shaped by working in his father's store, thoughtful reading of *The Catholic Worker* and papal encyclicals, and attending discussions and lectures at Dr. Arthur Falls' first Catholic Worker house. His experiences with striking workers and as a labor organizer and leader made the issues compellingly real. His ideas of justice and democracy were tested in union halls, on picket lines at factory gates, and around negotiating tables. In these forums he was both observer, analyst, and an activist "insider." His awareness of the strengths and weakness of organized labor evolved as he participated in the fight for unions.

EARLY UNION INITIATIVES

Marciniak's co-founding of the St. Joseph House of Hospitality stemmed from his desire to feed and shelter the needy but soon led to advocacy and more direct action on behalf of poor workers. Among the first initiatives of the Blue Island band of Catholic Workers was the establishment of the *Chicago Catholic Worker* to give their struggling enterprise a vehicle to garner support and share a radical Catholic vision.[12]

The monthly consistently promoted Catholic social consciousness and offered local labor news to readers. Marciniak saw the need for Catholic involvement was especially acute because of the split between the Congress of Industrial Organizations (CIO) and the American Federation of Labor (AFL). In the 1930s, the CIO first emerged as a committee of the AFL, which represented craft unions. The CIO soon sought to organize workers according to industry rather than specific trades. Under the direction of John L. Lewis, the CIO separated member unions from the conservative AFL unions. Some of the CIO unions were strongly influenced by communists and socialists. Many clergy assumed that the CIO was antithetical to Catholic doctrine and feared membership in the union would jeopardize their parishioners' faith.[13] Marciniak, by contrast, supported CIO unions and urged Catholics to become insiders to ensure that Christian principles guided the labor movement in the industries that provided jobs for tens of thousands of Chicago's Catholics.

"What role will they [Catholics] play in the future of this great labor movement?" Marciniak asked rhetorically in the *Chicago Catholic Worker* in 1941. He called for action: "not pretty speeches about the encyclicals," but "an honest attempt on the part of the laity and clergy to apply the principles set down in the encyclicals [of Leo XIII and Pius XI]." He concluded his impassioned article with a call for readers interested in forming a branch of an Association of Catholic Trade Unionists (ACTU) in Chicago to contact him. ACTU had been established by John Cort, a former Catholic Worker at Day's house of hospitality in New York, to diminish communist influence in unions.[14]

In 1938, the *Chicago Catholic Worker's* Cogley reminded readers of Mundelein's warning that many anti-Communist utterances issued by people in finely upholstered chairs "are made for the protection of selfish interests rather than to save Christian civilization. Don't let any sweatshop rich pillars of the Church fool you. Communists are made... not born." He warned Catholics not to support anti-Communists who are makers of Communists," noting that the "dictatorial anti-labor policies of Catholic bosses...are no more Christian and Catholic than was the last financial deal of Judas Iscariot." The editor urged his readers not to waste their time "red-baiting" but urged them to become true "radicals" and noted: "Catholicism uncompromised is as radical as Christ Himself."[15] The best way for Catholics to influence the poor was to be with the poor, as were the communists:

We have listened from well-padded chairs in well-padded ballrooms to well-padded lecterns tell us of how much in sympathy with the poor we are; and we have sighed softly and maybe written a check the next morning...but all the time our place was with the poor, as one of them.

Cogley concluded that "long distance" sympathy would be useless in winning back the poor if the man or woman in ragged clothing was embarrassed to be given their rightful place in the front pews and Catholics busied themselves talking "Christ over banquet plates among ourselves. The Communist should shame us!"[16] Clearly, these were Marciniak's sentiments as well. Direct participation in the struggles was essential. He often remarked that "There is no great virtue in retreating to a cocoon. That kind of purity is for the faint-hearted."[17]

NEWSPAPER GUILD STRIKE OF 1938

Marciniak's call to action was tested in December 1938, when the Chicago Newspaper Guild, a CIO affiliate, went on strike against the Hearst Corporation's newspapers, the *Herald and Examiner* and the *Chicago Evening American.* Earlier in the year, Hearst management began to cut editorial positions in a series of mass firings. The *Chicago Catholic Worker* wrote a feature story about the dismissal of Guild workers in July 1939 and attacked Hearst for "his ruthless onslaught" against workers.[18] That action violated contract provisions and prompted reporters and other editorial staff to strike. The strike soon grew ugly with Hearst's "sluggers" beating Guild pickets with lead-filled hoses and baseball bats. Members of the Chicago Catholic Worker walked the line with the Guild pickets. They were supported by Father John Hayes, a Quigley Seminary teacher and a leading labor activist, and several other priests.[19] The rector of the archdiocesan seminary as well as liberal Protestant and Jewish leaders added their support.[20] Nonetheless, a silence surrounded the strike as the city's newspapers and radio stations conspired to block coverage. Only when the Archdiocesan weekly, *The New World*, reported the story and revealed the issues behind the strike was the silence broken."[21]

As the strike entered its fourth month, the *Chicago Catholic Worker* decried the intimidation and violence. It noted that "industrial tycoons" reacted to the idea of union or strike as ordinary people react to the word "leprosy." "Invariably the victims of any labor struggles come from the rank of workers," the monthly continued. Pointing to the 1937 Memorial Day Massacre at Republic Steel plant in South Chicago at which Catholic Workers had provided food and drink to the strikers and were eyewitnesses to the killing and beating of workers, the paper noted: "the local history of labor here in Chicago is a story of violence."[22]

While acknowledging that some strikers resorted to violence, the *Chicago Catholic Worker* made clear that "any study of the situation will show that labor has much cleaner hands in this regard than industry can boast of. Certainly, a man has a right, sometimes one might say a duty, to strike."[23] The strikers used secondary picketing at the entrances of advertisers' businesses, sound trucks in the neighborhoods, airplane streamers and parades in the Loop on a weekly basis to overcome the news blackout. Hearst fought back. Pickets were injured in "scuffles" on the picket line and then carted off to jail. Marciniak knew firsthand Hearst's tactic of sending circulation trucks to race their engines next to secondary picket lines to sicken union supporters. Even the Guild sound truck was pushed into the Chicago River to silence it.[24]

The Catholic Worker position in support of the Guild was clouded by a peculiar incident involving a series of articles about youth authored by Bishop Bernard J. Sheil, the head of the Catholic Youth Organization. Hearst had contracted for these articles prior to the strike for later publication. The disclosure that the articles would run in the Hearst paper as the strike raged perplexed the Catholic Workers and forced them to question Sheil's allegiances. They did not want to sit in judgment on the bishop's actions. Yet, they recognized that it would be "hypocritical and cowardly" to ignore the matter. Accordingly, they drafted a blunt telegram to the bishop regarding his proposed contribution to the Hearst paper and simultaneously published it in the *Chicago Catholic Worker*:

IN THE NAME OF CHRIST THE WORKER
WE HUMBLY PETITION YOUR EXCELLENCY
TO RECONSIDER PROPOSED YOUTH
SERIES FOR HEARST.
SUCH A SERIES APPEARING AT THIS TIME
WILL VITIATE THE CATHOLIC INFLUENCE
OF PRIESTS AND LAITY ON STRIKE FRONT.
ARTICLES UNFORTUNATELY SEEM
TO PLACE YOU
IN OPPOSITION TO STRIKING WORKERS.[25]

The editors expressed fear that the controversy would increase the already vocal attacks of the communists against the Church and hoped the bishop "would see fit to issue a formal statement to relieve the embarrassment and confusion."[26]

Bishop Sheil quickly denied alleged support of Hearst's Chicago *Evening American*. He explained that his series of columns had been submitted months before the strike and were under the control of the paper. In self-defense, Sheil rejected the allegation of support for Hearst as "preposterous" and affirmed his allegiance to the "heroic" strikers. He lashed out at Hearst management for violating the federal law which granted all labor the right to bargain collectively and labelled its action a "direct contradiction to the spirit and letter of the Encyclical [sic] of Leo XIII and Pius XI."[27]

The assurances of the bishop along with the support of the Catholic Workers and the clergy buoyed the strikers and their families as the strike dragged on. The striking reporters and editorial staff, however, were not able to secure an effective boycott of advertisers nor to secure the support of the skilled press operators, drivers and others covered by unions affiliated with the AFL. After 508 days the strikers won a face-saving settlement that provided for a nondiscriminatory hiring of Guild strikers.[28]

PACKINGHOUSE WORKERS ORGANIZING COMMITTEE, 1939

In the 1930s, tens of thousands of workers labored in Chicago's stockyards and packinghouses where cattle, hogs, and sheep were herded, slaughtered, butchered, and packed. The slaughterhouse conditions and workers' bleak lives, made famous by Upton Sinclair's 1906 novel, *The Jungle*, were much the same for the workers in the 1930s.[29] Post-World War I, efforts to organize the workers had been minimally successful because the largest companies among them— Armour, Swift, and Wilson—created company unions to blunt independent organizing efforts. In 1933, the National Industrial Recovery Act, Section 7(a), was enacted and gave unions the right to collectively bargain, and union organizers once again tried to enroll workers. Conflict arose between local labor leaders in Chicago pressing for industrial union-ism and those with the AFL, which resisted the indus-try-wide approach. In 1936, some members separated from the AFL and formed the Packinghouse Workers Organizing Committee (PWOC) as a step to becoming a CIO member union. Because the worker's hostility against Armour was greatest, that packer was targeted. The PWOC sought a national contract, rather than a local one, so that Armour could not break strikes by shipping work from one factory to another. Also, it demanded increased wages, improved working conditions, an end to discrimination against Black people and modified work speed-up regulations.[30]

Catholic Workers and a few neighborhood priests were critical to the organizing efforts. Despite intimidation and violence by packinghouse management, the PWOC efforts progressed.[31] Frank McCarthy, a CIO organizer, stopped by the *Chicago Catholic Worker* office to talk about unionism and noted how important the friendliness of the priests had been to the effort. "'You'd be surprised how much effect a sermon on the encyclicals can have toward waking up the sleepy Catholic worker to get into the union,'" McCarthy noted. He added that the help of a Polish daily paper edited by a priest, the vocal support of Fr. John Hayes, and seminarians who volunteered at St Joseph House were invaluable. The *Chicago Catholic Worker* supported the CIO as the best hope for better working conditions and told packinghouse workers to read the encyclicals and join the union.[32] The paper's words were backed up by deeds; Marciniak and other Catholic Workers joined the pickets for the PWOC. During one incident, Marciniak was arrested for leafletting and the police carted him off to the station in a paddy wagon. This incident gave him unofficial union credibility in his future endeavors.[33]

The PWOC made progress with Armour, but it wanted formal recognition of its bargaining rights. Armour's intransigence prompted the PWOC to summon a policy convention. Young Marciniak was among the sixteen thousand delegates and observers who jammed the Chicago Coliseum in anticipation of a speech by John L. Lewis, the leader of the coal miners' union and driving force behind the CIO. Bishop Sheil, despite admonitions not to appear and threats on his life by powerful conservative labor officials and industrialists, joined Lewis on stage to demonstrate the alliance of labor and the Chicago Catholic Church.[34] In a short, ringing speech Sheil stated the Pope's position on the right to collective bargaining, a living wage, and the necessity for unions. Also, he cautioned workers to avoid violence and pursue industrial relations peace.[35] Years later Marciniak happily recalled Sheil's courage and the speech's importance in siding the Church with unions.[36] The convention unanimously authorized a strike if the company refused to meet with union officials.

Catholic Workers sided with the industrial workers at the expense of alienating Catholic leaders in the business community; they believed in Peter Maurin's aphorism that "rugged individualism" made "ragged individuals." A 1939 *Chicago Catholic Worker* editorial referred to John Steinbeck's *Grapes of Wrath*, noting that patently un-Christian individualism had seeped into the nation's philosophy, economics, and social relations, and even into its churches. Christians had forgotten Christ's message that He was the vine all others were the branches, that He came for all humankind, and what people did for the least of His children they did for Him. This conviction about the moral unity of all as enunciated in the doctrine of the Mystical Body of Christ drove the members of the St. Joseph House of Hospitality to be radical in their view of social solutions and to devote themselves to service to the poor and victims of the economic system.[37]

Between 1938 and the December 1941 attack on Pearl Harbor, the *Chicago Catholic Worker* sided with labor unions, alerted readers to the issues in strikes, and encouraged and supported boycotts. It challenged its wealthy readers to treat all employees with dignity and fairness and called on union leaders to solve internecine conflicts and to end the separation of the skilled and industrial unions as antithetical and impractical to solving workers' problems. The paper was a constructive force for change through its efforts to educate workers so that they might take the place of the communist union leaders.[38] During those years with the Chicago Catholic Worker, Marciniak also helped in the formation of Chicago's ACTU, he taught in the labor schools set up by Bishop Sheil,[39] and supported boycotts of the city's finest merchants for paying subsistence wages and for their practices of racial discrimination and anti-Semitism.[40]

Marciniak's idealism and activism were tempered. He knew that the road to success would be a long one requiring willingness to "earn leadership the hard way of patient continuous service." The *Chicago Catholic Worker* acknowledged that communists controlled the policies of some unions and noted that Catholics, now awakened to the Church's social teachings, had little influence because they had not served in the union trenches. It warned that ambitious Catholics who tried to "muscle in from the top and impose their ideas" too often blundered and became a "discredit to the Church's interest in labor."[41]

THE CATHOLIC LABOR ALLIANCE

When St. Joseph House of Hospitality closed in December 1941, Marciniak soon undertook another initiative to sustain his economic and social justice mission. He directed his energy to creating a new enterprise that would pursue peace by making sure that the rights and needs of workers were known, supported, and respected. Even though the breadlines had faded, the conditions of workers were still problematic. He wanted to build on the ideas of ACTU but wanted a wider base from which to advance labor's cause. Marciniak conceived of an alliance of labor *and* professionals unrestricted by religious affiliation.

Appealing to those familiar with his past accomplishments he secured funds to begin the Catholic Labor Alliance (CLA) and its publication, *Work*, in July 1943.[42] Although not formally an Archdiocese of Chicago entity, the CLA had the tacit blessings of Archbishop Samuel Stritch because Rev. Daniel Cantwell, the CLA chaplain, ran interference for the organization. Rev. Joseph Morrison, Rector of Holy Name Cathedral, gave CLA free rent in the former sewing room located on the top floor of a Cathedral High School building at Chicago and State Streets. The location was convenient, but the four flights of stairs provided a workout for the youthful editor. He sometimes skipped lunch just to avoid climbing the stairs again.[43]

The first edition of *Work* announced CLA's mission: "to work for democracy at home as well as abroad" and to cooperate with all wage earners in its realization. Marciniak invited all those interested in pursuing a "democratic and just America" guided by the norms of economic morality outlined by the Vatican and pledged "to work for democracy at home as well as abroad and to cooperate with wage earners for the realization of their objectives." CLA's founders were spurred on by communistic influences in the labor movement and the rapacity of certain businesses, both of which threatened to affect the stability of the nation. Because labor unrest threatened the war effort, the rights of labor were "shackled" by federal legislation such as the Smith-Connally Act (1943),[44] which posed a threat to "fair play in a democratic and just America."[45] The Alliance sought to work out in America a socio-economic order according "to the universally applicable principles" of *Rerum Novarum* and *Quadragesimo Anno*. *Work* would be politically non-partisan; and, Marciniak explained, it neither would form a third labor movement to disrupt existing AFL or CIO unions."[46]

Marciniak's conviction that workers' organizations were still the "paramount prerequisite for industrial peace" informed the CLA's mission. Industrial democracy and peaceful industrial relations were, he believed, "only a dream" because merely twenty-five percent of the workers were organized and had yet to secure collective bargaining rights. The bloody record of America's industrial history gave slight hope of a mature industrial social order until union membership was both expected and accepted. Further, *Work* alleged that most mainstream newspapers misinformed and confused workers rather than helped them and, for this reason, it planned to "teach rank and file workers with a program of education and at the same time to bring the rights of the workers to those who are uninformed about these rights." CLA held, he explained, "the best interests of capital and labor are served by a mutual recognition of each other's rights, as a basis for cooperation and industrial progress.... Industrial peace on just terms is the goal to strive for."[47]

Work outlined CLA's program: 1) a newspaper dedicated to covering and analyzing news that affected workers, 2) schools to educate workers, and 3) a commitment to apply the principles of the papal encyclicals to social and economic problems. The labor schools facilitated collective bargaining by training workers to represent their own interests and understand their employer's. This education was a pressing need because, outside the Communist circles, it was practically non-existent in Chicago. Marciniak respected the successes of ACTU in New York and Detroit, however, the CLA never became an ACTU affiliate, even though Marciniak did attend its annual meetings. The heavy emphasis by some ACTU chapters on Catholic voting blocks, anti-communism, and close alliance with the AFL were an obstacle to Marciniak's broader goals. He wanted CLA to be a more inclusive entity open to all religions with unionists and managers communicating with each other to advance understanding and partnership. He believed that exclusion of owners and managers would slow prospects for genuine progress in the struggle for justice.[48]

Work would provide a broad range of issues that directly and indirectly affected worker welfare. Marciniak pledged to cover not just union issues but news on such topics as the "plight of the sharecroppers, the suppression of the Farm Security Administration, the taxing of public housing projects, [because] all of these may be in a real sense workers' problems."[49] The paper covered both local and national labor disputes, economic injustice, racial discrimination in the workplace, union programs, and leadership changes and the divide between industrial and trade unions. Finally, it carefully monitored the economy, tracking inflation and worker incomes and public policy topics such as housing, national health care and urban renewal—all matters that affected the workers' quality of life. The new publication was distributed by volunteers at factory gates and to those on picket lines, carted by the bundle to Catholic high schools and parishes, and mailed to subscribers.[50] Under his guidance circulation for *Work* grew to 15,000 copies monthly through street corner sales and subscriptions that were local and national.

BROTHER MARCINIAK

Marciniak began his labor career on the picket lines in 1938 leafleting for the Chicago Newspaper Guild and continued his connections with the Guild after founding *Work*.

In September 1943 he joined the Guild and was issued membership card No. 20013.[51] He was a fully participating guildsman. He was far from being a "pie card" member, the union slang of derision used to describe employees who used their card only to make a living and did not support union principles. For seventeen years Marciniak served in a variety of roles in both the local and the national newspaper union and enjoyed the fraternal regard of his fellow members. From this affiliation he experienced first-hand the challenges the labor movement faced, the benefits of comradeship, and the opportunity to network locally, nationally, and internationally.

While launching CLA and teaching at Loyola, he became an organizer for Chicago's Guild and set to work convincing all newspaper employees of whatever classifications to join the Guild. In 1947, Marciniak was elected Vice President of the Guild as well as elected to its eight-person delegation to the American Newspaper Guild's (ANG) national convention. At the Fourteenth Annual Convention, delegate Marciniak was elected to serve on the Finance Committee. In succeeding conventions, he was elected to serve on committees and chaired the Constitution Committee. The latter was appropriate for he had risen frequently to make points of order on procedural matters and gathered applause for clarifying and improving critical resolutions. He was never shy to speak his mind even if it were to oppose resolutions made by ANG's presidents.[52]

At the ANG convention at the Sir Francis Drake Hotel in San Francisco in 1948, "Brother Marciniak" (all delegates used the fraternal address on the convention floor) began to establish his leadership when he urged the delegates to support Secretary of Commerce W. Averell Harriman's request to release the Guild's president to serve as Labor Information Specialist in Europe to garner support for the Marshall Plan. Marciniak told the delegates that three weeks before the convention, he had attended a meeting of CIO representatives in an "off the record" meeting soliciting the Guild aid to help "determine the political and economic character of Western Europe."[53] He emphasized to applause that releasing their president was "an honor and opportunity for the American Newspaper Guild." In 1952, Harriman addressed the ANG convention to thank the delegates for helping to limit communist influence in Europe through the work of their president's service as the Labor Information Specialist, stating: "I think it very doubtful the journalist unions of western Europe would have broken away to form a free International Federation of Journalists [if it were not for the service of the ANG president], and that has had a vital effect on newspaper reporting in Europe."[54]

From 1949 through 1953, Marciniak served as Executive Vice President of the Chicago Newspaper Guild, ever trying to increase membership. He had successes with the Chicago *Sun-Times* and Chicago *Daily News* with nearly 600 members combined. One of his responsibilities was to serve as mediator and contract negotiator. His greatest nemesis was Robert McCormick, the powerful publisher of the Chicago *Tribune* who used his in-house unions to thwart Guild efforts. Regarded by fellow unionists as a "fire eater,"[55] Marciniak was called upon to negotiate a contract with the *Wall Street Journal*, which had recently purchased the Chicago *Journal of Commerce*. He was ready to fight and grew red-faced when his demand for a substantial pay increase was immediately rejected only to respond a couple of minutes later "we have a contract." To Marciniak's surprise the business paper's publisher believed the Chicago compensation scale was low and had proposed to exceed Marciniak's demand. For once he did not have to fight.[56]

Marciniak's work as a contract negotiator extended beyond a quest for a living wage. In 1954 he called for specific language in the ANG's collective bargaining policy to prohibit discrimination based upon race, religion, or creed. ANG should be consistent with the CIO's non-discrimination policy and make it explicitly clear to publishers that the Guild's commitment to that principle was integral to all contacts, he emphasized[57] Two years later he seconded the resolution of the Human Rights Committee to "bind publishers to human rights in hiring" and stressed the need for locals to incorporate the language in their contracts.[58]

Not only was Brother Marciniak extremely sensitive to due process in contract negotiations, but he also demanded the same in the Guild's relationship with its own staff and defended employees against arbitrary administrators. Ordinarily cool and collected, he often was the one who would call for a ten-minute parliamentary recess so people could sit down and calmly discuss solutions rather than talking on the floor and solving nothing.[59] Yet, when he served as an advocate for a staffer's trial held in evening session of an ANG convention, his patience failed him. He protested that he had not been given adequate time to prepare the defense, as well as being forced to gulp down his pea soup and sandwich and leave his pie "unfinished." He had been piqued earlier in the session when denied the microphone to secure clarifications on staff arbitration. Rising to his full

5'8" height Marciniak pealed, "I am not a midget." He would not be ignored when it came to defending the underdog or Robert's Rules of Order.[60]

When he married Virginia in 1953, Marciniak wanted a consistent source of income and relinquished his duties at the Chicago Newspaper Guild to serve as full-time editor of *Work*. However, he sought and won an at-large membership that would put him on the governing board of the ANG. His campaign flier highlighted his record, including: walking the picket line during the Hearst Strike of 1938; six years as Vice President of the Chicago Local; four years as an organizer for the Chicago Local securing contracts for the workers in the *Wall Street Journal's* Chicago office, commercial employees of the Chicago *Daily News* and the *Milwaukee Sentinel*; his experience negotiating for papers in Chicago and Milwaukee and smaller Guilds in Sheboygan, Wisconsin, Waukegan and Joliet, Illinois and Gary, Indiana; and his service as a six time delegate to the ANG. He promised an aggressive agenda to double membership in the next decade, work more closely with other white-collar unions, build administrative capacity in more locals and "devise programs for ANG tailored for 1953 and for a newspaper union rather than rely on trade union practices devised to meet 1890 problems."[61] He was elected and continued to make strategy and policy contributions until 1960.

THE TAFT-HARTLEY LAW

During WWII, labor and management cooperation improved to support war production. Individual interests were subordinated to the collective interest of patriotism.[62] However, when the war ended, workers realized that they had worked long and hard but had not shared in the profits as had their employers. In the effort to recover wages lost to inflation and to secure improved working conditions, industrial relations tensions increased as did the number of strikes. In response, the National Association of Manufacturers (NAM) led an effort to change the New Deal labor laws that had empowered employees and sought to return a freer hand to management. Working with Representative Fred Hartley and Senator Robert Taft, NAM drafted and secured the introduction of legislation that would roll back the rights and recognition that labor unions had achieved.[63] The battle over the Taft-Hartley law and the aftermath of its passage prompted Marciniak's spirited response.

In May 1947, Marciniak called for President Harry Truman to veto the labor bill and called for a joint congressional commission to study *"the underlying causes of labor trouble and to prescribe remedies for proven abuses."*[64] Using techniques learned from labor and community organizers, he criticized the Taft-Hartley law and its backers by lambasting specific organizations and corporate leaders.[65] He identified NAM as the "enemy," personalized it, and cast it in its most threatening form. Marciniak criticized the trade association's rank duplicity, editorializing that the manufacturers falsely claimed their goal was to stop abuses when their real intention was to stamp out organized labor. The bill sought to "whittle down" protections in the New Deal Wagner and LaGuardia legislation and he warned that if NAM got its way "union security will be wiped out, national unions will be weakened, collective bargaining will be short circuited." Even though NAM stated it wanted "equality," its proposals clearly favored management. *Work* recited the words of an unidentified labor advocate: "the only place to find that kind of labor management peace was in Alcatraz."[66] Marciniak cautioned readers about the NAM tactics to mold public opinion through its "expertise in propagandizing." NAM's advertising and publicity budget of $3 million was used to run a series of ads in 73 daily papers with a circulation of more than 23 million and 92 weeklies, 113 radio stations.[67]

Work exposed the incongruities of NAM's position and took Congress to task for having a double standard of thundering against labor monopolies, on one hand, and soft-pedaling the dangers of economic monopoly that threatened democracy, on the other. Marciniak supplied data by industry: 45 of the largest transportation corporations controlled 92 percent of the business; 20 banks controlled 27% of all loans and investments; 200 of the largest non-financial corporations controlled 52% of all corporate assets; three auto companies controlled 89% of the industry; and, most damning, 79 of the 100 largest corporations were indicted or under federal investigation for monopolistic practices. In major economic sectors, competition was dead, and monopoly and oligopoly reigned. *Work* told its readers that the 80th Congress' failure to regulate big business anti-competitive practices "can only mean that the Senate and House of Representatives publicly pay homage to "free enterprise" but privately pledge allegiance to industrial and financial dictatorship.[68]

As Congress considered overriding Truman's veto of the Taft-Hartley legislation in June 1947, Marciniak was at an ANG convention speaking in support of a resolution calling on the House and Senate to sustain the veto.[69] After Congress overrode the veto, he took another tack and challenged all the parties to work together for industrial peace. Specifically, Marciniak called on government to honor its obligation to fairly administer the language of the law and urged the president to appoint officials to the National Labor Relations Board (NLRB) who both understood labor relations and were friendly to organized labor. He cautioned employers not to use the law as a green light to push workers around. Rather, he urged corporations to resolve disputes in collective bargaining, warning that using law as a club would create long-term employee "distrust and suspicion." His most pointed words were for unions. Organized labor must work within the framework of the legislation and not encourage protest strikes and political work stoppages. Rather, he also exhorted labor to test the constitutionality of the new law and get out the vote for candidates sympathetic to worker rights. Finally, he pleaded for an end to the disunity between the AFL and CIO's 60,000 member unions suggesting that their split may well have given Congress the opportunity to pass the law.[70]

On the first anniversary of the Taft-Hartley law, *Work* reported on its impact. While there had been fewer strikes, the National Labor Relations Board had to double its staff to manage a record case load. Most troubling was the one-sided application of the law: twenty-two of the twenty-four injunctions sought were against unions and the NLRB gave priority only to the cases against unions—not one brought by labor against management. *Work* concluded by quoting Rev. Charles Owen Rice writing in the *Pittsburgh Catholic*: "The frighteningly evil thing about this law is that while pretending to be in the public interest, while professing to 'protect' the worker from union leaders, it deprives the public of protection which a strong union movement provides in our corporation-dominated industrial system."[71]

The following year, Marciniak editorialized against Taft-Hartley as a "roadblock to social progress and justice" and concluded, "Let's remove it and get on with the businesses of building an economic and political democracy."[72] This conclusion was a succinct statement of Marciniak's belief about the restrictive labor law. He held tightly to the conviction that all deserved social and economic justice and without them America would never achieve its potential as a democracy. He persisted in his opposition when the American Newspaper Guild met in Columbus, Ohio, the capital of Senator Taft's home state. Brother Marciniak called for a suspension of rules to take up a resolution on the Taft-Hartley law. Representing the Chicago delegation, he noted the group was in position to speak on the effects of the Taft-Hartley law upon labor relations and trade unionism in the country. "We have a strike in the City of Chicago that has lasted eighteen months. We have 1500 printers out on the bricks, a concrete example before our doorsteps of the effect of a piece of legislation on trade unionism." Marciniak then brought before the Convention a resolution he had helped to draft on behalf of the Chicago delegation and prefaced it with: "I don't think I have to make any long speech as to why the law should be repealed." He just read the resolution:

> Two years of experience under the Taft-Hartley law have proved to the American Newspaper Guild that it is a law which was designed to, and in fact has, burdened and oppressed labor in its normal and legitimate operations. The law has seriously interfered with the Guild's effort to extend the benefits of collective bargaining to unorganized employees, and with the improvement, even the maintenance of the economic standing of the working newspapermen.
>
> We are convinced that the Taft-Harley Act is an utterly impossible foundation on which to build sound and beneficent labor relations. It is not designed to that end. Patchwork amendments will not alter its basic nature. The Taft-Hartley Act must be destroyed, root and branch and the principles of the Wagner Act restored.
>
> That can be accomplished only by the passage of the Thomas-Lesinski Bill without crippling amendments which reenact Taft-Hartleyism in fact if not in name.[73]

The resolution concluded with a call for the ANG's full support of the Thomas-Lesinski bill without amendments and sent it to the Senate and House of Representatives.[74] The Thomas-Lesinski bill, however, died in Congress.

THE STEEL STRIKES
OF 1952 AND 1959

In the post-war years, an ongoing theme in *Work* was the failure of worker's wages to reflect their contribution to production. Using U.S Bureau of Labor statistics, the paper emphasized that when inflation occurred workers lost purchasing power, as corporations raised their prices and increased profits. Between 1939 and 1947 worker wages increased 121 percent while corporate profits after tax increased 265 percent.[75] *Work* particularly pointed out the imbalances it observed in the steel industry. The industry's pricing was most critical to inflation control because its output was used in 40 percent of all manufactured goods. In January 1950, *Work* called for an investigation of U.S. Steel Corporation (USS), the nation's largest producer. The major producers led by USS had raised prices and thereby drove up consumer prices. The paper's vigorous support for the congressional investigation emphasized that there was "no justification for such a price boost at the present time" and it threatened an "inflationary price boost."[76]

Work called on Congress, newspapers, and public opinion to unite in a campaign to compel a price rollback. Backed by financial data, the paper listed reasons for its position. Marciniak placed a photo of the prosperous United States Steel executive, Benjamin F. Fairless, on the front page and laid out the rationale: the company had made more than $133 million in after tax profits and now wanted to add $80 million more. He rejected Fairless' justifications for the increase explaining that government studies indicated that slated production innovations would lower costs.[77]

Marciniak raised a fundamental moral question and challenged Fairless to address it. Fairless had admitted that steel demand was great, and *Work* asked him if he had the right to "make as much money as it [the steel industry] possibly can without any thought as to what these high prices and high profits will mean to the general welfare?" The allied question was whether industry has a "moral obligation to take a cut in profits when a price increase might unbalance the country's economic system?" Answering its own questions, the paper responded: "Our position is that Big Steel's high profits should be limited by the common good. We see no emergency which could force U.S. Steel to boost its prices."[78]

When the United States committed to fight communism in Korea in June 1950, President Truman attempted to control prices, wages, and raw materials. His early efforts failed to manage the cost of consumer goods and housing when resources were diverted to rearmament. He created a new agency to coordinate wage and price controls. Steel workers determined to prevent a repeat of the WWII scenario that resulted in inequities with workers' wage increases below the inflation rate and corporate profits greater than that rate. Their unions choose an industry-wide strategy, rather than a company-by-company approach, to secure wage increases.

In January 1952 as the prospect of a protracted steel strike loomed, *Work*'s associate editor, Robert Senser, explained the issues in the dispute in a feature, "What Steel Dispute is All About." He contended the price of steel was the central issue. The workers sought a raise to catch up with inflation and to reflect their own contribution to the rise in productivity. Senser reported that United States Steel's Fairless declared he would not bargain collectively. Fairless preferred a decision by Truman's recently created federal Wage Stabilization Board (WSB) allowing the steel producers to raise prices to cover the direct and indirect costs of a wage increase. When WSB's head, Roger L. Putnam, denied steel's request to tie a price increase to any wage increases but offered an avenue for a minor increase, Senser agreed and cited a government study showing the industry could offer workers a 30 to 40 cents per hour increase, meet all expenses, and still make a "'fair and equitable'" profit.[79]

As the likelihood of a strike loomed, the Catholic Labor Alliance stepped up its economics education efforts. In April, Marciniak shared his perspective to help citizens make up their own minds on the conflict that threatened the nation's war effort. Americans were fortunate in that government agencies had done independent studies to judge the merits of disputes on wages and prices and make specific proposals to settle the conflict without wrecking price and wage controls. He noted that the federal Office of Price Stabilization determined the steel industry's proposed increases were excessive and appropriately denied the manufacturers' request for large price increases. Marciniak believed the Wage Stabilization Board had authorized a "reasonable compromise" because anticipated worker productivity would benefit the industry.[80]

In spring 1952, the CLA's annual Msgr. John A. Ryan Forum[81] addressed the issues of inflation and industrial relations. The March forum was entitled "How Can We Win the War on Inflation" and the May session, "Bridging the Gap Between Management and Labor." Marciniak had secured none other than WSB's Roger L. Putnam to give the last lecture.[82] By the time Putnam took the stage at the Morrison Hotel to address improving industrial relations in April, President Truman had taken the unprecedented action of seizing the nation's steel mills to ensure production and prevent a labor strike.[83]

Immediately two steel companies filed papers in the United States district court to prevent the seizure and, while the legal battles ensued, they launched a war of words to sway public opinion.[84] Headlines compared Truman to a dictator and numerous editorials called for his impeachment and the introduction of federal legislation giving government the power, not to just delay, but to end a strike.

As the publicity war raged, *Work* provided a distinctly justice-based perspective. In May, it ran a full-page advertisement mimicking the steel companies' advertisements that had featured editorial copy from several national dailies that condemned the seizure. *Work's* ad reprinted editorials from Catholic publications with the notice: "This is not an advertisement of the 'Steel Companies in the Wage Case.' It is published in the public interest by *WORK*." Among the papers cited was the *Pittsburgh Catholic*, which noted that the unions had earnestly sought to avoid a strike by postponing it several times and agreeing to accept the decision of the stabilization agency while the steel companies had acted jointly to reject a settlement because they could not dictate terms. It concluded:

> Seizing the plants was a drastic move, but no more drastic than the situation demanded. Some persons call the seizure 'socialistic,' but this is inflammatory

INSISTING ON WORKER RIGHTS

nonsense. The plants remain the property of the owners; the profits go to them; and the government control will be withdrawn as soon as the strike issues are settled, and continuous operation assured. The whole thing is the exercise of the government's right and duty to protect the welfare of the people.[85]

In June 1952, the Supreme Court ruled the seizure unconstitutional, and the workers walked out. The economic impact was soon felt as steel reserves were denied for consumer goods and directed to production of tanks, trucks, and mortar shells. The unions tried a divide-and-conquer strategy with minor successes, but Big Steel stood by its pledge to limit pay and weaken the unions. Consistently, Work supported the unions and pointed to inconsistencies in the approach of Big Steel.[86]

During July, hundreds of thousands of manufacturing workers were laid off for lack of steel. Many businesses struggled, even farming. Produce rotted in fields because manufacturers had no steel to make the cans necessary to preserve food. Most significantly, on July 23 the U.S. Army had to close its largest shell-making facility for want of steel. Truman had enough; the next day he ordered Philip Murray, President of the United Steelworkers of America, and Fairless into his Oval Office and escorted them to the Cabinet Room to settle their differences. That afternoon the two leaders came to terms that were the same as the union had sought at the start of the strike.

When the strike ended, Marciniak angrily wrote that it had been an unnecessary tragedy that dragged on too long. In particular, he chided Big Steel for its "gentlemen's agreement" forbidding individual settlements by smaller companies. He also chastised the press, radio, and television with trying to shape public opinion by withholding information or misinforming the public and contended: "Had the public been given the truth, it would never have tolerated the way Big Steel held out against the unions for higher steel prices."[87] When the dust settled, Marciniak reported on Murray and Fairless' joint peace mission to those in the mills observing that the strike had not been a "picnic" and the task of bringing harmony and cooperation would not be either.[88] Events would prove Marciniak to be correct.

In 1956, there was a repeat of the steel worker/management conflict, however, it was briefer than the previous strike. Management was quicker to make concessions on wages, health and pension benefits unemployment compensation and worker protections but it paved the way to major conflicts in 1959. Management recouped the costs of its concessions with price increases but resolved to take back elements it had conceded. It focused especially on Section 2 (b) of the industry-wide contract, which limited management's power to adjust work rules, including the number of workers per task and the use of new equipment that would reduce hours and employees.

Prior to the 1959 negotiations, steel producers hired Madison Avenue public relations agencies to trumpet their concern about inflation in the hope of swaying public opinion and gaining a bargaining advantage. Further, they adopted a much more formal approach to negotiating by using attorneys and engineers to bargain and abandoned their previous use of plant managers who would fraternize with union members away from bargaining table. An industry weekly noted: "This is an apparent effort to make up quickly what was bargained away in the past 18 years."[89]

In response, the steelworkers' union hired its own publicists in the hope of garnering support to protect its workers from the threats of automation and work-rule speed-up actions that threatened to shrink the number of jobs of its 500,000 members. Bargaining positions hardened and the contract ended on July1, 1959 triggering a lengthy strike which disrupted steel production and all steel reliant industries.

Once again, *Work* stood with the workers. The strike was not simply an issue of a 15-cent hourly wage increase. The paper pointed out the manufacturers could afford this since they had shown a profit of 8.7percent even while operating at only 60 percent capacity. While workers sought a share in the profits, arguing that these profits resulted from their productivity, more importantly, they wanted job protection. In the previous ten years, sixteen per cent of the steel workers' jobs had been eliminated and continued productivity increases threatened to cause more job losses. The union did not directly fight technological change but sought to cushion its impact on the workforce.[90]

Work contended that management must not unilaterally amend work rules and praised Kaiser Steel, the only company to break with fellow steelmakers by negotiating a settlement that included a solution to the work rule conflicts. Marciniak penned a feature calling for management to learn from Kaiser's use of panels of management and labor representatives empowered to negotiate changes. The article also highlighted the constructive and preventative benefits of mutual agreement committees in several other industries. Marciniak believed that the panels were the only solution to the growing industrial relations challenge posed by the impacts of automation. These negotiations, he emphasized, should be addressed early and away from the bargaining table.[91]

From July through early October 1959, the steel strike negotiations were fruitless and then collapsed when the union rejected management's proposal as "totally unacceptable".[92] The strike's crippling effects on the economy compelled President Dwight Eisenhower to invoke the eighty-day injunction provision of the Taft-Hartley Act to force workers back to the mills. Immediately, the union sought to have the Act declared unconstitutional. The Supreme Court upheld the law on November 7 and ended the 116-day strike.

The "cooling off period" imposed by the injunction gave breathing room to negotiate the strike issues but this was not a solution to on-going labor issues. Marciniak warned: "Collective bargaining in the steel industry has become bankrupt" and catalogued the staggering billions of dollars that the strike cost steelmakers, and the steel dependent auto industry, and the hundreds of thousands of workers idled. Further, he feared the injunction would end with workers once again going back to the picket lines and that the government would have to back compulsory arbitration to end the strike as well as lead to a pattern of interventions.[93] The anxious steelmakers realized that they needed to prevent government intervention in an election year. On January 15, a new short-term contract was agreed to that retained Section 2 (b) and gave a cost-of-living increase. The strike had no clear winner. Labor got work rule protections it wanted but it would take two years of wage gains to cover the losses suffered in the strike. Steelmakers, while able to recover losses with price increases, found that they now had to face new competition. American steel buyers had tapped foreign sources of steel during the strike and the European and Japanese competitors entered the United States market during the strike and would stay.

The Supreme Court decision to uphold the Taft-Hartley gave companies a weapon in their battles with unions. A Chicago *Tribune* editorial noted that the Taft-Hartley law was not the definitive answer to paralyzing strikes and continued: "A better way must be sought that will avoid the frightful losses, if possible, to do so. Meanwhile, the Taft law has shown that it is the only way yet devised of restoring industrial peace when stubborn men are reluctant to agree on terms."[94]

Marciniak disagreed. More than ever, he held to the belief that labor and management must work together. Before and during the 1959 strike, Marciniak had argued for a national "summit conference" of union and management leaders away from the bargaining table.[95] His urging did not move the White House to act; it tried to keep a distance. Soon after the strike, he and others who had pressed for a collaborative path to industrial peace got their wish. Secretary of Labor, James P. Mitchell, announced a White House conference to be followed by "conferences on industry levels where employer representatives and employee representatives can sit down outside of the bargaining table and talk about common problems in the industry." For this Marciniak was pleased.[96]

LATER LABOR ENDEAVORS

Unions had reached their peak of influence by the 1950s but faced other major problems. They came under attack for fostering featherbedding, corruption, and racketeering,[97] inefficiency, and the migration of jobs to southern states supporting "right to work" legislation and a new generation of workers who seemed unwilling to sacrifice their spare time to keep the labor movement alive. Marciniak knew from his service on the American Newspaper Guild and more than twenty-three years engaged in the labor movement that challenges lay ahead. In March 1960, he drafted a thoughtful *Work* feature "Yesterday's Goals Outmoded: How to Chase Union Blues," which he sought to stem the gloomy talk about the future of unions. He argued that the prophets of doom made two mistakes. The first was looking backwards to the old days of militant unionism and the second was the failure to try to anticipate the needs of the 1960s and 1970s. Reflective of the changing times was the Catholic Labor Alliance's change of name to the more inclusive name, the Catholic Council on Working Life (CCWL).

Marciniak produced an annotated list of fifteen actions based on a democratic rather than an autocratic philosophy of union management, an expanded vision which would aggressively expand recruitment among white collar and lower paid workers and pay more attention to the workplace problems rather than internal and partisan politics. His greatest emphasis was on restoring the creative aspect of work and focusing on the dignity that comes from "creating good and useful things, in serving the people who buy the goods and services, in working with responsibility." He

98

continued, "If unions can reinstate a pride in work, they will have done much to earn the loyalty of workingmen."[98] His was not a romantic view of work. Rather, it was that of an idealist who conceived of work as a life calling that enabled a person to participate in the completion of God's creation. This would be a major theme in his future endeavors.

Marciniak undertook one of his final projects for the Catholic Council on Working Life in 1959 by the convening of a national conference on migrant labor. As early as 1946 he reported on the abuses suffered by migrant labor in *Work*. When few people paid attention, he told of Puerto Rican women who worked sixty-four hours a week as domestics for fourteen dollars and never earned enough to buy warm clothes for the knifing cold Chicago winters nor to repay the labor agency commission charges for airfare.[99] Likewise, the paper exposed the plight of agricultural workers who followed the seasonal harvests of produce, grains, and cotton. Marciniak noted that the agricultural migrants were unprotected by minimum wage legislation, ineligible for workers' compensation, and relegated to housing in cramped camps; and their children were unschooled and became members of labor crews in the first decade of life. America's migrant workers also paid a price in depressed wages and often had to wait to the end of the growing season to be paid. In 1950, the conditions in Michigan were so bad the Puerto Rican government appropriated $117,400 for the aid of beet workers and prompted a federal investigation that resulted in higher wages and food preparation services for workers during the harvest season.[100].

In November 1959, the Catholic Council on Working Life convened the National Conference to Stabilize Migrant

Labor, bringing together 300 growers and canners, educators, union leaders, heads of community associations, and
federal, state, and local officials. The intent was to have frank
and full discussions by all the participants in the effort to
improve the conditions of the half million Americans and
half million Mexican migrant laborers. The sessions included
a discussion of the economics of migrant labor by a University of California, Berkley agricultural economist, moral
issues by Archbishop Robert E. Lucey, a former member
of the Presidential Commission on Migratory Labor, and
practical issues by a series of growers, public welfare agency
staffers, and public officials, including James P. Mitchell,
the U.S. Secretary of Labor. The conference was conceived
to "harmonize" various farm interests under the banner of
seeking the ways and means to provide "regular employment, steady income, stable family life and adequate labor
supply."[101] Marciniak hoped that having all the dominant
interests meet and discuss the issues that affected migrant
labor in one gathering it would lead to more comprehensive understanding of the issues and support for reforms at
the local and national level. At its conclusion the influential
labor advocate, Msgr. George Higgins, noted the conference
was "a step in the right direction but there is still a long way
to go."[102]

A summation of the conference proceedings by Marciniak entitled *Toward a National Policy for Migrant Labor*
was published in pamphlet format for broad distribution by
the CCWL to educate people on the economic, social, and
ethical issues relating to migrant workers and their labor.
The principal conclusion was that the immigrant worker
program needed to be revised and that federal protections

instituted for citizen migrants, including the right to organize and workers' compensation insurance, and health and safety protections.[103] As he hoped, national and local attention was directed to the plight of migrants through stories in newspapers, and reports on television and radio. Significantly, Chicago's Archbishop Albert G. Meyer, now cardinal designate, announced the establishment of a national office to protect and promote the welfare of Catholic migratory workers, making it a special priority of the American Catholic Church to care for the welfare of its poorest members.[104]

JOURNALIST AND TEACHER

Marciniak was an agitator and advocate. He was also a journalist and teacher who educated and challenged the workers on the streets and in factories as well as the priests in the rectories and the managers in their offices. Overtime, he added to his vocabulary the words of theologians, philosophers, and economists as he sought to define the issues and secure lasting change.

As a Catholic Worker, Marciniak believed in the importance of individual responsibility. However, as the forces of business became stronger and more united in the battles over labor legislation after World War II, Marciniak turned to political, sociological, and economic frames of reference more than the personalist lens emphasized by Dorothy Day. He realized workers could not win any battle without government support. His early engagements had been on the picket line fighting individual companies such as Hearst and Armour. His later ones became broader including the National Association of Manufacturers, Big Steel, and government policies that diminished worker rights. With the increasing power of large corporations, Marciniak saw an ever-growing sense of urgency for political action, including testing the constitutionality of laws in court, using the ballot box to overturn the anti-labor legislation, and supporting government interventions such as in the seizure of the steel mills.

Between 1938 and 1960, Marciniak was one with the working people in the bread lines, on the picket lines, at his desk composing headlines for *Work*, and influencing his own union. He fought for all workers so that they could have a decent life and the blessings of American Freedom. Unions with participatory governance offered the best hope for just outcomes and provided a counter to unfettered economic self-interest that was destructive of democracy. Marciniak's contributions to the fight for labor rights were both in word and action. His reasoned and passionate discussions of the moral and social issues raised by 20th century industrialization enlightened workers and managers. The organizations he created and forums he convened advanced economic justice. The engagement in the fight was for Marciniak a moral imperative and a social responsibility characterized by a mature optimism.

NOTES

1   *Work*, September 1945.
2   Ibid. and *Herald American* cited in "Work Trades Blows with Herald-American Editor," Ibid., October 1945.
3   Ibid.
4   Ibid.
5   https://www.papalencyclicals.net/leo13/l13rerum.htm.
6   Paragraphs 57-58, *Quadragesimo Anno* (May 15, 1931) | PIUS XI (vatican.va).
7   Shanabruch, *Chicago's Catholics*, pp. 128-154.
8   "Why A Paper?" *Chicago Catholic Worker*, August 1941.
9   Mundelein's speech to the Holy Name Society, January 2, 1938, cited in Kantowicz, p.208.
10 Aaron I. Abell, *American Catholic and Social Action: A Search for Social Justice, 1865-1950*, (University of Notre Dame Press, Notre Dame, Indiana, 1963); Steven M. Avella, *This Confident Church: Catholic Leadership and Life in Chicago 1940-1965* (University of Notre Dame Press, Notre Dame Indiana, 1992); and Kantowicz, *Corporation Sole*.
11 For an account of Catholic labor leaders see Kimball Baker, *Go to the Worker*, and Francis Joseph Sicius, "The Chicago Catholic Worker Movement 1936 to the Present" (unpublished doctoral dissertation, Loyola University, 1979) and "Young Man with a Cause."
12 Cogley served at *Commonweal* from 1949 to 1955 and *The New York Times* from 1965 to 1967.
13 See Abell, pp. 255-263 and Jay Dolan, *The American Catholic Experience: A History from Colonial Times to the Present* (Doubleday and Company, Garden City, New York, 1985), pp. 401-407.
14 "Wanted! Catholic Labor Leaders," Ibid., July 1938, p. 4. ACTU was founded by John Cort, a former Catholic worker, to educate and coordinate Catholic workingmen and women in the American labor movement. See Baker, pp. 53-83.

15 "Enough Rope," Ibid., September 1938.

16 "To the Poor...To Christ!," Ibid., November 1938, p. 2.

17 William Droel to author, August 2, 2021.

18 "Hearst Gets Them Coming and Going." See also: Harlan Drae-ger, "Determined to Unite," *Program Magazine Fifty Ninth Annual Convention, The Chicago Newspaper Guild* (July 1992), p. 8.

19 For information about Fr. Hayes and the Catholic Worker Movement see Baker, pp. 30-52.

20 "Slug Guild Pickets at Hearst Plant," Ibid., p. 1. (The account was written by Jack Gibbon Morris, a member of the Guild. In March, the paper explained this unusual action: "In order to give the striking workers a just hearing, denied them by more powerful sections of the press, we turned over these columns during the past two months to a striking reporter on the *Herald and Examiner*." Ibid, March 1939, p. 1.); "Nationwide Interest Aroused as Guild Strike Enters on Fourth Month, Ibid., March 1938, p. 3; and Barbara Warne Newell, *Chicago, and the Labor Movement: Metropolitan Unionism in the 1930's*, (University of Illinois Press, Urbana, Illinois,1961), pp.186-193.

21 Cited in "Guild Strike Gets Church Support," *Chicago Catholic Worker*, February 1939.

22 Ibid, March 1939. The following year, Marciniak attended the memorial for the Massacre at the Auditorium Theater and there met and established a friendship with Paul Douglas, a labor economist at the University of Chicago who became a Chicago alderman and U.S. senator.

23 "Strike Breaking Racket now on a Big Business Basis," March 1939.

24 Draeger, pp. 8-9.

25 Cited in "Nationwide Interest Aroused, as Guild Strike Enters on Fourth Month," Ibid., March 1939.

26 Ibid.

27 Cited "Bishop's Letter to Strikers," Ibid., April 1939.

28 "Newspaper Strike at Half Year Mark," Ibid., June 1939, p1 and Newell, p. 193.

29 P. David Finks, *The Radical Vision of Saul Alinsky*, (Paulist Press, New York, New York, 1984), pp. 14-15 and Dominic A. Pacyga, *Slaughterhouse: Chicago's Union Stock Yard and the World It Made*, (University of Chicago Press, Chicago, Illinois, 2015).

30 Newell, pp. 152-165.

31 "Victory at Yards Despite Terrorism," *Chicago Catholic Worker*, December 1938.

32 "CIO Organizer Pays Us a Visit," in Ibid., July 1939.

33 Dan Herr, "The Chicago Dynamo," *The Sign*, September 1962.

34 Sheil is reported to have had a bodyguard as his life was threatened. According to the account in the *Chicago Catholic Worker*, "Little does the general public know of the pressure that was brought upon the Bishop to prevent his speaking at the CIO mass meeting." The Chicago Federation of Labor, the Hearst papers and meat packers had publicly asked the bishop to decline the invitation; and in reports to the papers, it was revealed that in the days preceding the talk, His Excellency had constantly been besieged by anonymous threats to his life." See Kantowicz, pp. 195-196 and Sicius, pp. 159-164.

35 "Strike Threatens Yards as Armour and Co. Refuses to Bargain with Union" *Chicago Catholic Worker*, August 1939, and "A Month Marched...," Ibid.

36 Steven M. Avella interview with Msgr. Daniel Cantwell and Edward Marciniak, December 1983, p. 7. The Interview transcript is in the Interview Files, Archdiocese of Chicago Archives. The *Chicago Catholic Worker* expressed grave fear that violence would take place. Even though there was little doubt as to the PWOC election victory, it reiterated the bishop's plea to exhaust all peaceful means before calling a strike and pointedly referred to the Memorial Day Massacre of steelworkers in South Chicago just two years before. See: "Strike Threatens Yards." August 1939.

37 "'Rugged Individualism'" and 'Ragged Individuals,'" Ibid., August 1939.

38 "Catholic Union Leadership Must Be Earned: No Short Road to the Top," Ibid., November 1940.

39 One of the first Labor Schools met weekly at St. Joseph House of Hospitality.

40 Sicius, pp. 164-170.

41 "Catholic Union Leadership Must Be Earned: No Short Road to the Top," Ibid., November 1940.

42 Sicius, pp. 221-222.

43 Riegle Interview, p. 14, and Avella Interview with Cantwell and Marciniak, p. 3.

44 The Smith Connally Act allowed the federal government to seize and operate war production industries threatened by or on strike by labor unions and forbid unions from contributing to elections for federal offices.

45 "A Program of Action," July 1943 and Bob Senser, *Our Lady of the Sacred Heart*, "The Story of the Catholic Labor Alliance," (May 1949) reprinted pamphlet by CLA, Marciniak Papers, Shelf 1, Position 1.

46 "A Program of Action," p. 1-2.

47 Ibid.

48 Ibid. and Baker p. 128. Marciniak regularly attended the ACTU national meetings and sustained a lifelong connection with its founder, John Cort.

49 *Work*, "A program of Action," July 1943.

50 Numerous people who had volunteered in the CLA offices commented on the formative experience they had helping to get out the paper in letters they sent to Marciniak as part of the 1990 "All City Salute". See Marciniak Papers, Position 1, Shelf 2.

51 Marciniak's Guild membership card is attached to the copy of his letter of resignation in 1960. His membership card contained proof of his monthly payments until that date. Marciniak to Secretary-Treasurer Perlick, June 23, 1960, Shelf 1, Position 3.

52 See *Proceedings of the Fourteenth Annual Convention*, (1947) pp. 12, 20, 52-53, and 85-87 and *Proceedings of the Fifteenth Annual Convention* (1948).

53 *Proceedings of the Fifteenth Annual Convention* 1948, p. 48.

54 *Proceedings of the Twentieth Annual Convention (1953)*, p. 62.

55 Harlan Draeger, "Determined to Unite," Program Magazine of the 59th Annual Convention of the American Newspaper Guild, (July 1992), p. 8.

56 Cited in Ibid.

57 *Proceedings of the Twenty-first Annual Convention,* (1954), p. 110.

58 *Proceedings of the Twenty-second Annual Convention,* (1955), p. 57.

59 *Proceedings of the Twenty-first Annual Convention,* (1954), p 74.

60 *Proceedings of the Twenty-third Annual Convention,* (1956), pp 47-48, 57-92.

61 A flyer entitled "Chicago Newspaper Guild Committee for Marciniak," 1953. Marciniak Papers, Shelf 1, Position 3.

62 Industry councils were formed with labor unions and management working together to plan for production.

63 Philip Dray, *There Is Power in a Union: The Epic Story of Labor in America,* (Anchor Books, New York, New York, 2010), pp. 496-502.

64 "Congress Goes on the Union Busting Campaign, *Work,* May 1947. See Thomas R. Greene, "Catholic Views of Post-World War II Labor Legislation," *Journal of Church and State* (Spring, 1991) pp. 301 – 327.

65 Marciniak had been involved with the PWOC picketing and been actively involved with Saul Alinsky, the community organizing legend, in creation of the Back of the Yard's Neighborhood Council. Alinsky offered Marciniak a position, but he declined. John Cogley's future wife did work for the fiery organizer. The BYNC supported *Work* and advertised its support in the paper. Dan Herr, "The Chicago Dynamo," *Sign,* September 1962, p11-12; Robert Senser, "The Story of the Catholic Labor Alliance," reprint of *Our Lady of the Sacred Heart Magazine,* May 1949, Marciniak Papers, Shelf 1, Position 1.

66 *Work,* "Congress Goes on Union Busting Campaign," May 1947.

67 Ibid., June 1947.

68   "Congress Must Act to Limit Power of Huge Monopolies, June 1947, p. *Work* carried the fiery speeches and sermons of one of America's most vocal economic justice advocate, Archbishop Robert E. Lucey of San Antonio, for additional support. Lucey declared that the bill would not bring economic peace nor protect the worker rights to associate. The legislation would "hand cuff" labor, weaken unions by cutting wages and "'cut and chisel at liberties with impunity'" and grant new powers to government to issue injunctions that would not be effective. Referring to Europe's totalitarian regimes, the archbishop stated: "We have seen the results of government control abroad, and it always invites rebellion. Government should lead both labor and management in cooperative battle against depression, instead of treating the problem as a fight for spoils. "Archbishop Blasts Taft-Hartley Bill," Ibid., p. 5.

69   *Proceedings of the Fourteenth Annual Convention* (1947), p. 12.

70   "Labor Relations Under the Taft-Hartley Law," July 1947. Because of his work as a union organizer and delegate to the ANG, Marciniak was acutely aware of the conflicts between trade and industrial unions.

71   "About the Taft Hartley Law, It Deprives the Public of Protection," October 1948, p. 6. See also: "Taft-Harley Law-Six Week Later," Ibid., August,1947.

72   "A Law Can Go Too Far," January 1949. Marciniak did not tire of trying to expose flaws in the Taft Hartley law. He published a detailed summary of the report by the American Catholic Sociological Society characterizing the law as a "step backwards." The Society held the law was based upon repression rather than cooperation and led backwards to "'government by injunction for settlement of labor-management disputes.'" It hampered labor union organization and thus strengthened management's hand. Allowing management to seek an injunction in court to settle disputes was regarded as too powerful a weapon. See: "The Taft-Hartley Law Is a Step Backward," March 1949.

73 *Proceedings of the Sixteenth Annual Convention*, pp. 24-25.

74 Ibid., p. 25.

75 "What Is Happening to Uncle Sam's Economic System," October 1948. See also: "Facts on Wages and Profits," December 1947, and "Thirty-five years of Factory Worker's Wages – In Dollars and Purchasing Power," March 1948. Marciniak used graphs and cartoons to show readers the disparity in wages and profits so that the gap was visual as well as factual.

76 "U.S. Steel Should Be Investigated."

77 Ibid.

78 Ibid.

79 Ibid. Senser (1921-2015) was a graduate of Loyola University and served *Work* in the roles of reporter, associate editor, and editor. Thereafter, he worked as *Work*'s associate Editor and Editor. He continued his career in labor affairs as a labor attaché in the Foreign Service and sustained his concern for workers struggles, especially exposing sweatshop abuses in Asia. Retrieved July 16, 2021. https://adamsgreen.com/tribute/details/3494/Robert-Senser/obituary.html.

80 "A Citizen's Viewpoint on Steel," Ibid.

81 The CLA annually hosted forums at the city's major hotels to give Chicagoans an opportunity to hear national leaders, further its educational mission and to draw attention to its work.

82 "World Peace, Inflation '52 Ryan Forum Topics," Ibid., February 1952 and "Economic Stabilizer to Speak on Ryan Forum," Ibid., April 1952.

83 Truman had tried several tactics including convening union leaders and steel producers at the White House and turning the matter over to his stabilization agencies, but these efforts had failed. The president did not want temporary options such as provided by the Taft-Harley Law. Accordingly, when all prospects for resolution ended and the union notified the steel makers that it would call a nationwide strike, President Truman ordered the Secretary of Commerce to seize the mills to ensure steel production. "The seizure of steel," *New York Times*, April

13, 1952, *(1923-Current File)*. Retrieved from http://search. proquest.com/docview/112350856?accountid=28733.

84 Bruce E. Altschuler, "A Look Back at the Steel Seizure Case, *Journal of Supreme*; 2008 (Vol. 33, Issue 3) pp. 341-352, and Arthur H. Garrison, National Security and Presidential Power: Judicial Deference and establishing Constitutional Boundaries in World War Two and the Korean War," *Cumberland Law Review*, 208, (Vol. 39, Issue 3), pp. 660-667.

85 Cited in *Chicago Catholic Worke*r, May 1953.

86 See: "Why are the Big Steel Companies Holding Out?" Ibid., July 1, 1952. See also: Ibid., May 1952, p. 7.

87 "Lop-Sided News Reports Hinder Steel Settlement," Ibid August 1952. p. 1.

88 "Murray, Fairless Tour Mills on Peace Mission, Ibid., September 1952, p. 12. The costs had been great: the average steel worker had lost $600 in wages; 10,000,000 tons of steel had not been produced and prices of the metal increased more than $5.00 at ton.

89 Thomas Campbell, *Iron Age*, cited in *Work*, What Triggered the Big Steel Strike," September 1959.

90 "What Triggered the Big Steel Strike," Sept 1959, p3. See Jack Metzgar, *Striking Steel: Solidarity Remembered* (Temple University Press, Philadelphia, Pennsylvania, 2000), pp. 17-92.

91 "Lessons of the Strike: Fire Preventions Squads Needed for Labor Cries," November 1959.

92 "Talks Break Off in Steel Impasse," *New York Times*, October 6, summarizes the position of each side.

93 *Work*, "Bankruptcy May Bring Compulsory Arbitration," December 1959. The country's output in product and services had declined by $ 6 billion in only 77days of the strike measured in the third quarter. Steel companies lost more than $3 billion and auto production plummeted by 746,000 vehicles as manufactures laid off 200,000 workers for want of steel. The federal government lost $755 million of income taxes from

workers alone. *Chicago Tribune*, "Steel Strike Rips Economy Like H-Bomb," December 15, 1959.

94 "Who Won the Strike," January 5, 1960.

95 *Work*, March 1958. Marciniak emphasized that the management and labor leaders of substance should be invited to a presidential summit conference; further, he emphasized that professional spokespeople from the National Association of Manufactures and the AFL-CIO should be barred. He believed that the conference should be recognized as an "official" proceeding but that the officials would not officially represent anybody but themselves. Finally, he urged that such meetings to be off the record and that the attendees be charged with seeking "solutions other than compulsory arbitration." Ibid, "Bankruptcy May Bring Compulsory Arbitration," February 1960.

96 Cited in *Work*, "The White House Will Put These Heads Together," December 1960.

97 In the 1950s, *Work* devoted a substantial portion of its labor coverage to union leader corruption which ranged from racketeering and kickbacks and pension fund manipulation. Marciniak believed that workers had to become more involved and demand honesty. He was especially critical of the Teamster leadership and its corrupt practices. Only when the unions cleaned their own house, he argued would the threat of government limitations on unions be lessened.

98 *Work*, March 1960.

99 *Work*, "Slave Labor 1946 Style," Oct 1946; "Puerto Ricans Imported to Chicago for Slave Wages," January 1947, and "Employers Keep Importing Cheap Labor," February 1947.

100 *Work*, "Rich Harvest But Poor Pay for U.S. Migratory Farm Workers," September 1950 and "Sugar Beets Not So Sweet for Pickers," October 1950.

101 *Work*, "Migratory Labor Conference to Be Held in Chicago November 21 and 22," October 1959.

102 *Work*, November 1959 and "Growers, Unionists, and Public Seek Common Ground on Problems," December 1959; and *New York Times*, "Aid to Immigrants Urged," November 22, 1959.

103 (Chicago, 1960), the pamphlet is in the Marciniak Papers, Shelf 1, position 2.

104 *New York Times*, "Catholic Plan Aid to Immigrants," November 24, 1959; *Work*, "Focus on Migrants" December 1959.

Chapter 3

Advocating for
Economic Democracy

*In the long-run we are going to have to more than tinker
with the American economic engine;
we are going to have to overhaul it."*

Edward Marciniak[1]

Ed Marciniak faced challenges that come to all who
enter the public arena to advance a cause—be it income
equality, racial justice, environmental conservation, or others. His challenges came from those who regarded his ideas
as a threat to the status quo as well as those who regarded
him as too timid when radicalism was necessary to effect
change. Ed navigated in-and-around those allies who shared
part of his agenda and around opponents whose motivation
was not always what they said. His mission was to find the
surest path to the goal.

From the last years of the Great Depression through the
1950s, at a time when capitalism and communism were the

dominant ideological forces in the world, Marciniak developed a Catholic-based rationale for economic democracy founded on a partnership of workers, owners, and the public. While unwilling to engage in military combat in World War II, he did not shy away from a contest of words and wills in his mission to improve the condition of workers, even as the language and objectives of the battles between capitalists and communists changed. Employing the weapons of his analytical mind, acerbic tongue, and a network of political, religious, business, and union leaders, Ed helped shape the discussion of economic justice and influenced the development of practical solutions. He sought a reordering of society's priorities focused on the "common good" over individual benefit.

A Catholic position on capitalism and communism had been outlined by Pope Leo XIII in 1891 in the encyclical *Rerum Novarum* and became the framework for much of the Catholic discussion that was to follow for the next century. The pope argued for the right to private property as a means of securing a good life for individuals and against the state as the owner of all means of production. Conservative clergy relied on the encyclical to condemn communism, while progressive American Catholics relied on the text to guide their work for social reform and mount an effective challenge to the anti-religious tenants of socialism.

American bishops, such as Chicago's Archbishop James E. Quigley, denounced the irreligion of European forms of socialism yet supported unions.[2] Bishop Peter J. Muldoon of Rockford, who had been both chancellor of and auxiliary bishop in Chicago, served on the American Federation of Catholic Societies Social Service Commission and worked to ensure that Leo XIII's encyclical was widely circulated and applied.

When America entered World War I, Muldoon led the National Catholic War Council, which in 1919 issued "Social Reconstruction: A General Review of the Problems and Survey of Remedies," commonly known as the "Bishops' Program." It gave guidance for reforms both immediate and more distant. The Bishop's Program called for legislation that ensured a living wage for workers and protection of the rights of workers to deal with management through their own chosen representation. The program envisioned that workers would eventually have an ownership share of the means of production. This later proposal was based upon distributism, a late 19th century economic theory relying upon the principles enunciated in *Rerum Novarum* and supported and developed by influential British Catholic authors G.K. Chesterton and Hilaire Belloc. With the publication of Pius XI's *Quadragesimo Anno* in 1931, the theory gained added authority.[3]

JUSTICE AN ANTIDOTE
TO COMMUNISM

Ed Marciniak opposed communism and simultaneously challenged capitalism as it existed in America for being inconsistent with the teachings of the Catholic Church. He did not condemn capitalism; he called for its reformation. Large propertied interests, investor funds, and the traditional free enterprise system of unrestrained competition with the winner taking all were inconsistent with papal principles, he believed. Capitalism, as practiced then, relied on individualism and absolute ownership of property, with little thought of its social use. Marciniak attributed many of society's ills to the absence of restraints and curbs and opposed a misguided conception of individualism that ignored basic social responsibilities. Capitalism relied upon an order that separated the interests of labor from that of owners resulting in concentrations of wealth in the hands of a limited number of powerful persons and groups. His position to rebalance power, which is to redistribute it, was consistent with many Catholic social actionists.[4]

All through the 1940s, Marciniak dealt with the themes of communism, socialism, and capitalism. When he helped to guide the *Chicago Catholic Worker*, it was forthright in its opposition to communism but identified with many of the goals of the communists. He shared the perspective of the Bishop Robert Lucey of Amarillo, Texas, speaking to the National Catholic Social Action Congress in 1939: "The threat to our Christian democracy comes not from the radical and zealot but from the apathy and lethargy of a Christian people. The major threat is not in the communists; it is us." Instead of denouncing and opposing it, Lucey emphasized that actual social justice was the best means to defeat communism.[5]

Ever a believer in the power of united action, Marciniak founded the Catholic Labor Alliance (CLA) in 1943 to be a vehicle for labor professionals, workers, and business people to support workers' rights and infuse principles of justice and dignity into the workplace.[6] CLA's animating objective was "to bring the spirit of Christ into the working world," not by replacing organizations already in existence, especially labor organizations, but by developing men and women to be good unionists and good employers in their existing organizations.[7] The goal was to have Catholics be a force for Christian principles in the workplace. Chief among its undertakings, besides its influential monthly paper, *Work*, were monthly social action forums where Christian principles were discussed by workers in neighborhood sessions; the annual Msgr. John A. Ryan Forum, a series of lectures climaxed with addresses by top union officials as well as business and religious leaders; and labor education courses sponsored jointly with Bishop Bernard Sheil's School of Social Studies.[8]

Shortly after the end of World War II, Marciniak grew anxious that the United States was on the verge of a "red-scare" movement that might wipe out all the economic and social gains resulting from the cooperation between employers and employees necessitated by the war effort. Marciniak advised that the basic opposition of Marxist Communism to Judeo-Christian beliefs should not blind people. He contended that many "so-called" Christians misplaced their charity and exhibited indifference to injustice with their tirades against communists. He wrote that many honest people and organizations were "smeared with the red label and their good work hindered by loose language and distorted statements."[9] Pointedly, he charged that many businesspeople and racketeering union officials hopped on the anti-communist band wagon to hold their ill-gotten gains or their grip on power. Communists might try to frame the contest between communism and fascism or communism and capitalism, but Marciniak counseled otherwise: "The modern world must choose all right, but not among communism, fascism, or reactionary capitalism. It must choose between all of these and Christian democracy. For it is only in a Christian democracy that the rights of all men are respected in laws, customs, and social relations."[10]

In November 1946, *Work* published "A Declaration of Economic Justice," signed by more than 100 Catholic, Jewish, and Protestant leaders throughout the nation. Among the signatories were Marciniak, Rev. Daniel Cantwell (CLA chaplain), and Msgr. Reynold Hillenbrand (former seminary rector).[11] Marciniak provided an explanation for the document noting the leaders took "sharp issue" with those Americans who divorced religion from life. He noted that the document was a not a complete statement of the Catholic position on economic or moral positions but was "a minimum, rock-bottom program which should be endorsed by all men who hunger for justice and are willing to work for it."

The Declaration proclaimed eight propositions. First, moral law must govern economic life; that is economic problems are not solely technical but also theological and ethical. Second, material resources are God-given and entrusted for the "welfare of all and not the benefit of the few." Accordingly, private property comes with a moral obligation "subject to the restrictions for the common good." In some cases, the authors believed government ownership was appropriate because of the resource's relationship to the common good. While advocating for private ownership, controlled, or owned or direct ownership forms, the signers held that private property should be distributed as broadly as possible to individuals or cooperatives. Third, the purposes of economic life are to develop natural resources and skills for the benefit of all, distribute the benefits equitably, provide everyone employment according to their abilities and needs, and to develop "human personality with others in work and ownership."

The Declaration also dealt with profits. The fourth point emphasized that "the profit motive must be subordinated to the moral law, that is, human needs and dictates of social justice." The fifth declared that the common good necessitates the "free association" of workers, farmers, employers, and professional people to govern themselves democratically for their own welfare subject to the common good. Attuned to contemporary discriminatory practices, the signers stated: "it is their [associations'] moral duty to admit to their membership all qualified persons without regard to race, creed, color, or national origin."

The last three propositions related to the role of government. Point six declared that the cooperation of the functional groups among themselves and government "must be substituted for the rule of competition." It explained that the economy is meant to foster a democratic partnership rather than a competitive enterprise in which "competitive economic individualism, private monopoly, or excessive governmental intervention...all of which are unacceptable under the moral law." The seventh tasked government with intervening in economic life "whenever necessary to protect the rights of individuals and groups and the advancement of the general economic welfare." The final statement addressed international economic life by noting the existing system fostered monopoly and exploitation of natural resources by powerful groups and states and called for all national governments to assist all states to "provide an adequate standard of living."

The *Chicago Tribune*, not surprisingly, sounded an alarm. The city's Republican newspaper, which had a long history of anti-Catholic and anti-union coverage, reported on the substance of the document, and carried a six-paragraph editorial denouncing the signers and labeled them "pious demagogs," "fellow travelers," "latter-day prophets," and "false prophets" and characterized the documents as "stupid," "vicious," and "absurd."[12]

Marciniak considered the *Tribune*'s editorial a "display of rhetorical pyrotechnics"[13] and pursued the CLA's mission to ensure that the unions were strengthened by training workers to assume union leadership and giving them practical skills in labor management relations. The goal was to infuse Christian values that would lessen the impact of communist organizers, not to have a Catholic union. *Work* believed that the interests of capital and labor were "fundamentally the same—even though too often capitalists and workers function as if their interests were conflicting."[14]

The guiding principles for Marciniak's thought were summed up by Pius XI's 1937 encyclical, *Divini Redemptoris*.[15] The encyclical was written to expose the threats of Bolshevism and counter the influence of atheistic communism in Spain and Mexico. Pragmatically, Marciniak did not emphasize the flaws of communism, believing them to be obvious. Rather, *Work* focused on the positive aspects of the encyclical. As anti-Communist rhetoric heated up as the Russian threat in Eastern Europe grew in the late 1940s, *Work* reprinted the portion of *Divini Redemptoris* (paragraphs 49 through 58) that concentrated on Christian responsibility under the headline: "A Positive Approach to Communism."[16] In this section, the pope emphasized that charity must support justice. For employers to give to charitable causes while depriving workers of a just income was unacceptable. "The wage-earner is not to receive as alms what is due in justice," he stipulated. He recognized that employers were "saddled with the heavy heritage of an unjust economic regime," which too often was misguided and used the right of private property as a weapon to "defraud working people of (their) just salary and (their) social rights." The ideal demanded commutative justice, the contractual exchange of equitable goods and services and fulfillment of obligations. Further, Pius explained, it required social justice or genuine participation in the industry by employees and employers. All must be accorded dignity and receive the resources necessary to be free from privation and, in addition, be suitably protected by public and private insurance for old age, illness, and unemployment. The Pope called upon employers, organizations, and workers to join and create vehicles for mutual collaboration as had been called for in the earlier encyclical *Quadragesimo Anno*.[17]

As it embraced these guiding principles, *Work* tried to translate them for its American audience, knowing few people would read the full text. Marciniak committed himself to the Pope's call for Catholic action that "must organize propaganda campaigns on a large scale to disseminate knowledge of the fundamental principles on which…a Christian Social Order must build."[18] Underlying his perspective on the social order was Marciniak's conviction that all were one in the Body of Christ and that acts of one affected the well-being of all, as enunciated by Pius XII in *Mystici Corporis Christi*.[19]

A CRITIQUE OF
ANTI-COMMUNIST FERVOR

In a 1947 editorial, Marciniak challenged the anti-communist movement believing it posed one of the biggest dangers that the nation would soon face. He noted the "red-scare" threatened to wipe out "our great economic and social gains." In the name of anti-communism, he warned that wild, distorted charges were being made "with plenty of steam but not much in the way of fact" and they hindered the work of good men and organizations. The central reasons for these charges were the selfishness and greed of persons and entities trying to "protect ill-gotten gains" and "protect a corrupt economic system." Even racketeering labor bosses jumped on the anti-communist bandwagon. There were lots of people, he wrote, "interested in pouring hundred-dollar bills into the anti-communist campaign, not because they are interested in social justice, but because they want to preserve a way of life that lets them fatten their pockets at the expense of the poor."[20] In the same issue he provided examples of false charges against the progressive CIO and its leader and refuted them.[21] Marciniak dealt with these same issues at the annual meetings of the American Newspaper Guild. There he opposed the ouster of those who espoused communism; however, he offered no defense of those whose actions were against the national interest.[22]

In coming years, Work sustained its opposition to rabid anti-communists who used "red" as a flag to whip up support for the existing economic system and sustain its legal protections. Marciniak expressed grave reservations about proposals then circulating to take the Communist Party off the ballots for public and union positions. Banning the Communist Party was, he editorialized, "an easy way out for a lot of (people) who do not have the guts, the zeal, and the hunger for justice that requires (everyone) to work positively, daily, and perseveringly for economic justice and charity." Workers needed to assume the responsibility to build strong unions and a new social order, to read up on the Church's social principles and be active in their unions rather than spending their nights playing poker or relaxing on the sofa. A blanket ban on communists in office was, he explained, "a substitute for a diligent, unselfish devotion to a reconstruction of the social order."[23] After the CIO expelled communist dominated unions in 1949, he cautioned that both the CIO and American Federation of Labor faced serious responsibilities to organize the un-organized; to eliminate racial discrimination and push for civil rights; to fight for broader programs of worker security; to unite the divided labor factions; and to press forward with experiments in labor-management cooperation.[24]

Marciniak ridiculed the public figures who had heated up the rhetoric "throwing around the labels, *socialism, statism, and communism*, at the drop of a hat."[25] He worried that almost every effort to reform social and economic issues was being "smeared." With irony, he chided paranoid conservatives and warned his readers that someone would soon discover that Santa Claus wore red and be labelled as a threat. What most galled him was that "anti-communism" had become a substitute for patriotism:

> Like a lot of ordinary people in the United States, we think that our economic and political system needs some change to make it serve the public good. We aren't socialists. We aren't communists. We aren't capitalists either. We're simply Americans trying to find a Christian answer to some of our vexing social and economic problems. [26]

Many American Catholics who were eager to show their patriotism were strident anti-Communists. To these, Marciniak spoke when he railed against the steady diet of anti-Communism that was the staple of parish Communion breakfasts throughout the nation. In an article that included excerpts from leading Catholic voices calling for balance, he expressed grave concern about the hatred for communists that was being instilled in the young.[27] He gave an example of such mind poisoning by recounting that he had overheard a young boy in a theater respond to a news reel about a communist by exclaiming, "'I wish I could kill him.'" This hysterical "anti" attitude enabled the Catechetical Guild, a St. Paul, Minnesota publishing house, to sell two million gory comic books about communism. Regrettably, Marciniak noted, another comic book that provided a positive explanation of Christian principles on labor relations sold only 100,000.[28]

According to Marciniak, the public seemed confused about the difference between social reform and the term "socialism." Clearly the Vatican had condemned materialistic socialism and most Christians also rejected socialism as a form of government on the grounds that it did not recognize the dignity of individuals.[29] However, Marciniak noted in a 1950 column that "socialism" had elements with which Christian teachings agreed, including a belief that people were more important than profits, that the human person took priority over money, and that private property rights were not absolute. "This brand of 'socialism' is good Christian teaching that is old as the Bible," he wrote. Unfortunately, rugged individualists and "'free enterprisers'" regarded this as socialistic. Supporting his case, he cited a National Catholic

Welfare Conference (NCWC) statement that man, as a member of a community, had "duties of commutative justice and duties of social justice and charity."[30] Interventions that provided public housing and family allowances, child labor and fair employment legislation, old age insurance, and the like were "at the very heart of the Christian social teaching on the obligation of good government."[31]

The editor of *Work* acknowledged the successes of the "free enterprisers" in labeling as "socialist" those Americans who were dissatisfied with the way the present economic system was run. These critics labeled social reform of any kind, including support for union cooperatives or employee/employer partnerships, as socialist. However, Marciniak argued that the choice open to Americans was not "socialism" or "free enterprise," it was "economic democracy."[32]

When Senator Joseph McCarthy waged his campaign against communists in the 1950s, many Catholics supported him and his attacks on "leftists" and "commies." Marciniak regarded the strident cries against "creeping socialism" and "Liberty against Socialism" as political rhetoric designed to win votes. He endeavored to put government intervention into a context by pointing out that so-called "socialistic" programs had helped build the economy for the common good. He cited government leases for mining and grazing rights, public subsidies for railroads and airlines, government interventions in international and domestic affairs through court injunctions in labor disputes. The charges of socialism were now being hurled because "Uncle Sam has taken an interest in not only business but also the common man." Unfortunately, these hysterical extremists threatened to cause the nation to take a step backwards.[33]

Marciniak strongly believed there were times for government interventions. But in keeping with the Catholic principle of subsidiarity, he adamantly opposed government doing what individuals and local groups should do for themselves. To make his position clear, he published his own tests for socialism, stating that no government action can be regarded as socialistic: 1) if it is designed to serve the common good; 2) if it provides a needed service and is something people cannot do themselves; 3) if it strengthens families, businesses, unions, and voluntary organizations; and 4) if it is not based upon a blind trust in government's ability to solve economic problems.[34] His position on government programs and incentives for public housing illustrated his perspective on "socialism." *Work* took on critics who regarded government intervention in real estate as a failing to see that it was in the public's interest that decent housing be provided for low paid workers so that they could live with dignity and contribute to society.[35]

Repeatedly during his editorship Marciniak focused on the failures of Christians to stem the successes of communism by applying the principles of the gospel and the ideas expressed in papal encyclicals and in the writings of American Bishops. *Work* printed comments of episcopal leaders such as Bishop Francis Haas and Cardinal Francis Spellman of New York on the need to blunt communism not with words but with works of justice and charity. Simply denouncing communism was akin to denouncing murder and blasphemy. It did little to detour its proponents, Haas argued in 1950. It was better to remove the injustices that were "red meat" to the communists than to scream at them.[36] Marciniak shared the words of Cardinal Spellman that the widespread and un-alleviated poverty, racism, and class set against class were against the teachings of Christ. Spellman emphasized that all had a "'permanent obligation to concern ourselves with the work of justice in society'" and that there could be no effective steps taken for peace until people recognized the injustices that abounded in society.[37] The editor, however, continued to worry that these sentiments might be dismissed even by Christians as communistic ideals.[38]

Marciniak's patience with anti-communists was tried the following year by Louis F. Budenz, a former communist labor activist who became a vocal anti-communist. In an article in the popular and broadly circulated *Catholic Digest* Budenz attacked the Americans for Democratic Action (ADA) for its rebuke of Senator McCarthy. The ADA had been founded by liberal labor, civic, and political leaders in 1947 to support election of officials committed to advancing progressive economic and social policies. Among its notable founders were former First Lady Eleanor Roosevelt, noted Harvard economist John Kenneth Galbraith, United Auto Workers leader Walter Reuther, and theologian Reinhold Niebuhr. Marciniak called Budenz's linking of the ADA with the Communist Party "gutter journalism" and opined that the ADA "should be entitled to an honest opinion without being red-labelled even if it does dare to criticize the Senator."[39]

A letter to the editor from a reader in Menominee, Michigan recounted an exchange with Budenz about Marciniak's comments noting Budenz stood by his facts and position on ADA.[40] Marciniak published the reader's letter and then launched a defense of his support of the ADA explaining that "It was founded to counterattack

communist infiltration of the American liberal movement"
and to "provide anti-communist liberals with a meeting
ground for a constructive political program that would be
free of fellow-travelers." He noted that in a "political line-up
the ADA would be classified as left of center, just as Senator McCarthy would be pegged right of center." The salient
point he emphasized was "that being right of center doesn't
make McCarthy a Fascist any more than being left of center
makes the ADA communist."[41]

He was disturbed by Budenz's position that the ADA
could not be "vigorously anti-communist" and have liberal
members such as Eleanor Roosevelt. He pointed out that
the late Bishop Francis J. Hass was an original board member and then shared: "I attended the founding convention of
the ADA in Philadelphia. I can testify from personal experience that while the leadership is not conservative, it is not
communist. In fact, it is anti-communist." He believed that
it was possible to be a good Christian and a loyal American, be against the Budenz variety of anti-communism, and
simultaneously be "vigorously" anti-communist. He added:

There is a kind of totalitarian sensitivity among some
anti-communists which disturbs me: It suspects the
loyalty of anyone who dares question Senator McCarthy's methods or Mr. Budenz' judgment.

I personally think that congressional committees have
a right and duty to investigate communists in government. I am also frank to say that I don't like the way
in which much of this investigation has been carried
on. It could have been improved and more effective in

the reputation and rights of loyal public servants.... Just as it is vitally important to discover who the communist fellow-travelers are in government, it is equally important to make sure that all social reformers are not smeared as communists. If the day arrives when social reform is equated with communism, the communists have won a great victory.[42]

A DISTRIBUTIST CRITIQUE
OF CAPITALISM

In a 1946 editorial, Marciniak wrote that industrial peace with justice would require "more than merely tinker[ing] with the American economic engine, we are going to have to overhaul it."[43] He employed *Work* to unabashedly support social reform initiatives and argue persuasively for minimum wage legislation, public housing, and national health insurance among other "socialistic" initiatives. However, the one initiative that Marciniak supported continuously and with greater and greater frequency after World War II was the creation of industrial councils to bring together workers and owners. This he believed would enable all to live with dignity without stifling competition as well as to protect property.

The papal encyclicals, *Rerum Novarum* and *Quadragesimo Anno* pointed to the failures of free enterprise but did not condemn it wholesale. As a professor teaching courses at Loyola University and in CLA's labor schools, Marciniak was keenly familiar with these documents and fully embraced their ideas. Guided by his religious convictions he read voraciously and sought to come to terms with capitalism. As did most social reformers, he saw its weaknesses and identified with the school of thought that sought mechanisms to control the defects of unfettered free enterprise. As were the founders of the Catholic Worker movement, he was attracted to Distributism.

In a thoughtful draft of an article,[44] Marciniak began with the declaration: "As far back as I can remember, I have tagged myself a distributist." He believed in a society in which, citing the definition of the Distributist Association of the United Kingdom, "property and power are as widely and as fairly distributed amongst all people."[45] While Distributism was concerned with the distribution of wealth, property, and economic power, "not all distributists agree on the methods, but they are all of one mind that it must be done."[46]

Marciniak approached the challenges of industrialism as a social and economic system with the ingredients of factories, mass production, credit, technologies, and cities. He was not enamored of the Catholic Worker back-to-the land initiatives nor those of the Catholic Land Movement in Great Britain, but did not criticize those options;[47] however, he subscribed to many of the ideas enunciated by Hilaire Belloc regarding small business and decentralized controls.[48] He was clear: "I believe that (people) can use, organize, and direct these ingredients in a Christian way for the good." However, he saw a great need for a reconstruction of the current form of "industrialism" (he used the terms capitalism and free enterprise interchangeably).

Critics of industrialism viewed it as a Frankenstein-like monster; however, Ed suggested that the system was much more like an alcoholic. He made clear he hadn't given up on curing the sick system. He explained that he wanted to find a way to "sober up industrialism, to find the right cure." He acknowledged that the habit of addiction was not cured overnight and that the process of the "cure" was "long, slow and painful." Then he added, "We know, too, we ourselves [sic] not completely free of the intoxicating habits of modern industrialism: self-love and self-interest."

Capitalism's flaw, Marciniak posited, was that it grew up without the virtues of temperance, justice, prudence, or courage and the "guiding hand of Christian inspiration," even though Christians often led the enterprises. Rather than focus on individual reformation, he believed the failures in the system must be addressed. He listed five major problems: 1) irresponsibility, 2) centralization, 3) mechanization, 4) concentration, and 5) disintegration.[49] "I am here concerned," he wrote, "not with the question of making (people) Christian, but with the problem of making society Christian, even though it is obvious that both are essentially related."[50]

Systematically, he laid out each element and suggested solutions. Industrialism failed as it ignored the idea of responsible stewardship over a person's property and what he did and created with it. Marciniak noted that workers had little say about the products they made and the corporation's policies. The average worker, he declared, was "voiceless when it comes to making sure (their) industry serves the common good." Collective bargaining rights won by the labor unions as well as plans to provide stock purchases and profit sharing were "a step in the right direction" giving workers a voice in the affairs of business.

Marciniak devoted greatest attention to centralization, specifically dealing with the urban problems that he would devote himself to in his future career as an urban planner. The "monster-sized" cities, slums, and industrial organizations, and "our family warehouses" (in genteel circles, one calls them "skyscraper apartments"), he believed, swallowed up humans. He lamented the average person was overwhelmed by "noise, smoke, speed, and density." Rather than make families live in the shadow of steel mills on the edge of garbage dumps, he called for a decentralization to give families space to breathe and find community and peace. He encouraged superhighways and rapid transit and held out hope that the ideas of industrialists like Henry Kaiser, who planned to build smaller plants all over the country rather than mammoth auto plants, would be adopted. He acknowledged that most Americans believed that "efficiency and bigness were inseparable twins" but argued that experience was showing that small business units could be more efficient than large ones. As he had expressed as a graduate student, he was distressed at the growth of corporate farming which treated agriculture as just a way to make money rather than a way of life. "We need more family farms and fewer factory farms," he concluded.

The third and fourth points, mechanization and concentration, received less development, not because they were less important but because the issues were more commonly acknowledged. Mechanization had deleterious effects on workers, Marciniak believed, because the engineers and experts were primarily focused on product and profit rather than the safety and well-being of the persons operating the machines. Overspecialization, he contended, made it "hard for the workers to do a human, decent day's work" as the tempo of the assembly line was conducive to "neither calm nerves nor good health." Workers should have a say in the machinery that they used, Ed said, so they might better utilize their skills and reduce the dehumanizing aspects of industrialism. Concentration of wealth and power made property ownership difficult to achieve for the average worker. Marciniak called upon government, unions, and civic and business organizations to devote their efforts to assist in making home ownership a possibility for American workers so they could have a stake in the community where they made their living.

Finally, Marciniak held that an individualistic society fostered disintegration. There was a clear need for coordination to ensure that every element of society worked together to promote the common good. "Because society has lost its organic character," he wrote, "society is gradually being torn apart by class and racial conflict." The means to avoid this disintegration was to "restore" partnership to American industry with employers and employees working together on the problems of society. Significantly, he noted that partnership was not "a benevolent paternalism, but rather a real partnership in which working (people) will become co-responsible with management in solving the economic problems of industry."[51]

A CALL FOR ECONOMIC DEMOCRACY

This formula of equal partnership with labor and capital accepting joint responsibility for the policies of industry was contrary to the conservative movement that accompanied Cold War anti-communist rhetoric. World War II emergencies had produced government-imposed controls on business and placed limits on labor's right to organize and strike. Corporate leaders called for an end to the wartime control measures, and many Catholics joined them, sharing an antipathy to apparent socialism. Despite such conservatism exhibited by some Catholic clergy and the new middle class who were moving to the suburbs, there was still a contingent of older Catholic social actionists such as Marciniak who did not change course.

Pope Pius XI's encyclical *Divini Redemptoris* (1937) reinforced *Quadragesimo Anno* in stating that workers deserved a share in the work product. He supported an approach to capitalism that considered the interest of all parties in the economic system and stated: "...a reign of mutual collaboration between justice and charity in social-economic relations can only be achieved by a body of professional and interprofessional organizations, built on Christian foundations, working together to effect...the Corporation."[52] In 1941, Philip Murray, President of the CIO, met with President Franklin Roosevelt and proposed a form of industry planning by groups of managers and workers in the critical defense industries as a means to increase productivity and avoid strikes and labor disturbances. He labelled his proposal the "Industry Council Plan" and it called for councils of management, labor, and consumers chaired by a government representative to ensure coordination in key industries. The White House did not accept the plan; however, when the war ended many Catholic social actionists focused on the idea of industry councils as a way to implement the goals of *Divini Redemptoris*.[53]

In 1946, the Social Action Department of the bishop's National Catholic Welfare Council (NCWC) issued a statement calling for the establishment of industry councils, arguing that social justice demanded organized labor and organized management come together in an occupational group system that included all interested parties. These groups would seek to modify competition by maintaining standards of fairness regarding production by enabling labor to have a voice in industrial policies and decisions and by excluding the need for political and bureaucratic dictatorship like that of communist collectivism.[54]

For more than ten years Marciniak's Catholic Labor Alliance campaigned to educate workers about the Industry Council Plan. One of its annual events was the Labor Day Mass that filled Holy Name Cathedral with Chicago's union, business, and political leaders. In 1947 Marciniak arranged for both Rev. Raymond McGowan, Director of the Social Action Department of the NCWC, to give the Labor Day Mass sermon and for his assistant director, Father (later Monsignor) George Higgins to do so the following year.[55] Higgins, a Chicago priest assigned to the NCWC, proclaimed to the hundreds of labor, business, and political leaders who jammed the cathedral: "We should be looking towards the establishment of a system of organized cooperation between labor, management, and the government—a system of democratic planning for the general economic welfare." He explained that this system of organized occupational groups, or industries, with labor and management working together with the cooperation of government representatives would work out all "major economic decisions of the industry: wages, prices, profits, production schedules and similar decisions." Such a system, he contended, would reduce conflicting interests of the various industrial classes, place industrial direction in the hands of the most competent, and limit centralized political control as a necessary safeguard. Higgins told the leaders that collective bargaining for fair wages and working conditions led to necessary labor militancy but now there was a need go a step further:

> The time seems now to have arrived when it [militancy] should be not supplanted, but supplemented by associations or conferences, composed jointly of employers and employes [sic], which will place emphasis upon the common interest rather than the divergent aims of the two parties, upon cooperation rather than conflict.[56]

The call for partnerships as envisioned with industrial councils was not just a program of the American bishops. Philip Murray, head of the United Steel Workers and early advocate for industrial councils during World War II, sustained his support arguing that it was not socialistic as business described it. In a Chicago address in 1950, he emphasized that the Industry Council Plan is "democracy at its best and the only alternative to either socialism or fascism." Murray stressed that American labor did not believe government could solve economic issues alone and added: "Neither do we believe that it can be solved by management alone or by labor alone."[57]

Marciniak strongly agreed with the NCWC and the CIO, and he advocated for industrial councils in news reports, editorials, and addresses. Further, Ed engaged in spirited debates on workers' rights to share in decision making in the workplace. His critics included Rev. Robert

C. Hartnett, S.J. and Rev. Benjamin L. Masse, S.J., respectively Editor and Associate Editor of *America*, one of the most widely read national Catholic weeklies. The two Jesuits interpreted Pope Pius XII's address to the International Congress of Social Studies and the International Social Union to imply that labor did not have a "strict" right to share in economic decisions. Marciniak was quick to urge a less limiting interpretation regarding economic "co-management." He argued that workers had a right to co-management even if the owner was not morally required to grant it and said that a "productive enterprise is not merely an economic institution.... It is also a social institution—the joint effort of capital and labor." Because of this social dimension, he contended that neither labor nor capital had exclusive rights to manage:

> To say that workers do not have a strict right to share in management may easily be interpreted by the enemies of labor to mean that workers are thereby denied the right of social co-management. The ultimate consequence of such a position would be a denial of the right to strike for just wages, the right to collective bargaining, and finally the right to form unions. If workingmen have the right to bargain collectively and the right to strike, it is because they also have the right to co-determine, to co-manage those conditions of employment which affect them directly.[58]

The Industrial Council Plan (ICP) had caused business opposition because it was being viewed from a narrow economic perspective. Writing to Rev Francis J. Corley, S.J.,

Editor of *Social Order*, Marciniak expressed concern that prices were monopolizing the discussion of the industry council idea, focusing on the economic order rather than the social order. He explained that free enterprise economists believed that any degree of government regulation was "total regulation" and distorted reality. Pope Pius XI's encyclical was, he noted "primarily concerned with social order reform rather than economic reform. And I'm afraid that if the economists start taking over the encyclicals they will be dehydrated." For Ed, the relationship between employer, employee, government, and industry were "first and fundamentally social relations and not economic ones."[59] The real issue was not about prices but "under what circumstances does the industry council have the right and the duty to concern itself with prices," he wrote in a second letter. When prices were too low or too high, they jeopardized the common good. The industry council, he believed, "may not sit idlly [sic] by and let prices go their free, merry way regardless of the consequences to the common good.[60]

According to Marciniak, the ICP had been misinterpreted and misunderstood by teachers and students who have "interpreted, explained, and tried to apply its structure in the United States." In an untitled draft of a speech,[61] he sought to be positive and constructive in clearing away the "fog, wrong emphasis, and misunderstanding" that surrounded the plan. ICP, he argued, was not a panacea or a chemical formula or geometric theorem. It was a call to selfless acts and faith in the oneness of all, a conviction that all were members of a single family and children of one God, one in the Mystical Body of Christ. The call by the pope for industry councils was a beginning. The development of the ways and means, he believed, relied not on more papal pronouncements but on the initiative of lay people. Apart from the American Catholic Sociological Society and a few dissertations, literature on the ICP was short on originality and, he wrote, "seldom comes to grips with the difficult economic problems involved." Further, he realized, there would not be a plan created of whole cloth, but that the process of developing a plan would be fragmentary and take time.[62]

Finally, Marciniak did not consider ICP "a special project of, by, and for Catholics." He regarded it as unfortunate that the ICP was presented as a "papal plan." and argued that in trying to reconstruct the social order "our approach should be that the ICP is a good thing, and therefore Catholic; not just that it is Catholic, therefore a good program." He pressed Catholics to search out proposals among Protestant and Jews and utilize their ideas. He concluded by emphasizing that while "Christianity may have all the answers, it is not true that Christians have all the answers.... No less here than elsewhere is humility a virtue for Christians."[63] His broad view in addressing issues by appealing to the role of the laity and ecumenicalism would soon enough apply to other statements and declarations.

In October 1954, Marciniak's friend and mentor, Dorothy Day, wrote about her son-in law David Hennessey's disagreement with the backers of the ICP for supporting co-management. Hennessey named well-known Catholic action advocates, including Msgr. Higgins and Marciniak. Hennessey argued that co-management was just a means "to make the best of our present capitalistic system." Hennessey regarded capitalism as "intrinsically atheistic" and believed that co-management worked from the top down and the "co-ownership" ideal espoused by distributists worked from the bottom up to ensure the means and product of work were controlled and shared by workers.[64] He concluded by implying that the supporters of co-management were not distributists and therefore were at variance with the pope.

Marciniak very strongly disagreed and, as he rarely seemed to avoid debating ideas, responded. At the top of the undated notes prepared for his debate with William Buckley, founder of the *National Review,* upon the publication of Buckley's *God and Man at Yale,* Marciniak had printed in bold letters: "BETTER TO WIN A FRIEND THAN AN ARGUMENT."[65] He did not seem to follow his own advice in this case. His response to David Hennessey, while reasoned, was also stinging and personal. First, Marciniak admitted he and his colleagues were "supporters of the industrial council idea (please note my use of the 'idea' for 'plan')." He continued: "To put me in my place, David claims he's a distributist and I'm not…because I back the industry council idea. But David is dead wrong, because I am a distributist and a disciple of the industry council idea."[66]

Marciniak continued to prove his point and argued that distributism and industry councils were not mutually exclusive. After giving his definition of distributism, he parenthetically commented that: "David can't complain about the orthodoxy of my source" as it came from the publication of the Distributist Association of the United Kingdom, and "he's always peddling the Association's pamphlets." Marciniak noted that not all distributists agreed on every method, but they were of one mind on the aim of distributism: to see that property and power were widely and fairly distributed.

He then reiterated his position on distributionism as stated in his previously referenced article, using the exact wording for major portions of his response. He chided Hennessey's "private exegesis of the distributist scriptures." He agreed that they shared a mutual goal of helping to assure the common good. Then he parted company:

> But I don't want to leave it to chance and whims of supply and demand. Neither do I want to leave it to the government alone. Nor do I want to leave it to the classes (landlords, labor, management, stockholders) to settle by private class brawls. The industry council idea calls for the responsible self-government on an industry wide, profession-wide basis. Workers, since they eat, so to speak, at the same table, ought to be cooperators in the common job of making sure that the industry to which they belong, and the national economy as a whole serve the public good.

Marciniak used the ailing coal industry, which had 100,000 unemployed miners at the time, as an example. He noted that what troubled the industry was the failure of labor, owners, and government to plan for the industry's overproduction and competition from other sources of energy such as gas, hydroelectric, and atomic power. He tartly concluded that "Hennessey's distributism would never help any coal miner" and reiterated his call that the industry council idea be applied to other industries such as shipping, textiles, and even to professions. He showed his exasperation one more time by concluding: "If David wants to criticize the industry council idea I have described here, let him go to it, but don't let him waste his time on the machino-factured version Dorothy Day reported in the CW."[67]

Marciniak's effort to clarify continued in his response to a priest whose letter Dorothy Day forwarded to him. A sense of ownership of the means of production, Ed responded, could be gotten by "bringing workers into a fuller participation in the economic way of a business" noting that unions, industry councils, recognition in the structure of the factory all contributed to the finished product. The moral problem of irresponsibility needed to be addressed and, he wrote, that "the problem begins at the top and runs down to the great mass of workers."[68]

Responsibility at the top would be restored not by management choice, Marciniak believed, but "by pressure and education from below." He conjectured about the course of action Hilaire Belloc would take about large business institutions.

> I don't think he would try to demolish them. I think that he would try to figure out some way of maintaining the distributist principle of personal responsibility at the lowest possible level, that is the human level.

> The CW article [his of November] is only concerned with structural reform and not the problem of personal moral reform. While the latter is most important, it cannot be in the long run accomplished without the former. That is why you have the encyclical on the Reconstruction of the Social Order.[69]

Work continued to publish stories about religious organizations, political groups, and leaders who voiced support for the Industry Council Plan, which had become more commonly known as "economic democracy."[70] The term was not important to *Work* but advancement of the movement was. However, the support was not without certain reservations because Marciniak was concerned about labor-management cooperation gone awry in industries where labor and management lobbied government to block imports, reduce legitimate taxes, and receive other favored treatment. "What has to be recognized," he acknowledged, "is that somewhere along the way their private interest may clash with the public good." He gave specific industry examples of collusion at the expense of the public and concluded that just because union and management cooperated on a project did not automatically "guarantee that the public good will result. The public has a right to protect itself against such organized cooperation.'"[71]

INTERNATIONAL COOPERATION

In 1959, Marciniak advocated for a much expanded vision of cooperation when he served as member of the U.S. delegation to the International Labor Organization (ILO), then an agency of the United Nations seeking to establish minimum and just labor standards. The organization, which had been founded in 1919 and based on the premise that a universal and lasting peace must be based on social justice, had for its motto, "Poverty anywhere is a danger to prosperity everywhere."[72] Msgr. George Higgins successfully secured an appointment for his friend and trusted ally as one of the United States' labor delegates to the conference. In May, Marciniak was issued his first passport, which listed him as 5' 8" in height with blue-eyed, brown hair, and no "visible marks." His photo captured the seriousness of a forty-three-year-old with a full face that reflected his age; however, Ed's hair was now cropped short, with no sign of his earlier pompadour and wave. The passport noted that he was an editor and "an adviser representing the workers of the United States to the 43rd Session of the Labor Conference to be held in Geneva, Switzerland, June 3-25, 1959." [73]

Eighty nations were represented by more than 1,000 delegates composed of government officials, employers, and union leaders. They met in the elegant columned Palace of Nations, formerly the home of the League of Nations. While most delegates were from industrialized countries, others were from South America and the new and struggling nations in Asia and Africa. Marciniak was appointed to the Committee on Collaboration.

The Committee on Collaboration was the largest and most representative in the conference, with 175 titular and deputy members. Marciniak was an active member of his committee and, in the absence of the workers' vice-chairman, he represented the workers in the plenary session. In the grand assembly chamber, he rose to summarize the report which called for the application of the principle of consultation and cooperation among, employers, employees, and government. On behalf of the Committee on Collaboration, Marciniak urged the ILO to concern itself with the "area of economic life which lies between collective bargaining on the one hand and social legislation on the other. This is the area of consultation and co-operation at the level of the industry and at the national level." Ed noted that the ILO had already devised labor standards and advanced industrial relations through advocacy for collective bargaining to ensure economic freedom and improve working conditions in the past forty years. This now was, he told them, the "third phase" of the ILO's agenda.[74]

Marciniak explained that only recently had nations begun to explore and develop new social and economic institutions and continued:

This is why consultation looks so much to the future. It is a rather new development in the family of nations. In its deliberations the committee on collaboration has attempted to share the experiences of worker organizations, employer associations and governments with bipartite and tripartite consultations and cooperation on the industrial and national level.

He assured the delegates that the committee avoided "grand schemes" and "pious" declarations, seeking to be "practical in examining various forms of consultation and collaboration." Further the committee sought to be certain that the consultation and cooperation be conducted "without endangering the freedom of workers and employers' associations and without discrimination of any kind on the grounds of nationality, race, religion, or trade union membership." Marciniak concluded by asking for the adoption of the committee's recommendation and a draft memorandum that spelled out various forms that the examination called for by the resolution would take. He urged that next year's committee take "the opportunity to pioneer in the area of consultation and cooperation" on the national and industrial level. The recommendation was adopted on June 24th.[75]

Msgr. Higgins was pleased that the *Recommendation* was adopted and that Ed had been selected spokesperson for the workers at the plenary session and with his role as its main advocate. In a memo that he shared with Marciniak, Higgins praised his friend's role, noting that "there are few American labor leaders and few American Catholic social actionists who have done more than he to popularize the philosophy underlying this *Recommendation*." Higgins highlighted Marciniak's work as editor, contributor to numerous Catholic publications, participant in an array of Catholic and non-sectarian conferences throughout the United States and for untiring efforts promoting collaboration in the interest of the general welfare. He concluded his praise by saying that Marciniak's staunch support of the Recommendation was "eminently sound" regarding Catholic teaching and a significant step in the direction of the so-called Industry Council Plan as advocated in papal encyclicals and "in many other social documents in the field of Catholic social theory."[76]

TRANSITION

Work **continued to promote the industry council idea.** In August 1959, *Work's* editor took issue with those social thinkers who believed that the industry council idea was "as dead as a dodo." Robert Senser provided examples or cooperation in Great Britain, the United Auto Workers' profit-sharing plan in the United States, and the ILO's recent reception of the "third phase" and other favorable examples of cooperation.[77] Nonetheless economic democracy as a philosophy did not gain traction despite the endorsements of prelates and union leaders and a small number of business leaders.

Generally, business and labor seemed to hold tight to their special interests and were hesitant to support cooperation and planning on an industry-wide basis. In time the powers of the unions seemed to diminish as did the drive to sustain the fight for the visions set forth in the encyclicals on economic justice. The Catholic Labor Alliance's name change to the Catholic Council on Working Life reflected an effort to be inclusive of all, but it lost some of its militancy in the process.[78] The Taft-Hartley law had permanently impacted labor's militancy and ability to bargain effectively, and the post-war rise of a Catholic middle class of more and more non-industrial workers influenced the work of Chicago social actionists such as Marciniak. He never gave up his intense advocacy for the dignity of workers and their rights to organize and bargain collectively—matters he had fought for at the Chicago Catholic Worker and Catholic Labor Alliance. But after more than twenty years in the labor arena, Ed now embarked on a new phase of political action.

In 1960, Marciniak left the Catholic Labor Alliance to become Executive Director of the Chicago Commission on Human Relations, where he continued his vocation of advocacy and agitation with a focus on racial justice. To honor the new appointee for his more than seventeen years of civic leadership, a committee of 60 prominent Chicagoans hosted a dinner on October 5 at the Morrison Hotel. The co-chairs were Meyer Kestnbaum, Chairman of Hart, Schaffner and Marx, where Eds mother had once worked as a seamstress; Stanley M. Johnson, Executive Vice- President of the Illinois

Federation of the AFL-CIO; and James C Downs, Jr, Chair of the Board of the Real Estate Research Corporation. The principal speaker at the testimonial was Marciniak's long-time friend and Catholic social activist, Senator Eugene McCarthy of Minnesota[79]

Telegrams and letters poured in honoring Marciniak, and a few of these were read at the event. Among them was one from George Meaney, then president of the AFL-CIO, who stated: "I am glad to add my voice to those of this distinguished gathering in paying tribute to the long and devoted service of Ed Marciniak, not only to the Catholic Council on Working Life but to the labor movement. Unselfish service like his represents the cause of labor at its best." He also received telegrams from James P. Mitchel, United States Secretary of Labor, and Arthur Goldberg, who had represented the striking newspaper workers in 1938 and was general counsel to the steelworker's union and would soon become the Secretary of Labor for President John F. Kennedy.[80]

Even after he entered government service, he kept his hand in labor issues by prodding unions to end segregation and Catholic schools and hospitals not to be obstructionists in the face of union organizing, [81] as well as supporting efforts to protect migrant workers. While he devoted his energies to securing racial justice and making cities livable as Chicago's Deputy Planning Commissioner and later as president of the Institute of Urban Life at Loyola University, Marciniak remained an unceasing voice calling for Catholic social action and understanding and appreciation of the dignity of workers and an authoritative agitator for their interests.

When the last issue of *Work* was printed in 1961, Msgr. Cantwell explained that the Catholic Labor Alliance stood for an industrial democracy with full worker participation. "What moved us was the desire to see freedom and human dignity spread. To use the government when necessary is wisdom. We have never believed that government is bad."[82] Ed Marciniak's mission had not been fully achieved. Nonetheless, his guiding principles and convictions about economic justice and the dignity of work influenced many in Chicago and elsewhere as they advocated for social betterment.

NOTES

1   "Industrial Peace with Justice," *Work*, November 1946.

2   Abel, p. 150.

3   *Ibid.*, 289-231.

4   In December 1949, *Work* featured a column by William Smith, S.J., the Director of the Crown Heights Labor School (Brooklyn) and Editor of the *Crown Heights Comment*. Below Smith's column, "Does the Church Approve Capitalism?" Marciniak added, "We like Father Smith's approach to the question and are glad to give him space in *Work*," p. 6.

5   Cited in "A Month Marched By...," *Chicago Catholic Worker*, August 1939.

6   Sicius, p. 221-222.

7   "The Catholic Labor Alliance, What It Is—And Isn't," *Work*, September 1952.

8   *Ibid.* Over the years featured speakers at the Ryan lecture series included: Archbishop Robert E. Lucey and Bishop Francis Haas; President of the American Federation of Labor, Phillip Murray; President of the United Auto Workers, Walter Reuther; Civil Rights leaders such as Dr. Ralph J. Bunche and Roy Wilkins; two United States Secretaries of Labor; and other leading labor advocates and elected officials.

9   "Dangers of Communism," January 1, 1947.

10 Ibid.

11 *Work* did not list the signatories; however, the Chicago *Tribune*, October 1946, published the names of signers from Illinois. https://search-proquest-com.ezp3.sxu.edu/hnpchicago tribune/docview/177364426/5F24BEAEC1624F8EPQ/ 1?accountid=28733.

12 "Religious Heads Offer Guide to Economic Life," October 17, 1946, https://search-proquest-com.ezp3.sxu.edu/hnpchicago tribune/docview/177364426/5F24BEAEC1624F8EPQ/ 1?accountid=28733, retrieved September 14, 2019 and "Pious Demagogs," October 18, 1946.

13 *Work*, November 1946.

14 "Class War," February 1947.

15 In 1959, when asked to submit a list of ten books he considered necessary for "anyone who wants to understand his social responsibilities as a Christian in today's world," Marciniak included Pius XI's *Divini Redemptoris*. Among other books listed were Dorothy Day's *The Long Loneliness*, Gerald Vann's *The Heart of Man* and Graham Greene's *The Power and the Glory*. "'Must' Books" Listed by Social Activists," *Work*, September 1959.

16 *Work*, July 1948.

17 Cited in *Ibid.*

18 *On Atheistic Communism*, paragraph 59, http://www.papalencyclicals.net/Pius11/P11DIVIN.HTM

19 In July 1947 *Work* published the address of Pope Pius XII to an American delegation to the International Labor Organization Conference. In it the pontiff noted the Church would always defend the worker against any system that would deny him his inalienable rights, which were derived not from civil society but from his humanity. "On Improving the Condition of the Workingman," July 16, 1947, cited in *Work*, January 1948.

20 *Work*, "Fighting Communism," January 1947.

21 "Anti-Communist Magazine Goes of the Beam on CIO Charges," cited in Ibid., The Anti-Communist paper, *Today's World* had been circulated in several Chicago parishes the preceding month and featured an attack on the CIO for only slapping the wrists of Communists who once dominated some of its member unions. It noted that "'Philip Murray goes through the motions, actually he does nothing to clean out the Kremlin's agents....'"

22 *Proceedings of the American Newspaper Guild*, 1954, pp. 74, 89, and 106.

23 "Inviting Apathy," *Work*, April 1947.

24 "Seeing Red," *Work*, November 1949.

25 "In Defense of Santa Claus," December 1949.

26 Ibid.

27 "A Certain Kind of Anti-Communist Diet is Poison," *Ibid.*, July 1950.

28 "Accentuating the Negative," Ibid.

29 "A Short Road to Nowhere," Ibid., May 1950.

30 Cited in Ibid. The acting Chair of the NCWC at the time was Samuel A. Stritch, Archbishop of Chicago.

31 Ibid.

32 Ibid. See also, "Socialism and the Archbishop," Ibid., December 1951.

33 "'Creeping Socialism'—Is It Real or Just Vote Bait," *Work*, November 1952.

34 Ibid.

35 "Government-Subsidized Housing Is Not Socialism" *Work*, June 1952. See Chapter 4 for an elaboration on the issue. The feature article by Patrick Malone notes that $16-million-dollar subsidies by federal and state were used to acquire and clear blighted buildings on Chicago's South Side, and this was described as "'free-enterprise' in housing" by government and business leaders. New York Life bought the government land for $2 million and developed Prairie Meadows. This transaction prepared the way for the development of Prairie Meadows, a $39 million middle-class housing project. *Work* noted that the real estate lobby was critical of government subsidies but that even conservative senators, such as Robert Taft and Averell Harriman, were supportive.

36 "Accent 'Do' Instead of 'Don't' In Social Teaching, Bishop Urges," April 1950.

37 Cited in "Smearing Social Justice with Red Paint," *Work*, August 1954.

38 *Ibid.* See also, "Is Your Brand of Anti-Communism Half-Baked: An Editorial for Anti-Communists," Ibid, June 1954.

39 *Work*, "Budenz, 'Catholic Digest' and ADA," November 1953.

40 *Work*, "He Defends Budenz...." December 1953.

41 Work, "...And We Defend Work," December 1953.

42 Ibid.

43 "Industrial Peace with Justice," November 1946.

44 There are a rough draft and a final draft of his position on Distributism, both undated. The first draft with numerous revisions indicated Marciniak's struggle to clarify the essence of the theory and his editorial precision. The final draft is quoted. Marciniak Papers, Shelf 1, Position 2.

45 In the first draft Marciniak cites the reference, *Man Unchained*, by Charles Hope in a publication of the United Kingdom group and notes that is available through the Distributist Book Stall, in West Virginia. The bookstore was an enterprise of David Hennessey, Dorothy Days' son-in-law.

46 Marciniak did not capitalize the terms "distributist" and "distributism." When citing his writings, his lower-case use is followed here.

47 See: *Flee to the Fields*, a reissue of a 1934 collection of essays introduced by Hilaire Belloc by members of the Catholic Land Movement. (Norfolk, VA: INS Press, 2003).

48 See: Hilaire Belloc, *The Servile State*, first published in 1912 and reissued in 1946. This is a history of European Capitalism and a rejection of big business supported by government with his advocacy for distributism as the best alternative. (New York: Cosimo Classics, 2007).

49 These terms are like those used by European Distributists.

50 Marciniak, Final Draft, Shelf 1, Position 2.

51 Marciniak Drafts n.d. Untitled first and second draft. Marciniak Papers, ACC, Shelf 8, Box 1. The essence of this draft is incorporated in Marciniak article that appeared in the *Catholic Worker* in November 1954.

52 "On Atheistic Communism," Paragraph 54. cited in Ibid., July 1948.

53 See: Craig R Prentiss, *Debating God's Economy: Social Justice on the Eve of Vatican II*. (University Park: Pennsylvania State University Press, 2008).

54 "We Need Industry Councils," *Work*, October 1946.

55 Father Raymond McGowan, the director of the Social Action Department was slated to give the sermon in 1947. "Labor Alliance Sponsors Annual Labor Day Mass," *Work*, August 1947.

56 "Union-Management Peace Thru Industry Councils," *Work*, October 1948. The Chicago Federation of Labor newspaper published the sermon as well.

57 Cited in "Murray: 'A Man with Ideas,'" *Work*, December 1952. The article was written by Rev. Daniel Cantwell, chaplain of the CLA, to praise the wisdom and leadership of Murray. See also: "Industry Council Plan vs. Bread and Butter Unionism," September 1953 and "Annual Wage Industry Councils Are Still the Major Union Goals," *Ibid.*, February 1953.

58 Marciniak Letter to Editor, *America*, July 15, 1950, Marciniak Papers, Shelf 2, Position 1. In a series of exchanges with Fathers Hartnett and Masse, Marciniak registered his opposition to their strict interpretation of papal statements because they gave comfort "to some rugged reactionaries who had already twisted the Pope's words as opposing the industrial council plan and profits for workers." Marciniak to Editor in Chief, *America*, September 7, 1950, Shelf 2, Position 1, Marciniak Papers.

59 Marciniak to Corley, February 8, 1951. Marciniak Papers, Shelf 8 Position 1.

60 Marciniak to Corley, January 16, 1951, Marciniak Papers, Shelf 8, Position 1.

61 He believed the address should more appropriately have the title: "How Not to Approach the Industry Council Plan" While undated, the draft seems to have been written between 1950 and 1952. Marciniak Papers, Shelf 2, Position 1.

62 Ibid.

63 Ibid. See also: Edward Marciniak, "Some U. S. Approximations to the Industry Council Idea," *American Catholic Sociological Review*, Vol. 17, No. 1 (March 1956), pp. 24-29.

64 "Distributism Versus Capitalism, pp. 1 and 6, https://thecatholicnewsarchive.org/?a=d&d=CW19541001-01&e=————en-20—1-byDA-txt-txIN————-, retrieved

September 13, 2019.

65 The debate was held before the Thomas Moore Association, a Catholic organization based in Chicago. Marciniak's eight pages of notes challenged Buckley's philosophy that individualism was the best guide for legislators and business executives and questioned the author's wanting "*laissez-faire* economics in a non-*laissez-faire* education." Years later, Marciniak reconnected with Buckley and their correspondence was playful, but their philosophies remained disparate. Marciniak Papers, Shelf 1, Position 1.

66 "Clarification on Distributism," *The Catholic Worker*, November 1954. https://thecatholicnewsarchive.org/?a=d&d=CW 19541101-01&e=————-en-20—1—txt-txIN-

67 Ibid. In the hand-edited first draft of the article, Marciniak deleted a reference to Dorothy Day "(if Dorothy Day publishes this script)." He seems to have thought better of this comment; however, he did include it. Marciniak Papers, Shelf 1, Position 2. In the December issue of the *Catholic Worker*, two letters were printed on the Hennessey-Marciniak debate. Lawrence Moran wrote: "Mr. Hennessey is directly practicing a program which follows his principles; Mr. Marciniak is expounding principles which can be put into practice only by the mighty of the earth." Page 4. https://thecatholicnewsarchive. org/?a=d&d=CW19541201-01&e=————-en-20—1—txt-txIN————-.

68 Marciniak to Father McShane, January 8, 1955. Marciniak Papers, Shelf 1, Position 2.

69 Ibid.

70 In May 1952, the paper editorialized that the Industry Council Plan seemed to have dropped from discussion but noted that it "may have taken on a different name—'economic democracy,' for example." *Work*, p .2. Marciniak delivered a paper to the American Catholic Sociological Society Convention in 1954.

71 "'If's' and 'Buts' about Industrial Cooperation," *Ibid*, April 1954.

72 Cited in "They Seek Peace with Justice," *Work*, July 1959.

73   Passport, issued on May 12, 1959. Marciniak Papers, Shelf 5, Position 2. His passport reflected international tensions with Russia and forbid travel to Hungary. He sought and received a visa permitting him to visit Poland where he had relatives.

74   "Remarks of Edward Marciniak, worker adviser, United States, and spokespeople for the workers in the Committee on Collaboration in Plenary sitting of the 43rd session of the ILO. Marciniak Papers, Shelf 1, Position 3. See also: Proceedings of the International Labor Organization, 1959, pp. 550-551.

75   Following Marciniak's report, the representative of Yugoslavia stated the communist position that a tripartite solution was not necessary in nations where industries were nationalized and workers already participated in economic decisions. "They Seek Peace with Justice," *Work*, July 1959.

76   Higgins, Director of Social Action Department, National Catholic Welfare Conference, n. d., Marciniak Papers, AAC Shelf 1, Position 1.

77   "Industry Councils –Far from Dead," *Work*, August 1959.

78   Avella, pp. 182-183.

79   Press Release, Catholic Council on Working Life, September 2, 1960. Marciniak Papers, Shelf 1, Position 1. Senator McCarthy had been the principal speaker at the Ryan Forum in January 1960. "Senator McCarthy Speaks Jan 30 on Ryan Forum," *Work*, January 1959.1. McCarthy sent Marciniak a letter after the event, noting it was an honor to participate and "wonderful also to have a sense of participation in the Chicago Catholic Action movement again." McCarthy to Marciniak, October 25, 1960, Marciniak Papers, Shelf 2, Position 2.

80   Mitchell to Marciniak, October 4, 1960, and Goldberg to Marciniak, October 5, 1960. Marciniak Papers, Shelf 2, Position 2.

81   One of Marciniak's strongest statements was: "Ethical Guidelines for a Catholic Institution Faced by a Union," *Social Thought*, Spring 1984.

82   December 1, 1961.

Chapter 4

Promoting Affordable and Public Housing for Families

What makes a city great is how it treats its families,
particularly the poor and helpless.

Edward Marciniak[1]

On October 8, 1947, the sixty-sixth anniversary of what is commonly called "the Great Chicago Fire," the city's chief fire marshal announced with a degree of satisfaction that only eighty-eight people had died in fires so far that year. Early in the morning of October 10, 1947, another cataclysmic fire raced through a tenement house in Chicago and upped the number of fatalities for the year to almost one hundred people.

The fire originated in the first floor stair well and the only interior exit and raced through a sixteen-unit apartment building on West Ohio Street creating panic. Two women died immediately and four other residents were injured as they plunged out of windows before firefighters arrived.

Some tenants were able to rush through the flames, others exited on a fire escape, and five jumped into a firemen's net, until the weight of a large man broke it. Two more women and six children died of suffocation or burned to death on the third and fourth floors before they could escape. Twelve other people were injured in the blaze. The fire department suspected arson.[2]

The coroner's investigation of the tragedy found that each room in the building was rented to an individual family with several families sharing the kitchen in their flat. It also reported that the surrounding neighborhood had been full of racial tension and acts of vandalism and that a dozen suspicious fires had been set recently. Furthermore, investigators reported that rents had risen by as much as 300-400 per cent once Black people had moved in.

Ed Marciniak wanted more information and sent a *Work* reporter to talk with community residents. One noted: "There are thousands of people in Chicago who wouldn't set a fire, but they would sign a restrictive covenant against Negroes. These people are guilty too." And another area resident explained if there were more housing, fewer restrictions, and "love in our hearts," such tragedies would not happen. "If only we could make these people realize that the ten fire victims were Negroes who had no other place to go—except into fire traps."[3]

Only a few months before the tragedy, the fire department chaplain of twenty-five years and pastor of Resurrection parish, Msgr. William J Gorman, confided to a *Work* reporter that the housing shortage was creating serious moral problems in all sections of the city. "This is no time to argue about the relative merits of public and private housing," he said. "The need is so desperate that we need to use every means to help." He explained that he had been in too many tenements in the Black and immigrant sections of the city and administered last rites to burn victims. "Even in the 'better' neighborhoods," he added, "some people are living in conditions not fit for a human being."[4]

The Ohio Street tenement disaster aroused Marciniak's anger and prompted a page one editorial. He expressed shock at the innocent life lost and that 300 people lived in a building big enough to house 50; but he shared his relief that more did not die. He also registered disbelief and disgust to learn that the tenants paid as much rent as the tenants of the fine Edgewater Beach Apartments with a view of Lake Michigan. He noted that rage was wasted unless it led to action: "Christian charity and brotherliness are not satisfied with well-meaning emotion and righteous indignation." Certainly, slum lords should be prosecuted for their many violations, he believed, but that was not enough. What was needed, Ed argued, was condemnation and demolition of slums and construction of decent housing. He called for action in the form of a 'Yes' vote on a forthcoming bond issue for land clearance and public housing.[5] This call for action was not his first nor would it be the last. He was acutely aware of the complexity of housing issues at the close of World War II; nonetheless, he committed the Catholic Labor Alliance newspaper to securing decent, quality housing for all, but most especially the lower income and the poor. As he had for labor rights, Marciniak both punched out editorials on his typewriter and nurtured relationships by buttonholing decision makers while attending countless meetings. Both the right to a job and to decent housing were essential and complimentary elements of his work in renewing the Kingdom for all God's people.

EARLY AFFORDABLE
HOUSING ADVOCACY

Marciniak possessed a keen sensitivity to and realization of the critical role of housing as shelter for families and as the foundation for healthy neighborhoods, the building blocks of livable cities. He knew that the poor were in constant search of quality affordable housing from his own experience. His father had moved the Marciniak family eight times, buying and selling homes until he could start his grocery business in Brighton Park, and Ed learned about neighborhoods and slums and tenements riding public transportation to high school, college, and graduate school. His experiences at the Catholic Worker house and sociology studies spurred his interest in urban affairs and the impact of policy in support of healthy communities.[6]

The need for decent affordable housing in the United States was a constant concern of reformers who worried about the overcrowding in run down, antiquated housing in the nation's largest urban areas. Franklin D. Roosevelt's 1937 inaugural address called attention to the problem when he said, "I see one-third of the nation, ill-housed, ill-clad, and ill-nourished." In Chicago, a 1939 housing survey found that 76,000 units needed major rehabilitation or were unfit for use. While this represented eight percent of the units, it did not specify the number of people crowded into them. Four years later, a Chicago Plan Commission survey found 242,000 substandard units within a twenty-three-square-mile zone south and west of the Loop.[7] The shortage of housing grew more severe after World War II commenced. Even as the economy improved during the war, there was little residential construction as building resources and labor were directed to war production and military service. When the war ended, the supply of housing was acute for veterans and their families as well as for the thousands of migrants who came to Chicago to staff the war production positions.

In September 1945, as the soldiers returned home, Marciniak launched *Work*'s campaign to address the mounting housing problem in an article entitled "On Postwar Housing: Where We Stand." He laid out the statistics about the State of Illinois, noting that 336,141 dwellings needed major repair, 773,764 were without private baths, 17,676 had no toilets, and 227,947 had no electricity. Acknowledging that Illinois' housing problem was part of a national problem, he demanded a permanent national agency to address the issue with special emphasis on the income groups that needed it the most. Specifically, he proposed that the federal government aid cities to buy, clear, and write down the cost of land for redevelopment, noting that land costs were too high for "middle-priced" housing. He contended the primary job of government was the long-term interest of all citizens, and this included new housing at price levels affordable to the middle and lower-income families. Marciniak advocated that building materials be restricted "to prevent a building spree in the upper income price levels" and pressed for an expanded program to provide public housing for the "lowest income group." Private enterprise had not built housing for those "families earning below $1500 a year [and] it would be unlikely to do so in the foreseeable future."[8] His suggestions were part of the public discourse on housing reform that included code reform and enforcement and subsidies for low-cost housing to cure the urban problems.[9]

Work reported on and vigorously supported local and national measures put forward by housing groups in the post-war years. Further, it called on citizens to press government to provide broad housing programs that contained community planning and concluded: "It is imperative that new housing be built according to good standards for air, light, and space, [and] that neighborhoods should not expand haphazardly without considering transportation, location of industry, recreation, education, health, churches, and community facilities. This will require joint planning by all."[10]

Marciniak often featured articles to inform people about housing conditions in hopes of affecting public sentiment and effect changes. *Work* featured a review by "A Chicagoan,"[11] of Louis A. Kurtz,' *Forgotten Neighborhoods*, which exposed readers to terrible conditions including garbage cans in front halls, babies nibbled by rats in their cribs, windowless homes, and bathrooms shared by seven families. The reviewer noted that 250,000 Chicago families lived in substandard housing. It is difficult, he wrote, "to forget them once you have seen them," and gave his own firsthand accounts of apartment conditions on the East 39th, Street, 42nd Street and Evans, and the 600 block of West Division. The units were without tubs and toilets but had bedbugs and roaches, dangerous wiring, exposed lath, pneumonia-producing standing water in the basement, holes in the walls patched with cardboard, and eight families living in a partially burned-out building without water or electric.

The reviewer reiterated Kurtz' praise of the National Public Housing Conference of Chicago (NPHCC) for bringing together leaders of business, church, civic, and labor groups to make people aware of what was needed to better house families and urged the *Work*'s readers to join "one of the most wide-wake bodies of citizens in Chicago today."[12]

Marciniak was joined in his efforts by Rev Daniel M. Cantwell, who taught sociology at the Catholic seminary and served as the Catholic Labor Alliance chaplain. Cantwell had gotten a master's degree in sociology from Catholic University, where he had studied with Msgr. John Ryan, whose writings on economic justice and ethics influenced a generation of social action advocates and for whom the Catholic Labor Alliance would name its annual forums.

Additionally, Cantwell served as a member of the board of the NPHCC. His column, "What's New in Housing," had the by-line: D.M.C. Both Cantwell's and Marciniak's editorials and news features highlighted the implications of policy issues and stressed the need for action. The paramount issues were the affordability of new housing and the need for public housing for low-income families.

BUILDING CODES

The campaign for affordable housing pitted Marciniak and Cantwell against a portion of the Catholic Labor Alliance's core constituency, the building trades. Nationally, 15 million new homes were needed and, according to Cantwell, the failure to build resulted from the construction industry pricing itself out of the market. The average worker could not or would not mortgage their future for the inflated price of housing. While tradesmen were being saddled with much of the blame, Congress began investigations into labor's role in the housing shortage. The cost of building materials had risen dramatically, as had safety measures written into revised building codes. Moreover, labor conflicts produced slowdowns such as reductions in bricks laid per mason. For this reason, Cantwell pressed Congress to bring together labor and management to find more productive solutions and urged labor unions to willingly plan for year-around employment with off-site building techniques. In particular, he called for honest and enthusiastic "experimentation" with prefabrication and new building methods. "The common good of millions of families inside and outside the industry demand this," he concluded.[13]

In November 1945, Chicago's City Council responded to pressure of the housing crisis and considered revisions of the building code to lessen construction costs. The aldermen had drafted the prewar code to protect the interests of trade unions and building product companies. Now they turned to a respected architectural firm to diagnose the problems. After two years, the consultant submitted a thousand page document, which resulted in two more years of aldermanic foot-dragging and lobbying by special interests exacerbating the matter for those seeking affordable housing. *Work* provided a critique of the objections by labor interests and added its support for the new code's focus on the performance of materials and construction techniques in case of fire and other safety concerns.[14]

After lengthy debate on December 30, Mayor Martin H. Kennelly secured a compromise that was expected to stimulate new home building. The compromise permitted limited use of prefabricated homes and wallboard in designated outlying districts *if* the building materials used were able to meet performance standards in limiting the spread of fire, weight bearing load, and stability tests.[15] This made Chicago's code one of the nations' most progressive codes for it now specified material performance and it protected union interests in residential and office construction in the core portions of the city.[16]

AFFORDABLE HOUSING

The issue of housing for low-income people proved even more difficult to solve because it involved political ideologies and racial and class prejudices. Slum housing characterized by overcrowded, rundown, unsanitary conditions was the breeding ground of crime and social dysfunction. However, as the populations of the cities exploded with migrants and immigrants, housing shortages forced the newcomers to crowd together wherever they could. Most often this was in the older neighborhoods surrounding the city centers already populated by society's outcasts.

As he had in the past, Marciniak appealed to religious and distributive justice principles in the application of housing policy and practice. In November 1945, *Work* featured a full-page editorial advertisement that urged immediate action to house veterans and their families: "It is not only a civic duty. It is a moral duty as well. Clearly all of us are obliged by the virtue of social justice to do what we can— even with some inconvenience—to remedy this pressing need of shelter for the men and women who are returning from Europe and the Pacific. And if we have any charity in our hearts that inconvenience will be easy."[17]

NPHCC estimated 97,000 veterans would return to Chicago between September 1945 and February 1946, and soon thereafter another 240,000. Thirty-two thousand veterans and their families would need to be housed by February, and by the time they all returned a total of 109,500 vets and their families would be unprovided for. *Work* reported on the housing group's rally and concluded with the testimony of a participant, Army Lt. Erling Eng, who angrily stated that the entertainment and parades that greeted vets were fine, but he demanded to know "what about us when the band music dies down?" He emphasized that the temper of the vets was one of impatience and told of one who had survived 250 days in a prisoner of war camp and now planned to picket an apartment building that rented a five-room unit to a single occupant. Also, Lt. Eng dismissed the claim of supply shortages, as they were never a legitimate excuse for failure, and noted that in the Pacific, "We learned that you can always get the men and materials to do what needs to be done. If America could make a two-billion-dollar atomic bomb in war," Eng challenged, "couldn't it provide homes for the men who fought for the nation?"[18]

In the spring of 1946, *Work*'s columns and editorials challenged the real estate and building industries, trade unions, and government to take immediate action to help veterans obtain decent, affordable housing. *Work* questioned the Chicago Plan Commission's consideration of a Chicago Real Estate Board proposal to grant a ten percent increase in rents, making decent housing even more unaffordable.[19] The paper's harshest criticism, however, was directed at Illinois' governor, Dwight H. Green. In early 1946, the governor had met with veterans and civic and labor leaders who sought a special legislative session to deal with housing. He declined to schedule the special session.[20] When bus loads of delegates went to Springfield to attend a conference of the Emergency Veterans Housing Committee, the governor dodged the group.[21] Eventually, Green proposed legislation that offered a bonus to Illinois' vets at a base rate of $10.00 a month and $15.00 for overseas service.[22] Editorially, Marciniak attacked Green, a former U.S. District Attorney known for his toughness prosecuting Chicago gangsters, for sidetracking plans for veteran housing:

> Must we see the complete breakdown of family morality before there is a housing crisis? Must we see veterans living in tents in Grant Park before there is a housing shortage?

> The special bonus session has fooled no one. A bonus without decent housing is a fraud, a political stunt. A bonus made available now while the housing shortage grows worse and the inflationary spiral in housing rises higher is in reality a bonus to the real estate and building industry. The sad fact is that a house which in 1940 would cost $6,000 would now cost a veteran $9,000 according to the latest figures of the National Housing Agency. It represents a rise of 52.2 percent since 1940.

Mr. Green, we want a special housing session without further buck-passing. We want to know what is
behind this rise in prices. We want to see Illinois grant
local communities the power to proceed rapidly with
the condemnation of slum property and to undertake
a large-scale housing program.[23]

The housing problem could not be solved at the local
and state level alone, because most levers of power were
controlled by the federal government. In his 1944 State of
the Union, President Roosevelt shared his Economic Bill
of Rights, which included "the right of every family to a
decent home." Harry S. Truman adopted his predecessor's
domestic agenda seeking to address the housing problem.
The most comprehensive and balanced legislation addressing America's housing issues came from the collaboration
across the U.S. Senate's partisan aisle. Senators Robert
Wagner (D. NY) and Allen J. Ellender (D. LA) and Robert
Taft (R. OH) jointly introduced housing legislation. The
bill addressed slum clearance and urban renewal projects;
increased authorizations for mortgage insurance, and funding for public housing units; research on housing and building technologies; and farm dwelling assistance. [24] As the
Wagner-Ellender-Taft Housing Bill (WET) was debated
in December 1945, *Work* reprinted an article from the
American Federation of Labor's magazine outlining labor's
housing goals, to which Marciniak penned an editorial note
regarding the bill: "It must Pass."[25]

Six months later, little progress had been made on
veteran housing in Chicago because the city was unable to
secure a firm answer on the federal cost sharing for it on

temporary housing projects. *Work* decried the holdup due to a lack of a coordinated effort to build houses and a lack of a real housing industry as participants in the process were focused solely on their own immediate interests. A column by "A Chicagoan" explained that there were material producers, craft unions, contactors, and real estate agencies; and it sardonically added, "Each group is out to get all that the market will yield—that is, to bleed the consumer." This attitude destroyed real imagination and dimmed the prospect to eliminate the shortage. The only hope was coordination, and the column concluded: "What we are saying adds up to another reason for writing your congressman to urge passage of the Wagner-Ellender-Taft general housing bill, already passed in the Senate but languishing in the House."[26]

Over the next three years, *Work* informed readers of the progress of legislation and consistently lent vigorous support for the W-E-T bill to that of the U.S. Conference of Mayors, many labor unions, and the Truman administration.[27] A provision in the bill was authorization of loans to assist municipalities for acquisition of slums and blighted areas. A city could then make the parcels available for public or private use. The bill also provided for a permanent national housing agency, a housing research program, funds for local urban planning, and substantial changes to the operation of lending institutions and the Federal Housing Administration, including a program for moderate income families and cooperative housing. A coalition of real estate developers, financial institutions, and chambers of commerce effectively opposed public housing, declaring it was "socialistic."[28] In July 1946, the National Real Estate Board and the National Association of Home Builders killed the bill in the House.

Marciniak scolded the special interests and lamented that those favoring the W-E-T. bill did not show equal zeal."[29]

Because public and low-income housing shortages remained unresolved in the new year, the National Catholic Conference on Family Life took up housing and wage issues when it met at the Stevens Hotel, Chicago's giant convention hotel on South Michigan Avenue. Among the speakers were Cantwell, who spoke on family housing, and Marciniak. who examined Catholic teachings on wages and prices. They were joined by scholars from the University of Notre Dame as well as Catholic leaders including Monsignors Raymond McGowan and George Higgins from the National Catholic Welfare Conference. As they argued that economic and public policy issues were inextricably tied to moral considerations and impacted family welfare, the speakers held both government and private enterprise responsible for ensuring the production of affordable and safe family housing.[30] The Conference approved the following declaration on public housing: "We advocate a home building program in which private capital and government will cooperate to provide decent homes for people." Further it added, "We are convinced that without going into economic experiments that are at variance with our traditions, government can assist private individuals and provide millions of needed homes. For that sector of our population which in present conditions cannot procure for itself decent housing we advocate reasonable expenditures from the public treasury."[31]

It is not clear to what degree Marciniak and Cantwell shaped the conference declaration, but it mirrored their position. *Work* was not shy in advocating for expanding government intervention in housing and, in its April 1947 issue, pressed for federal progress with the resubmission of the Taft-Erlander-Wagner (T.E.W), renamed with Taft first because the Republicans won control of the Senate. Marciniak regarded the legislation as essential to ending the overcrowded and substandard living conditions for more than twenty million Americans and emphasized that it was "juvenile nonsense" for the critics of the legislation to term it "socialistic" and "communistic." In fact, it was dangerous because such talk gave credit to communists for a legislative proposal that "is as just as the American bill of rights." Besides, he noted, Senator Taft, whose bill was under consideration, was an "old-time conservative" without "leftist" leanings.[32]

While Taft's anti-union legislation sailed through Congress and mustered the votes to override a veto in June 1947, his housing legislation languished in the Senate while the House torpedoed a federal program allowing local authorities to sell bonds for public housing projects. Cantwell penned a column to express his outrage: "There are apparently no limits—ethically or morally—to which Congress is unwilling to go to push government out of the housing field."[33] Congress' failure to act, just as Governor Green's failure to act, threatened vital housing options at a time of urgent need.

THE CHICAGO HOUSING AUTHORITY

The one agency that had the greatest prospect of helping to meet the needs of the city's poor and low income was the Chicago Housing Authority (CHA). The Authority was a municipal nonprofit corporation created in 1937 to provide housing for the low income and poor and was governed by a board appointed by the mayor. At its inception, the CHA was administered by Elizabeth Woods, a respected social reformer who had led its efforts to provide public housing. Using federal assistance, the CHA had built several thousand family units in four low-rise projects. Three of the projects were for whites and one for Black people. This segregation complied with the federal regulations requiring tenants to be of the same race as those in the immediate area where the housing was located. The Jane Addams Houses on the westside, Julia Lathrop Homes on the northside, and the Trumbull Park Homes on the far southside were completed in 1938 and were for whites. The Ida B. Wells Homes on the near southside, which was the largest project and opened in 1941, was for Black people. The CHA built housing for families of the workers who had filled the wartime manufacturing jobs. When the war ended, the units were made available to all low-income applicants.[34] The CHA also immediately sought to provide temporary shelter for veteran families by acquiring 2,500 trailers. With a loan from the City of Chicago, it also purchased 500 flimsy plywood "demountable houses" to be located on vacant land owned by the city and the Cook County Forest Preserve. While the city's Emergency Temporary Housing program pledged 6,000 of these units, only 3,400 were built for the vets, using old military barracks, Quonset huts, and the trailers and demountables.[35]

So, housing was unaffordable both for veterans and for other Chicagoans. They could not save the money for a down payment on a modest home, even in the suburbs where land was much cheaper. Rents approached fifty percent of a worker's income. This spurred the CHA to build new apartment housing for the hardest pressed. Its planners identified additional vacant land throughout the city so projects could be initiated without waiting for assemblage of sites and demolition of structures. Racial prejudice and aldermanic objections, however, would block these plans.

At this early juncture, Marciniak began to assemble what would become a decades-long expertise in all aspects of public housing. The CHA's plan to build the permanent public housing for the poor was met with harsh criticism by neighborhood leaders, who claimed the rickety eyesores built for veterans were not welcome in their own communities. Marciniak was quick to respond to the critics: "Obviously, some type of housing is better than none at all." This statement appeared in a *Work* editorial for Labor Day 1945, entitled "Blind Opposition." The expanded press run was handed out to the 1500 civic, business, political, and labor leaders who attended an annual Mass at Holy Name Cathedral. Ed's greatest ire was directed at private enterprise which "never in Chicago (or elsewhere) provided low-income groups with decent housing." He praised the CHA for making a good start on building public housing despite the "potshots" from the *Chicago Tribune* and other opponents. In the same issue of *Work*, Cantwell's column "Public Housing Is Not 'Temporary'" reaffirmed Marciniak's oft-stated position that that public housing was not socialism. Rather, Cantwell stated it was government's responsibility to "make up for what private builders had never done for low-income families, even in good times."[36]

A 1948 report of the Public Housing Association documented the dramatic failure of private enterprise to meet the need and showed that Chicago lagged the rest of the nation in response to the crisis. Chicago builders had promised 30,000 units in 1947, but they produced fewer than 6,000 units. Marciniak feared that Chicago was fast becoming a "second rate" city, and noted: "Never, except for the days of the great fire in 1871, has Chicago had a shortage of housing comparable to that which it has today." In fact, the city was losing ground as more housing units were demolished the previous year than were replaced with new construction. The report blamed the foot dragging of the city council's housing committee for bottling up the CHA's plans and the state's failure to staff the Land Clearance Commission—the entity responsible for site acquisition authorization. The report also charged negligence in failing to create an agency to rehouse people displaced by slum clearance. *Work* also highlighted the city's lack of non-profit development corporations capable of using the newly created legislation to build low-cost housing.[37]

Both the Chicago *Sun-Times* and the Chicago *Daily News* shared the same position as *Work*'s on the need for public housing and its criticism of Republican legislators who blocked Senator Taft's bill from getting to the House floor for a vote. The *Sun-Times* editorialized that federal aid to public housing was as "socialistic" as federal aid for highway construction. Further, it pointed out that to get rid of the slums and avoid new ones, new housing had to be built by someone and to date private enterprise never had done that. Echoing Cantwell and Marciniak's position, the daily paper concluded: "Without public housing, therefore, slums just cannot be eliminated. That's the kind of 'socialism' you find in public housing which gives low-income people a chance for a decent life, which pulls out the roots of urban crime and juvenile delinquency, which cleans up the festering blight of modern cities."[38] In *Work's* update on housing, it commended the *Daily News* for its series on Chicago housing pointing out the desperate need for a slum-removal program, and went on to press for Taft's legislation which would provide essential funding to clear the blighted land surrounding downtown and make available to Chicago an estimated $125 million. For Chicago to take on the burden alone was regarded as a "manifest impossibility."[39]

Work also scolded the National Home Builders Association meeting in Chicago for its recent declaration that public housing was a program "of exorbitant cost, shoddy results, and inevitable waste."[40] The paper quoted the findings of Alderman Robert E. Merriam, former director of the Metropolitan Housing Council, that there was "no indication of malfeasance in the office or misappropriation of funds or misuse of authority."[41] Merriam's report had little impact on city council opposition to the CHA, because most white aldermen were fearful of racial turnover in their communities and sought to control the location of public housing in their wards. Containment of the racial boundaries, as Arnold Hirsch documents in his history of race and housing in Chicago, was the critical factor.[42] The issue was more than a Chicago issue as Cantwell noted in his column entitled, "Letters That Need To Be Written," a rhetorical letter to President Truman:

> Your Civil Rights Report was greeted in the South with hostility. That was the way they felt about it. In the North we greeted it warmly and sanctimoniously.

Actually, that is not the way we felt about it. Our actions say something else.

We could clear the slums today in Chicago if it were not for race prejudice. If clearing slums meant only clearing white people, we could get under way with the job with comparatively little difficulty.

But actually, there is no place to move the Negroes who will be displaced. It is impossible to even begin. We must decide once and for all if that discrimination in housing will not be tolerated. We must create new neighborhoods, new physically and spiritually....

Everywhere in housing it's the same problem. The rights of Negroes to get good housing in a good and peaceful neighborhood is denied. The South has suffered under the denial for generations. Cities in the North are rotting away under it too. Don't take us too seriously when we raise holy voices against the South.[43]

In August 1948, Marciniak penned an editorial appealing for citizen support of Mayor Martin Kennelly to back up the CHA's selections for new housing sites. The CHA had operated under the guidelines of the former city administration, which directed the CHA to honor racial composition of neighborhoods for tenant selection. Marciniak editorialized that it was imperative for "the whole city to be considered the surrounding area." Furthermore, he argued that because of the great need for housing for Black people, the "proportions of Negroes to be admitted in projects in 'new' areas ought to be somewhat in excess of their whole population in the total city population." He calculated that percentage to be close to twenty percent. Such a policy he held would be "just" and "judicious" and "a great advance toward full American and Christian living."[44]

Marciniak urged housing developed on vacant land outside the slum area as much as possible. He added that these sites should be large enough to constitute new communities that would "not become lost in the surrounding wornout [sic] neighborhoods." He concluded his editorial with the recommendation that would limit the aldermanic prerogative on public housing site selection: "Actually, these decisions must be confided to the Commissioners and Executive Staff of the CHA. We are confident in their record that they will make them with an eye to justice and the good of Chicago."[45]

Through early August 1948, Mayor Kennelly moved forward with site selection planning in closed door meetings with aldermen and CHA officials, hoping to hammer out a solution for $18.3 million in public housing projects. When City Council convened on August 27[th,] 400 people jammed the council chamber and loudly booed and directed catcalls at the mayor and aldermen. Residents shouted, "We ought to throw you out" and "We'll never vote for you again," and a few spectators used profanity, forcing the mayor to frequently gavel for order and threaten to clear galleries. Kennelly's plan passed; however, the angry protestors waited for the mayor in the hall outside the council chamber forcing him to use a rear exit to return to his office.[46]

Marciniak praised the mayor and the CHA board for their unprejudiced plans to provide housing for all groups where it was most needed. A portion of the lands purchased

by the CHA could be cleared and resold to private enterprises to engage in genuine slum clearance; however, his
editorial added: "Genuine slum clearance means building
dwelling units to rent at prices the lowest income group can
pay." Many Chicagoans feared that the temporary relocation
housing would not be in the slum area where the people then
lived. Marciniak also questioned the uproar against three of
the selected sites in districts occupied by Black people and
added, "prejudice should not blind us to the fact that these
areas need rebuilding the most."[47]

On the eve of the November 1948 national election,
Marciniak published his own open letter "To the Next President of the U.S," appealing to whomever won to address
the urgent need for affordable housing. He paraphrased a
recent speech of Archbishop Patrick O'Boyle of Washington D.C. to a Catholic Charities convention, which called
for the American genius that produced more planes, ships,
and guns than ever dreamed possible to now concentrate
on solving the "housing log-jam." Admitting that building
houses normally was the work of free enterprise, the prel-
ate contended that for-profit builders had not evidenced a
willingness to come close to meeting the needs of the large
number of people living in the blighted areas and, therefore, government subsidies were necessary. Marciniak then
personalized the issue by stating that a small, new home
in Chicago costs $9,300 not including the cost of the land,
architect, and builder profits. He added: "That figure is no
lie, I know from my own looking around." Most people he
knew were unable to make a twenty-five-year commitment
for a hefty mortgage when they were not even certain if they
would have a job in five years.[48]

While Truman's upset victory over Thomas E. Dewey likely gave *Work's* thirty-one year old editor satisfaction, the economic justice and housing issues remained. Only months earlier *Tribune* editors had attacked the President for his housing agenda as a "program of socialism." Further, it objected to rent-control measures protected by Truman, believing the free market would create demand for new construction only when the artificially lower rents were free to rise.[49] In August of 1948, Congress did pass watered down housing legislation that reduced payments and extended mortgage terms for moderately priced houses; however, the law did not include urban renewal and public housing. Truman reluctantly signed the legislation despite its shortcomings and lamented, "In short, Congress in enacting this bill has deliberately neglected those large groups of our people most in need of adequate housing—people who are forced to live in disgraceful urban and rural slums."[50]

Marciniak assured his readers that the socialism "scare" of the home builders and *Tribune*-like propagandists was not a real threat. Nevertheless, he cautioned that using the "socialism" label was misleading and stressed that the real test of a program was: "What does this law mean IN ITSELF—regardless of what the Communists or Socialists say about it?" He pointed out that those who called any form of government ownership and control "socialistic" ignored the facts. "If that's true, this country has been socialist since George Washington's time," he argued and gave examples. For his Catholic audience he emphasized: "If government intervention is socialism, then Pope Leo XIII practiced socialism. As far back as 1891, he advocated such "socialistic" things as child labor laws, minimum wage laws, unionism, and social security." Ed also cited Pope Pius XI: "Certain forms of property must be reserved to the government, since they carry with them the power so great it can not be left to private individuals without injury to the public welfare." Marciniak concluded his argument by pressing readers to heed the Popes' pleas for justice: "Let's not permit the confusion about 'socialism' to block the way to that goal, especially in the 81st Congress."[51]

In 1949, the T. E. W. bill proceeded through the newly-elected Congress with provisions for slum clearance, urban redevelopment, and public housing projects, and it was signed by Truman. Marciniak energetically pressed Chicago's mayor to apply for 40,000 units, one half of Illinois' pro rata allocation in the housing act. Significantly, the bill provided mortgage financing for construction of single-family homes on the lots that had sat vacant for twenty years as the latter would be easier to manage.[52] Slum clearance and public housing would be more challenging. Housing expert Alexander von Hoffman noted that the public housing advocates had won the battle in Washington, D.C. but were soon opposed by a concerted special interest campaign at the local level.[53] In Chicago, it was not just a matter of "socialism," it had been and remained a matter of racial politics.

SLUM CLEARANCE AND REDEVELOPMENT

In the 1950s, redevelopment of the blighted areas and housing for the poor, especially the poor Black families, would be one of the Chicago's greatest challenges. The Black population had increased from approximately 278,000 in 1940 to

812,000 in 1960. In this period, the Black per centage of the Chicago's population increased from 8.2 percent to 22.9 percent. As Arnold Hirsch noted, "Chicago offered migrants work; however, the city was much less able to provide them with shelter."[54]

Once again, City Council balked at approving public housing sites and Marciniak sustained the drive to influence and mobilize his readers. In a front-page article, *Work* laid out the political and moral issues. The only way to get apartments for low-income families was for an agreement on a package of seven sites to be used for the first 10,000 units and for that to be the first installment of 40,000 additional units over six years. Putting all its eggs in one basket was "pretty dangerous," but it was necessary. If the city balked, it might lose out on this essential federal program. *Work* explained that three of the sites would be on vacant sites and four on slum lands but all must be approved as one package for the initiative to go forward. Furthermore, the densely populated slums could not be cleared until housing for displaced residents could be built on vacant land to begin the relocation process.

Marciniak forthrightly addressed the core issue, racial change in neighborhoods where there were no Black people. He noted that some of the people who would be in public housing would be Polish, Irish, Italian, and Black; however, most would be the latter and he acknowledged this might be a problem:

> For some white people, the coming of Negroes will make no difference. Some will even be glad about it, because their colored brother will be getting a better

chance, and because their neighborhood will better represent the great variety of people for whom Christ died and whom He invited to become members of His Mystical Body.

But some others will see the coming of Negroes as the signal to demonstrate how undemocratic and un-Christian they can be. These people are no longer as numerous as they once were. But there are too, too, many still.[55]

Work, emphasized that saving the housing program was a moral choice, and explicitly stated that "we are responsible for the way our alderman votes in the city council when the crucial vote on the housing sites comes up this month." This required readers to get to their individual alderman and "help" him to make up his mind to vote for all the sites. "It means," Marciniak continued, "there must be no deals among the aldermen, each promising the other to keep public housing out of the other's ward." He was insistent that each reader share his or her religious convictions with their alderman, noting that "there was a day when Christians took strangers into their homes, today we are asked only to take them into our neighborhoods."[56] He also called on the council members to do what was best for the entire city, not what was popular in certain neighborhoods or with special interests.[57] The editor persisted in his urging and was supported by the Cana Conference of Chicago, an organization for married couples that had active groups in most parishes[58]

As the aldermen objected to CHA housing in their wards, *Work* corrected misinformation circulated about public housing, appealed to human sentiment, and called for action. Rather than just report on the pathetic living situations, it published portions of moving letters from people who described their conditions that included inadequate or broken plumbing, lack of privacy, broken windows, gaping plaster holes, pneumonia-inducing dampness in fetid basement units, and rats biting children as they slept. The desperation was typified by one writer, who begged: "'Please help me get a place to live. I have three children and expecting another one. We live in one room just large enough for a double bed and a single one.'"[59] These pleas of the poor were never heard in the in the City Council chambers, however, as protestors jammed the galleries objecting to public housing.

In June 1949, the CHA Chairman, Robert R. Taylor, acceded to a compromise as a last resort to prevent the loss of funding for approximately 13,000 units. In substance, the CHA caved into the aldermanic prejudices. The deal, according to the *Chicago Tribune*, was "contrary to a long-standing position of the CHA and housing advocates who have argued that large projects in outlying vacant areas must be built first for relocating families before construction can proceed in the slum." The new plan called for the CHA to build elevator buildings on vacant land in the slums where tenants of blighted housing would be relocated, with more high-rise housing to follow, repeating the process. This compromise ensured a phased development of public housing, so the relocations had to move more slowly and forced the poor, mostly Blacks on the south and west sides, to live in slums for several more years.[60]

HIGH RISE PUBLIC HOUSING

The compromise by the alderman and the CHA also impacted the livability of the public housing for families. Marciniak was never a cheerleader for all types of housing. He harbored grave concerns about high rises, and he was scalding in his critiques. In late 1951, after a few CHA projects had been built, he penned a feature article he titled "Is Chicago's Future Up In the Air?" His subtitle set the tone: "These Frightening Skyscraper Homes." He introduced the article with a description of portions of New York City with block after block of 12-to-14 story buildings that were "monotonous, uninteresting, and depressing." Some belonged to the big insurance companies and others to the New York Housing Authority; their tenants ranged from low-income to high-income. He regarded them as "monuments to misplaced construction and architectural genius." Labelling the buildings "masterpieces of regimentation," Marciniak shared the observation of Lewis Mumford, the noted urban expert, planner, and architect, who found the only good thing that could be said about the public housing high rises was that they were "'better than slums.'"[61]

Observing the first CHA projects, the Dearborn Homes, Prairie Avenue Courts, and Ogden Court, which ranged in height from 7 to 14 stories, Marciniak caustically noted their "cliff dwelling" appearance. When a booster group trying to revitalize the South Side laid out a plan showing a mass of skyscraper dwellings, he was stingingly critical: "If we saw them in a picture of Moscow, we would recognize them for what they are, dungeons for regimented human beings." He was not thinking of the wealthy in the skyscrapers along Lake Shore Drive, who could live wherever they wanted and had few children; however, he was concerned for the poor-and-middle-income families with children who had few options.

> We are not wringing our hands over what has already been built. What we want to know is where is Chicago going to draw the line. What we suggest is that Chicago draw it right now, before we build anymore cliff-dwellings and skyscraper housing projects for families who want to raise children.

> If we are not going to rebuild the old neighborhoods for families with children, then we had better stop worrying about the flight of people from the city. Where else are they going to go.

Ed's advocacy was also for the older population who deserved surroundings that were more than a place to "commune with a deck of cards and a television." Wryly, he added, "even the poor commune with God." Architects and city planners had a responsibility to help the people who lived in the buildings to get to heaven as well.[62]

Marciniak's concerns were for the future of Chicago and its residents. He pointed out the flawed reasoning of those who argued that the high price of land required building higher in pursuit of getting the maximum number of units on each parcel of land to increase returns. He disputed that there was a compelling economic law driving Chicago's trend. The problem from his point of view was that high rises begot more high rises and increasing heights and set the expectation on the future value of surrounding land leading to more tall buildings and higher land prices. From his perspective, the builders were not farsighted enough to see that the shorter life of these buildings and the damage to the community. What might involve less public expense today, he believed, only deferred greater social and economic costs. The expense to build low rise garden apartments for human community now, "not hives for bees or cages for muskrats," he contended, would have benefits with longer lasting value. He prophetically concluded: "Right now we are building slums for the future—this time mammoth slums. However, much they soar to heaven and look like temples to man-made gods, they are not eternal."[63]

Marciniak's article drew an immediate and broad response, locally and nationally. The executive director of the South Side Planning Board responded that Marciniak failed to consider that the area's density made going higher a necessity as single homes and low-rise units with green space required more than twice as much land as was available. The planner accepted the self-imposed constraints of accommodating all the people then crammed into the slum and disagreed with *Work's* apparent assumption that a healthy environment required much lower rise housing solutions.[64] A letter of agreement with Marciniak's position came from Alderman Robert E. Merriam of Hyde Park, who would run for mayor of the city in two years. He noted that he was drafting legislation that would allow single family houses to be built on slum clearance land.

John Ducey, a housing expert who had formerly worked for the CHA and a Marciniak friend, reluctantly felt compelled to object to *Work's* characterization of high rises.

Ducey suggested that climbing stairs to the third floor of a walk-up unit with heavy groceries and a child in tow was not preferable to an elevator building for many. He observed "your real battle" is with density per acre and square mile and encouraged Marciniak focus on that issue.[65]

G. Holmes Perkins, the Dean of Fine Arts, University of Pennsylvania encouraged Marciniak to follow up and make a strong case in future editorials and advised him to present an alternative to cliff dweller housing. The most supportive response for Ed came from New York. Lewis Mumford, author of the acclaimed book, *The Culture of Cities*," who wrote: "I am in full agreement with your article on the appalling mistakes that your public housing authority is making in Chicago in servile imitation of New York." Mumford also buttressed Marciniak's points on the true cost of such housing, noting that the additional costs of finding solutions to the congestion caused by density was born by the community on an ongoing basis. On the social side, Mumford found such public housing to "disrupt" families and neighborhoods and to cause ill health. He concluded with the question: "Why are your fellow citizens so lacking in common sense and self-respect that they sheepishly imitate New York's worst sins and errors?"[66]

Accompanying the Mumford letters, Marciniak provided an editorial response reaffirming his concern for decent housing for poor families and discussed the need for long range, comprehensive planning for the metropolitan area. The city and CHA's planners were drafting plans with blinders by responding to the pressures to keep population density near the Loop to support commercial enterprises and keep the same number of people in the same small area. The planners, Ed contended, were caving into the need for action along with the pressure to prevent "the undesirables" from the slums from moving into new wide-open spaces in the metropolitan area." This latter defensive strategy had that very month resulted in the CHA's commitment to build the fifteen-story Oakwood-Lake Park project, a higher structure with a bigger footprint than its predecessors.

Marciniak heeded the University of Pennsylvania dean's advice to provide an alternative. He boldly urged comprehensive, long-range planning for the metropolitan area extending fifty miles from downtown. "Why not start thinking of Chicago as a vast expanse, which it really is," he asked. "If we think and plan on such a broad scale, can't we build all the homes we need for family living? But if we go on making midget-sized plans, is it any wonder we have to build more skyscraper housing?" Despite the pressures to get something done, he insisted on asking questions:

+ Why must we go on keeping so many people in so many small spaces?
+ Is there any sensible reason, socially or economically for building buildings into the air to create open spaces on the ground?
+ How could anyone prove that it is taste and not necessity which makes families who want children move into skyscraper housing? Do families with low or moderate incomes have any choice in the matter?
+ How wise is it to use expensive public services to build in large quantity and glamorize a type of

housing that makes having children less and not more attractive?

+ Who dares defend the proposition that skyscraper housing was ever seriously proposed as a particularly good place to rear child?

+ What will we do in Chicago? Will we think hard now? Or rue the future?[67]

CHA's director of information responded that "we are in full accord" with *Work*'s viewpoint on family life in elevator buildings; however, "our hands [are] virtually tied" by costs and limited building locations."[68] Marciniak was not satisfied, and he added a sharp editor's note that the new policy would mean the end of two-story rowhouses, which the CHA still regarded as ideal for families with children. If the CHA really believed this, he argued, they should "go into action." He listed the board members by name, including that of his friend John Yancy, a Black union leader who was on both the Catholic Labor Alliance board and the CHA board. The commissioners needed to make a case to the communities and city council "on behalf of the families with children," Marciniak pressed. "Let's not give up the fight now Mr. Commissioners. Defend the rights of family to a decent home in the name of democracy and in the name of God."[69]

But CHA policy would not and did not change, and thousands of units in elevator buildings would rise on the site of former slum housing on the north, west, and south sides of Chicago to house families. For the next fifty years, Marciniak would continue to oppose such structures.

Marciniak was most certainly distressed by the aldermanic shenanigans and the mayor's willingness to accede to them; however, he persisted. He continued to feature stories intended to shock his readers such as "6 More 'Murders by Fire' on Chicago's Conscience," which told of the death of three children and other residents of a converted stable on South Washburne, less than a five-minute walk from the former site of the St. Joseph House of Hospitality. What might have been good enough for horses had become slum housing.[70] His editorials railed against the greedy landlords who milked their properties for maximum income by subdividing units and failing to provide safe and healthy living conditions and against Chicago's bribe-taking building inspectors, who overlooked serious safety-and-health code violations. Pointedly, Ed challenged the mayor to clean house in the building department and give priority to overcrowded slum residents rather than building parking garages to relieve congested streets for downtown merchants. As well, *Work* also sustained editorials about the injustice of builders who used limited labor and materials to build expensive homes, taverns, theaters, and bowling alleys and ignored the working poor.[71]

URBAN RENEWAL

Illinois and the City of Chicago passed legislation that made slum clearance, land assembly, and eminent domain possible, as well as the conveyance of the cleared land to private entities pursuant to the Housing Act of 1949. Two major developments demonstrated the challenges that faced those who wished to renew the city and eradicate the slum and blighted areas. The first major project was by New York Life and other private entities who promised to build high rise housing for middle class residents on the southern edge of the Downtown. This project, known as Lake Meadows, received wide support from the business community and the mayor who feared for the central business district's future. Marciniak wrote little about the project in its earliest stages, other than to note that the public action to clear the slum land and sell it to the developer at pennies on the dollar was a form of socialism for the money interests who supported the project to protect their Loop businesses. He recommended that the same largess should be made more generously available for the families that were being removed and in dire need of decent housing. Marciniak's concern for the poor and powerless, however, did not exclude the task of rebuilding the city. When the project was completed, he supported the development's commitment to integrated living. A certain number of units were set aside for Black families who met income and other criteria, making them eligible for rent subsidies. However, there was a limited proportion of units for eligible non-whites, as the goal was to attract the sought-after white market.[72]

A second renewal project which was of much larger scale and operated under community conservation rules drew Marciniak's comment and involved him in a controversy that affected his relationship with the Catholic Archdiocese of Chicago. The University of Chicago had drafted the renewal project to stem the resegregation of the Hyde Park community, where the highly regarded University of Chicago (U of C) was located. The shortage of adequate housing in the black belt and the slum clearance for the Lake Meadows project forced Black people to find housing in adjacent communities. In the 1950s, Hyde Park experienced an increase of racial change on its western and southern fringes and the conversion of apartment units into smaller units to house more families. The growing economic and racial instability in the area around the university lessened its attraction for many whites, who had moved to the suburb and threatened the U of C's ability to woo star faculty and students to its campus.

The Hyde Park-Kenwood Community Council, a community organization, initially put together plans to improve the area by monitoring building violations and controlling rumors of violence. The university administration considered this inadequate, so it created, funded, and directed the South East Chicago Commission, a nonprofit corporation, to take advantage of new state laws that allowed local entities to plan and direct the conservation and renewal of their communities with city council approval. Over a period of years SECC drafted plans and garnered support to implement a major residential and commercial development project that would change the physical character and racial makeup of Hyde Park. The liberal Hyde Park community, which took pride in diversity, reduced its resistance to the plans and agreed to a project that would cause the removal of Black people and lower income whites. The goal of the planners was to upgrade the attractiveness of the U of C environment by eradicating cheaper housing occupied by the lower-middle class and increasing the supply of new, more expensive housing designed to give the university breathing space to expand.[73]

Rev. John Egan, who became involved in urban affairs through his connections with community organizer Saul Alinsky, had extreme reservation regarding the plan because of its disparate impact on the poor and Black residents who would have to relocate. He perceived that the plan not only affected those residents who were to relocate, but also the communities adjacent to Hyde Park that would experience increased pressure on their already taxed housing supply. Too often slum clearance and urban renewal had become "Negro removal," and so Egan spoke up. He made his case forcefully to both the archdiocese's cardinal and chancellor and secured their support as well as *The New World*, the Archdiocesan newspaper. Egan's primary argument was that the poor were unjustly burdened and had been given no voice in their future. However, in discussing the larger issue of the impact on churches and schools in the adjoining communities, he highlighted the welfare of those institutions.[74]

Marciniak officed in the same building as Egan and shared many of the priest's concerns for the poor as well as his view that housing was a metropolitan-wide issue, not a simple community issue. However, he believed, as did Cantwell, that the community leaders of Hyde Park had the right to vet a plan and see to its implementation. They believed that Egan's position was overreach by the Archdiocese into public policy and was ill-advised. Shortly after Egan testified at a public hearing, but before his fiery speech against the plan at a City Council meeting, Marciniak vehemently opposed Egan. His *Work* column read more like one of his editorials, even though it was not on the editorial page.[75] Entitled "Chicago's Hyde Park Renewal Plan—Preview of the City of Tomorrow," he commented on the "hubbub," noting that it might be either a triumph or a tragedy for Chicago.[76]

Marciniak feared that the "uproar" jeopardized the renewal plan designed to stop spreading slums. Moreover, he believed it could be a model for civic activism for other communities to engage in the essential work of community planning. While the discussion of the Hyde Park-Kenwood Renewal Plan advanced, Marciniak posited that it was important that the other forty to fifty neighborhoods "already infected by rotting slums caused by poor zoning, chaotic planning, overcrowded apartments, unenforced building codes, corrupt ward politicians, ungodly barriers of race hate, and lackadaisical property owners" engage in their own planning. He explained that thousands of Hyde Park property owners and tenants had contributed money and countless hours over nine years to do just that. Furthermore, Ed pointed out that the community had accepted public housing as part of the plan and had been a model of peaceful acceptance of Black people without a mass white exodus. Marciniak opined that no other neighborhood could claim such "a good record of devotion to Chicago's common good." He was quick to add that Hyde Park's rehabilitation solutions were specific to its needs, just as those of the Back of the Yards neighborhood's plan were specific to its needs.

The moral issues of planning were paramount for Marciniak. The relocation of families needed to be for "just and sufficient cause" and whether those thousands who suffered and lived in places "not fit for hogs or horses will be relocated to decent homes with minimum of discomfort." For Marciniak the last people to be pushed around should be defenseless poor. The fact that the city's relocation office had improved was significant; however, he believed that real responsibility rested with the more than five million people of the metropolitan area outside of Chicago. They were the ones who wanted new expressways that cleared slums so they could speed to the suburbs, they wanted clearance to build a medical center to care for the sick and crippled, and they wanted parking lots to house their autos in the downtown. All of these "civic" choices required the uprooting of thousands of families. The relocations that would result in the Hyde Park plan were "the heavy responsibility" of both the city and the suburbs.[77]

Marciniak acknowledged that many city-wide agencies had interested themselves in the Hyde Park plan including the Chicago Urban League, the Cardinal's Conservation Committee, the Church Federation of Greater Chicago, and the Cook County Industrial Union Council. They had offered ideas to improve the plan by cushioning the impact on the low income and poor, and Ed conceded their ideas deserved careful consideration. Nonetheless, he expressed a degree of consternation that the groups had not coordinated their efforts to secure a better hearing from the city and renewal planners. In the end, Marciniak wanted action.

> A city is not good without good houses for its families. It may display a wonderful lakefront, magnificent expressways, modern factories, handsome parks, and a dazzling skyline of office buildings. These are not enough. These are not the most important. What makes a city great is how it treats its families, particularly the poor and helpless.

> In Hyde Park public-minded citizens have been working towards this goal. Now all of Chicago should help them get on with the job.[78]

His goal of rebuilding the city and its neighborhoods with a broad sense of responsibility was consistent. Four years later, sociologist Rev. Andrew Greeley took a swipe at Marciniak for his earlier *Work* column in a review of Peter H. Rossi and Robert Dentler's *The Politics of Urban Renewal*. Marciniak responded to Greeley with his usual tart directness. "I am not getting involved in the pejorative nature of the comparisons you are making.... It is like saying that the historians who analyze the Pearl Harbor situation had a better understanding of what transpired than those who were on the firing line. You can't give merit badges to people with hind sight."[79]

When questioned about the Hyde Park redevelopment a few years later, Marciniak responded forthrightly, "No relocation program—involving low income families—can be accomplished without some mistake or injustices. And Hyde Park had its share." He noted, however, that the "overwhelming majority" of the families were relocated to safe, sanitary housing, and the hardcore cases were eased by the social welfare. One silver lining for them was urban renewal made public the human burden shouldered by these families that would have remained hidden from view.[80] The public process made it the public's responsibility to address the heartache and injustices as never before.

Tellingly, when asked to recommend books for people who wanted to pursue Catholic social action, Marciniak advised justice seekers to read *Exploding Metropolis*. The book is a compilation of articles from *Fortune* by noted urbanologists and city planners who stressed the need to make cities livable by examining the issues of slums and urban renewal, urban sprawl, downtowns for people—not businesses, and the uses and abuses of government power. It was according to its editor, William H. Whyte, "a book by people who love cities."[81] Marciniak was one of those people who loved cities, and he took it as his mission to make them more livable.

The issues of housing, planning, and development that provoked his journalistic attention in the 1940s and 1950s would be critical in his future endeavors as a public servant, scholar, and activist. While he did influence people and made lasting connections helpful to his advocacy for decent housing, his efforts with the CHA had not yet gained wide political support. Through his experiences and analysis, Marciniak came to believe that planning was one of the most important roles of government. City planning was more than just cityscape renderings and colorful maps; it required a thoughtful review of the consequences of the built environment and a public policy guided by a moral ethic. Ed Marciniak believed that the city planner's vocation was to enhance urban life, especially for its poorest families.

NOTES

1   "Chicago's Hyde Park Renewal Plan—Preview of the City of Tomorrow," *Work*, August 1958.

2   *Chicago Tribune*, "Fire Prevention Record Better," October 9, 1947; and "10 Killed in Tenement Fire," October 10, 1947.

3   "Rents Tripled for Negroes Fire Investigation Shows," November 1947.

4   Chicago's Big Need: Low Rent Housing," March 1947.

5   "Fire Disaster Demands 'Yes' Vote on Bond Issue," November 1947.

6   Illinois House Resolution HR1043, http://ilga.gov//legislation/fulltext.asp?DocName+09300HR1043.

7   Mayer and Wade, *Chicago Growth of a Metropolis*, p. 366 and Grossman, Keating, and Reiff, *The Encyclopedia of Chicago, p. 849.*

8   P. 7.

9   Alexander von Hoffman, "A Study in Contradictions: The Origins and Legacy of the Housing Act of 1949," *Housing Policy Debate*, Vol.11, Issue 2, pp. 299-306, https://www.innovations.harvard.edu/sites/default/files/hpd_1102_hoffman.pdf.

10   "Where We Stand," September 1945. The paper urged labor unions and churches to support of cooperative housing programs.

11   The reviewer was identified as "A Chicagoan." The directness and style as well as the detailed content seems to point to Marciniak or Rev. Daniel M. Cantwell as that reviewer. It was a common practice for editors to write articles and reviews without giving a by-line. "A Chicagoan" was often the author of occasional columns on policy issues affecting Chicago.

12   November 1945.

13   D.M.C.," Labor and Housing," *Work*, August 1947.

14   D.N.C., "Is the New Building Code as Bad as They Say?," Oct 1949; "Let's Not Confuse the Issue" and "What the Experts have to Say About the Proposed Building Code," *Work*, December

1949; and "Council gets New Building Code", *Chicago Tribune* November 12, 1947. When the Chicago Building Trades Council opposed the proposed version even though it had declined an opportunity to contribute to its revisions, Cantwell charged the trade groups with duplicitousness for their objections to the proposed code and false advertising designed to drum up opposition. In particular, the plasters' union opposed factory-made wall board as it dramatically reduced the costly, labor intensive lath and plaster construction and threatened union jobs. Cantwell attended the hearing and admitted there might be room for debate but not deceptions. He objected to the union's "unreasonable" demand to apply the safety measures necessary for a hospital or hotel to a single-family home. To add authority to its position, *Work* printed four letters to the City Council Committee on Building Code Revisions from respected architects, including the President of the Chicago Chapter of the American Institute of Architects supporting the code.

15 Work had carried stories about prefabricated buildings and even had argued for a steel component home manufacturer that sought assistance in taking over a now vacant Chicago factory that had previously made bombers for Dodge Motor company during WWII. See: *Work*, "Chicago's Housing Record is a National Disgrace," November 1946. See Also: "Prefabricated Housing, February 1947.

16 Compromise City Building Code Adopted Unanimously," and "How Chicago's Building Code Will Take Lead," *Chicago Tribune*, December 31, 1949.

17 "Needed: Housing for Chicago Veterans.".

18 Ibid. In a December 1945 the paper noted that City Council had appropriated $1,000,000 for 500 temporary dwellings to be transported to Chicago and that the Chicago Housing Authority had arranged to bring 2500 trailers to the city. Plans were being made for the conversion of the Dodge aircraft plant near 79th and Pulaski to be converted into living accommodations for vets and their families. Ibid.

19 "The Chicago Plan Commission," *Work*, April 1946. Chicago had rent controls mandated by the federal government, but the requirements ceased in 1946. Chicago passed legislation to keep rent control authority, but it was soon overturned by the Illinois Supreme Court in January 1947. See Wendy Plotkin, "Rent Control in Chicago after WWII: Politics, People and Controversy," *Prologue* 30.2 (Summer 1998), pp. 110-123 http://wbhsi. net/~wendyplotkin/Prologue.pdf

20 Green Studies Plea to Call Vet Home Session," *Chicago Tribune*, January 3, 1946.

21 "Sidetrack Housing Plan for Illinois Veterans," *Work*, May 1946. The article was written by June Gardner, who attended the session for the paper.

22 "Draft Illinois Bonus Plan," Chicago *Tribune*, April 17, and "Green to Call Legislature in Bonus Session," *Chicago Tribune*, April 24.

23 "Housing Session Long Overdue," June 1946. The following month Green ducked the issue. The governor ignored the call for a special session and advocated for "a restoration of unrestricted competition and the unleashing of private investment, rather than appropriation of public funds for public housing." Cited in A Chicagoan's column, "We Need More Housing," *Work*, July 1946.

24 See "Roosevelt's Economic Bill of Rights, January 11, 1944," http://www.worldfuturefund.org/Reports/Model/rooseveltbillofrights.html, April 28, 2020, and Von Hoffman, pp. 305-307.

25 "Good Housing for All Is Special Challenge to Labor," *American Federationist*, November 1945, cited in *Work*, December 1945.

26 "Why We Don't Get Houses, "*Work*, June 1946.

27 See "Unity in Housing," and "U.S. Needs More Housing; But Congressmen Keep Stalling," and "Federal Housing Program Fails to Pass Congress," August 1946; and "We Still Do Not Have a U.S. Housing Program," October 1946.

28 Ashley Foard and Hilbert Fefferman, "Federal Urban Renewal Legislation," Duke *Law Journal*, pp. 635-642, https://scholarship.law.duke.edu/cgi/viewcontent.cgi?article=2856&context=lcp and von Hoffman, pp.306-309.

29   "Federal Housing Program Lags; Who Is to Blame?" *Work*, September 1946. See also, "Congressional Bungling: We Still Do Not Have a U.S. Housing Program, October 1946.

30   "Housing, Wages, Topics for Family Life Meeting," *Work*, March 1947.

31   Cited in "Public Housing," *Work*, July 1947.

32   "Congress Given 2nd Chance to Ease Housing Shortage."

33   "Housing Moves Ahead," July 1947. This column was Cantwell's first under his own by line: " D.M.C."

34   Arnold Hirsch, pp. 12-13.

35   "Housing Note," *Work*, December 1945. See also: *Chicago Tribune*, "Homes in War Plants Urged to Ease Crisis, November 6, 1945; "Returning Veterans Plunge into Battle for Place to Live," Nov. 12, 1945; Council Votes Million to Aid Vets' Housing," November 20, 1945, and "Select 2 Sites for Emergency Vets' Housing," December.1, 1945. The first two veterans to move in did so on Christmas eve with Mayor Kelly and three aldermen on hand to welcome the vets. The rent was $32.50 per month.

36   September 1947. Also included was the copy of a New York monsignor's letter to the *New York Times* which emphasized the need for government sponsored public housing.

37   "For a 'Second-Rate' City, A First Rate Housing Program," May 1948.

38   *Sun-Times*, June 17, 1948, cited in Cantwell's column, "The People are Still Waiting," *Work*, July 1948.

39   July 1948,

40   Cited in *Work*, April 1948.

41   "Letters that Need to Be Written," April 1948.

42   April 1948.

43   Ibid.

44   "Chicago's Housing Program Needs Support of Citizens."

45   Ibid.

46   "Cited in "Council OK's Housing Sites Amid Tumult., *Chicago Tribune* August 28, 1948. See also Chicago *Tribune*: "Housing Figures meet Mayor in Effort to Settle Relocation," August 3. 1948; "Housing Authority, Council Again Fail to Agree on

Projects," August 6, 1948; Mayor Ok's 9 Relocation House Sites," August 12, 1948; ;and "Council OK's Housing Sites Amid Tumult," August 28, 1948.

47 "Slum Clearance," *Work*, November 1948.

48 November 1948. Marciniak still lived with his parents. There is no evidence of what his compensation was from his work directing the Catholic Labor Alliance, Chicago Newspaper Guild, and free lance writing.

49 "Who Gets the Houses?" July 1948.

50 Statement of the President Upon Approving the Housing Act. https://www.trumanlibrary.gov/library/public-papers/157/statement-president-upon-signing-housing-act-1949.

51 "Does Truman Victory Mean U.S. Is Going 'Socialist'?," December 1948..

52 "Housing Action," *Work*, June 1949. See also: "Proposed Federal Housing Bill Would Bring 'Dead' Real Estate Back to 'Life,' *Work*, April 1949.

53 Von Hoffman, pp 308-310.

54 P. 17

55 "10,000 Homes in 1 Package," February 1950. The deadline for action was March 1 or Chicago would lose it opportunity for federal assistance.

56 Ibid.

57 "Chicago Needs Public Housing: It's Your Ball, Aldermen," *Work*, March 1950.

58 "Cited in "87000 Chicago Families Need Public Housing," June 1950. By 1950 the Cana Conference groups met monthly to discuss family and social issues. *Work* printed a lengthy article from the Conference's organ, *Couplets*, which told worried families that public housing was not a threat to property values. It encouraged Cana members to consider that the high rise along the Gold Coast did not lose value being near the slums or public housing west of Clark Street and called on them to contact their aldermen to make decent housing available to the poor. *Work* carried a special side bar that relied on data from *Olcott's Blue Book*, the standard reference book on land values in

Chicago, and emphatically concluded there was proof that "values have increased in every area in Chicago where permanent public housing projects have been built, regardless of nationality or race of the occupants." Further it reported, this was true of "projects on vacant land as well as slums clearance property."

59 Cited in "Housing Misery Grows But City's Conscience Is Dull," June 1950..

60 "Compromise Housing Sites OK'd by CHA," June 17, 1950, and "Delay of New Public Housing Projects Seen, Sept 24, 1950," September 12, 1950. The article was written by a community activist who noted that that many of these make-shift homes had "no running water, no electric lights, no toilet, no baths." See also, "Experts Argue 3 Hours on Fire Death Verdict," *Chicago Tribune*, Oct 19, 1950.

61 *Work*, December 1951. Portions of the contents of Mumford's thoughts on high rises was shared with *Work* readers by Daniel Cantwell three years earlier. He quoted Mumford at length about high rise living and the urbanist's critique of them as unfit for people with families and the elderly. "You Can't Call A Skyscraper A Home," December 1948.

62 Ibid.

63 Ibid.

64 Morris B. Hirsh Cited in *Work*, January 1952. The writer manipulated Marciniak's contention to make it a matter of land use. Further, his argument was based upon a lot size that was 60 by 125 feet. This was more than what typical of a Chicago bungalow and raised ranch development in the preceding thirty years.

65 Ibid.

66 Cited in Ibid.

67 "An Editorial," January 1952.

68 Emil G. Hirsch to Editor, cited in "Our Readers Talk Back" *Work*, February 1952.

69 "Editors Note," January 1952.

70 The article was written by a community activist who noted that that many of these make-shift homes had "no running water, no

electric lights, no toilet, no baths." See Also, "Experts Argue 3
Hours on Fire Death Verdict," *Chicago Tribune*, Oct 19, 1950.

71 See *Work*: "First Things First," November 1950; "The People
Who Could Wipe out Chicago Slums," July 1953; "Fight on
Slums Needn't Be Lost—If People Care Enough: A Primer on
Housing," January 1959.

72 Hirsch, pp. 100-134 and pp. 259-261. Supporting the Lake
Meadows project and the subsequent Prairie Shores project,
which also had racial ratios, were Illinois Institute of Technol-
ogy and Michael Reece Hospital which were in the area. Also,
see Chapter 5 and 6 regarding housing and quotas.

73 See Hirsch, pp. 135-170 and Peter H. Rossi and Robert A.
Dentler, *The Politics of Urban Renewal: the Chicago Findings*,
(Free Press, New York, New York,1961), pp 66-101.

74 For an account of Egan's position and testimony see Margery
Frisbie, *An Alley in Chicago: The Ministry of a City Priest*, (Sheed
and Ward, Kansas City, Missouri, 1991), pp. 94-110; Avella,
pp. 227-236; and Hirsch, pp.164-167. Rossi and Dentler, pp.
220-239.

75 It is of note that Marciniak's August column appeared on page
three rather than the editorial page.

76 August 1958.

77 Ibid.

78 Ibid.

79 Marciniak to Greeley, March 21, 1962, Marciniak Papers, Shelf
1, Position 1. See also *The New World*, March 2, 1962, for the
review and Marciniak to Greeley, March 6, and Greeley to Marciniak March 17, 1962, Marciniak Papers, Shelf 1, Position 2.

80 Cited in Carl Larsen, "In Defense of Urban Renewal," *Chicago
Daily News* clipping in Marciniak Papers, Shelf 1, Position 1.
Larsen had been a newspaper reporter who became director of
public relations at the University of Chicago.

81 Editors of *Fortune*, (Double Day Anchor Books, Garden City,
New York, 1957), p. vii. Among its contributors were Francis
Bello, Jane Jacobs, Seymour Freedgood, Donald Seligman, and
William H Whyte.

Chapter 5

Fighting for Racial Justice

If charity is the bond that unites Christians,
then racial injustice and hatred
are the greatest evil.

EDWARD MARCINIAK[1]

Edward Marciniak was and has remained an enigma for his apparent temporizing in his work for civil rights as a public official. At a 1990 tribute to Marciniak at the Bismarck Hotel, Msgr. John Egan, a leader in justice issues in Chicago, said of Marciniak, "Ed never followed the parade. If there's a voice of conscience in this town, its Marciniak.... He never trims his sails." Marciniak's boss, Mayor Richard J. Daley, said of him: "I can always believe his answers.... His social conscience, his concern for others, is as deep as his knowledge of the city and its people."

But there were others who adamantly disagreed. Elinor Richey Soderberg, an African American free-lance writer, was so angered by Marciniak in 1963 that she wrote him the following postcard: "Sometimes when you are in your bed at night doesn't your soul ache for the lies you concocted for the sake of ameliorating a vicious democracy-crushing political machine?" A year after Marciniak died in 2004, Alderman Leon Despres of the 5th Ward, once a friend and supporter, portrayed Marciniak as an obstacle to racial justice, claiming in Despres' autobiography that he provided for Daley an "essentially political cover-up."[2]

Was Marciniak a pawn or a misguided do-gooder who got in over his head when Richard J. Daley tapped him to be Director of the Chicago Commission on Human Relations (CCHR) in 1960 as the civil rights movement built momentum? Or was he consistent in the mission he set out for himself as a young man to make Chicago a better and more just place for all? Why would an idealist such as Marciniak work for Richard J. Daley, who according to historian Roger Biles, held "atavistic racial views?"[3] At first glance there seemed to be an irresolvable conflict between this progressive social idealist and his service in Mayor Daley's cabinet. Paid public service required Marciniak to moderate his clarion voice for racial justice to be an advisor and mediator. When the "outsider" becomes an "insider," the primary question arises: "Will or must moral principles be compromised by taking on the role of policy and program maker?" Marciniak's role change caused consternation on the part of some in the civil rights movement.

The years Marciniak served as the Director of the Chicago Commission on Human Relations under Richard J. Daley between 1960 and 1967 were defining moments for Chicago and for Marciniak. His unique religious and socio-political perspective informed his work to end employment and healthcare discrimination and a segregated housing market. When Marciniak took the CCHR position in 1960, civil rights change appeared to be inevitable, but the nature and pace of that change was not inevitable. The evolving challenge of dealing with moral imperatives and political realities tested Ed in new ways.

CHICAGO AND EDWARD MARCINIAK'S SOCIAL CONSCIENCE

The Chicago of Marciniak's childhood days had continued its growth trajectory. Its population of 2.7 million in 1920 had grown to nearly 3.4 million by 1940 and reached its peak population of 3,620,962 by 1950.[4] Chicago was a city of opportunities and, except in the Depression years, the demand for workers to fill jobs in its factories, slaughterhouses, warehouses, railroad yards, and grand department stores remained. While the number of immigrants was reduced after restrictive legislation in 1924, the city continued to grow as a result of a dramatic increase in its population of Black people arriving from the South. These new arrivals were from rural areas where opportunities were limited by discrimination and the prospects of continuous, grinding poverty of the tenant farming system. They sought the life told in letters from those who had gone to Chicago and in the pages of the *Chicago Defender*, a newspaper sent south on the Illinois Central Railroad.

The city celebrated its cultural and economic development with its hosting the Century of Progress International Exposition in 1933-1934. However, the hastily constructed buildings on the shores of Lake Michigan could not hide the stresses and strains of poverty and its attendant physical and social maladies a short distance away. Unlike the European immigrants, many who were at times begrudgingly accepted and assimilated into the polyglot neighborhoods, Black people were residentially isolated even when they worked alongside of whites in the steel mills and stockyards and on the loading docks. In July 1919, the city had been convulsed by a race riot that lasted over a week and took the lives of 23 Black people and 15 whites and injured an estimated one to two thousand persons. As the Black population grew from 109,485 in 1920 to 492,265 in 1950,[5] the patterns of segregation grew more formalized and the movement of Black people into white neighborhoods would very often be accompanied by threats, property destruction, and violence. Even as the middle-class Black population grew with the increased number of professionals pursuing opportunities in Chicago and others counted among union workers, the restrictions did not fall away. The pressure increased. Midwestern cities such as Detroit, Cleveland, Milwaukee, and Chicago would be tested as the tensions mounted. After World War II, the demands for civil rights heightened as Black soldiers and factory workers realized their contributions to the war effort were not being reciprocated; discrimination in the workplace, education, and the marketplace persisted.

As a youngster growing up in the Brighton Park community, Marciniak was unlikely to meet Black people or be more than slightly aware of the terrible race riot that took place when he was a toddler. Most Black people lived in segregated overcrowded housing in the so-called Black Belt, five miles east of his home. However, when he began his commute on the public transit to the seminary high school, he certainly broadened his awareness of the diversity of the city's population. There was ethnic diversity, but no racial diversity in his Quigley Seminary's student body. However, as noted earlier, because of his religious training both at home and at the seminary, Marciniak more and more came to appreciate the unity of humankind and in college activities in the Sodality of Our Lady and Chicago Inter-Student Catholic Action (CISCA) he found a theological base in the Catholic doctrine of the Mystical Body which would infuse his sense of social justice.

Marciniak's friendship with Dr. Arthur Falls, founder the first Catholic Worker group in Chicago, was pivotal. It was Falls who had convinced Dorothy Day to place a Black workman alongside of a white workman on the masthead of her newspaper and who endeavored to end discrimination through his work with the Chicago Urban League and to gain a voice for Black people in the Catholic Church through his leadership of the Federated Colored Catholics. As a seventeen-year-old, Falls had experienced firsthand the terror of the riot of 1919 when white youth came into his South Side neighborhood intending to "burn out" Black people. He and his father sat guard all night protected by a broom stick and a coal poker, as their armed neighbors patrolled the neighborhood.[6] Marciniak's friendship with Falls and experiences at the Saint Joseph House of Hospitality and with union organizing work in the stockyards taught him about racial discrimination. These personal contacts and experiences led from awareness of race prejudice to a commitment to end racism, which he later called the "tape worm of the Christian body."[7]

In 1942, two years before Gunnar Myrdal published his influential book, *The American Dilemma: The Negro Problem in Modern Democracy*, Marciniak wrote his master's thesis on the attitude of Chicago Catholic college students toward Blacks and concluded that more education and actual interracial group experiences would be necessary if future generations were to be unbiased.[8] His findings led him to help organize the Chicago Council Against Racial and Religious Discrimination in 1943, a group on whose board he served for fourteen years. In 1945, he helped to create the Catholic Interracial Council (CIC) and served as its first secretary and remained an active board member until 1960. Along with Rev. Daniel Cantwell, Marciniak steered the Catholic Interracial Council to increase awareness of racial injustice in Chicago and to deal with employment and housing discrimination. Additionally, he was an active member of the National Conference of Christian and Jews (NCCJ) speakers' bureau, which sought to increase religious tolerance.

Marciniak was acutely aware of Catholicism's failures on race issues, and he tried to press for change through communication and education. He helped to gather CIC's first members. Among these were Augustine Bowe, a lawyer who would later become Chief Judge of the Municipal Court and the Chair of the Chicago Commission on Human Relations, and John Yancy, a Black Catholic who was Secretary Treasurer of the United Transport Union.[9] Marciniak experienced firsthand the hard-set attitudes that held sway in Chicago neighborhoods. In an interview, he recounted his experience at a parish meeting to illustrate the atmosphere of the late 1930s and 1940s: "It was a women's group and they invited me to talk, and I gave my straight talk and the pastor chewed me out for twenty-five minutes in front of the group saying, 'why don't you have the gumption of your Polish forbearers to stand up, just the way they did in the 1919 riot.'"[10] The implication being that white ethnics should resist integration.

At the time, Cardinal Samuel Stritch, who had a Tennessee background, was "equivocal" on race issues, preferring to avoid conflicts by removing pastors who supported segregation.[11] Nonetheless, Marciniak and Cantwell met with pastors who were clearly resistant to the integration of their parishes and schools. Among them was the pastor of St. Philip Benizi Parish, located on the city's near north side. He refused to admit Black students to the parish school. The strategy of the CIC was, Marciniak explained, "not to keep the peace but to advance race relations."[12]

Through his editorship of the Catholic Labor Alliance's monthly and as a member of the NCCJ speaker's bureau, Ed sought to develop an integrated approached to racial justice and social justice. At a meeting of the Catholic Press Association in Milwaukee, Marciniak spoke of a "Catholic Approach to Racism" and called on professionals who worked in the Catholic press to not only provide information and disclose intellectual errors but foster a "hunger and thirst after justice." This was the true "social vocation" of Catholics.[13]

In 1946, the young editor of *Work* told his friends from CISCA days he believed that "If charity is the bond that unites Christians, then racial injustice and hatred are the greatest evils."[14] That year Marciniak was startled to discover prejudice at his *alma mater* where he served as an

adjunct. The head basketball coach did not take Loyola
University's star Black basketball player, Ben Bluitt, on a
road trip to play at Texas Christian and Southern Meth-
odist Universities. Distressed and angry, Marciniak wrote
to Coach Thomas Haggerty and directly and forcefully
questioned his failure to protect the Black player from discrimination. He prefaced his letter to the coach by noting
his own pride in Loyola's "enviable reputation in the community as a staunch and consistent supporter of the Christian
position on interracial justice." Then he got to the point that
the University's reputation built upon fifty years of honoring the policy of non-discrimination was now jeopardized.
"Apart from the moral principles involved in the recent basketball incident," he wrote Haggerty, "Loyola's good reputation and honor were on trial." Because Haggerty acceded to
the requests of the southern schools not to bring the team's
only Black member to Texas, Marciniak told the coach that he
had "acquiesced to Southern Jim-Crow, making a mockery of
Loyola's moral integrity, and it appeared to be "rank prejudice."
Ed concluded that in his student days, "the Jesuits set me an
example of devotion to principle and personal integrity which
now prompt me to speak out instead of remaining silent."[15]

EARLY ADVOCACY FOR
RACIAL JUSTICE

Marciniak's passion for civil rights was evident in his civic
activities and as an editor at *Work* from 1943 to 1960. In
1944-45, he served as the state chairman of a campaign
for an Illinois Fair Employer Practices Law and sustained
his commitment through the years as a speaker in public

forums and testimony in Springfield.[16] In *Work*, he featured stories about the moral imperative of employers to end discriminatory hiring practices and for white workers to accept Black employees as they did white co-workers, and he sponsored Catholic Labor Alliance (CLA) forums to educate Chicagoans.[17] A consistent theme of the newspaper was the need for fair employment practices and laws that would open the doors for all workers regardless of race, religion, or nationality. He chastised the department store owners on State Street for having drawn "an iron curtain around themselves to bar Negroes as sales clerks," and praised Minneapolis' mayor Hubert Humphrey for showing leadership in persuading retailers to hire on ability and the New York State's Fair Employment Practices Commission legislation for its anti-discrimination legislation.[18] In 1950 when Carson Pirie Scott and Company, a storied State Street retailer, broke with the "whites only" tradition and hired 30 black sales clerks, Marciniak praised its action and commented:

It seems obvious that only with prodding from a Fair Employment law will any number of firms start giving Negroes an even break. The stores and offices which hire on a merit basis —whether on State Street or elsewhere— still amount to a pitifully small number. FEPC laws were largely responsible for educating Eastern department stores against discrimination against Negroes and other minority groups.[19]

As a follow up a year later, *Work* featured Carson Pirie Scott's successes and photos of Black salesclerks interacting with whites. It also condemned the Illinois State Chamber of

Commerce for its support for a voluntary fair employment program rather than formal legislation.[20] Marshall Field's department store was one of the most notorious in its resistance to hiring Blacks, and Marciniak put the store on his "taboo list." He would later caution his wife and children not to shop at the city's foremost emporium, an unwritten rule that would persist in the family household throughout his life.[21]

More central to *Work's* concern was the existence and impact of the dual housing market that caused more than 350,000 Black people in Chicago to live in crowded and substandard housing. Ed pointed out specific incidents of discrimination, failure by public agencies and private parties to respect and protect individual rights, as well as those rare instances wherein individuals and communities stood up to end discrimination in housing. Arnold Hirsch's *Making the Second Ghetto: Race and Housing in Chicago, 1940-1960* tells of Chicago's extreme residential segregation. Black people in Chicago had limited options due to restrictive covenants (agreements by homeowners never to sell to Black buyers) and the explicit prejudice that was demonstrated through acts of vandalism and violence at the edges of the ghetto that grew dramatically in the wake of the Great Migration. In 1946, *Work* reproduced a map showing acts of vandalism and violence against Black people. These incidents were at the edge of the so-called Black Belt, in what was termed "tension areas" because of the violence that occurred when Black families attempted to expand their housing options.[22]

Twenty-five per cent of all housing south of Roosevelt Road (which ran east to west at 1200 south) was restricted to whites only by covenants that were attached to the property. In an editorial, Marciniak criticized the Master of Chancery in Superior Court for ruling that whites have "'the inalienable right to do as they see fit with their property... and to pick their neighbors.'" This was "double talk" pure and simple, according to Ed, because it denied Blacks *their* rights. "Furthermore," Marciniak wrote that the anti-Negro agreements actually "violates the white (person's) 'right to pick (his or her) neighbors." He added, "We know many whites, including the editor of *WORK* [original emphasis], who want to live in an integrated, democratic neighborhood where (people) of all races can live together in peace."[23]

Restrictive covenants were morally wrong and produced terrible burdens on the residents of the ghetto and the entire city. A friend-of-the-court brief in the case that *Work* cited explained that restrictive covenants create overcrowding, disease, delinquency, crime, tensions, and other social ills as well as violate the state and federal constitution. (It is interesting that the Oakland-Kenwood Property Owners Association, which served a community at the edge of the Black Belt, voluntarily ended restrictive covenants because the property owners came to realize what really threatened them were not Blacks but "bad use of property, overcrowding, and exploitation.")

In 1948, an accord was brokered by Thomas H. Wright, the executive director of the Chicago Council Against Racial and Religious Discrimination, who noted: "It [the agreement] will prove that property values depend upon maintenance and correct use, not upon the racial origin of the occupant."[24]

Even though racial covenants were declared unconstitutional in 1948, segregation remained because Blacks and whites were kept separate by prejudice and market manipulation as both white and Black real estate brokers endeavored to promote sales. Black people were forced to live within constricted areas and, whenever the pressure for housing grew as the population increased, contiguous all white neighborhoods turned over racially in short order as panic-peddling realtors took advantage of prejudice and fear. Also, the prejudices of those charged with enforcement of the laws contributed to the dual housing market. For example, when returning African American veterans tried to move into public housing at the Airport Homes, an emergency housing project on the Southwest Side, they were intimidated while police fraternized with the white demonstrators.

The Council issued a report that noted: "Violence is tolerated or encouraged by people who are otherwise quite law-abiding.... It is futile to expect any solution until the churches have secured a general recognition of the sinfulness of segregation. With this must come a general acceptance of the right of every person to live in any section of the city." Accompanying the article, *Work* featured a woodcut drawing by Ade Bethune, whose work regularly appeared in *The Catholic Worker*, which showed Jesus standing behind a chain link fence with a Black family. The caption read, "SEGREGATING the Negro is segregating Christ."[25]

Marciniak believed in the power of reasoned studies to counter the misinformation that accompanied the fears of homeowners in the neighborhoods adjacent to the expanding Black population. He penned a lengthy article entitled, "When Negroes Move In, Does Property Depreciate?" It cited Belden Morgan, the past president of both the Chicago and Los Angeles chapters of the Society of Residential

Appraisers (SRA) and who had previously served the Federal Housing Administration. The appraiser noted that his investigation showed that vacancies did not increase, nor did property values decline, in multi-unit rental buildings in Los Angles when Black people moved in. Morgan did note that "hysteria" did cause lower property values when Blacks moved into a neighborhood, as if it were an "invasion." When everyone tries to sell in a hurry, he observed that owners lower their property value to make sure that they can sell before their neighbors. This creates a mass exodus that gluts the market and depresses prices. Using an analogy that was familiar to Depression-era owners, he explained, "It is like a run on the bank when people get panicky. Whites who hold on to their property are often able to sell at prices substantially higher than prevailed before the 'invasion.'" The appraiser warned that in many cases the deflated prices that perspective sellers were given were the result of prejudiced appraisers, not the market facts. Marciniak's article was accompanied by the same Bethune wood cut drawing that he used previously.[26]

Marciniak also believed in the value of a good example and lauded those individuals and community groups that demonstrated racial peace was possible. When demonstrators in the Fernwood neighborhood protested Black people moving into public housing, one community member organized a welcoming committee. *Work* praised the organizer but regretted that some demonstrators surrounded and intimidated the volunteers helping the Black people move in.[27] The Hyde Park-Kenwood Community Conference, the Oakland-Kenwood Planning Association, and Woodlawn Inc. were singled out for praise:

When a few Negroes moved into some other "white" neighborhoods in Chicago, 500 and more policemen were needed to keep peace and order. But during the past two years there have been no serious disturbances in the Oakland-Kenwood-Woodlawn area.[28]

Despite the efforts of a few groups, the problems of prejudice persisted and increased in most areas contiguous to the ghetto as Black people, especially the burgeoning Black middle-class sought better housing. Airport Homes, Fernwood, and Park Manor were among the South Side communities where Black people experienced violence. Marciniak criticized the leadership of the Park Manor Community for being followers rather than leaders. He lamented, "They have not led the people to see that racial hatred and prejudice violate the democratic principle of equal opportunity and the Christian teachings of brotherhood." He rebuked their silence, which he said was a tacit approval of discrimination. However, when two religious leaders in Park Manor took "thoroughly Christian positions," *Work* praised them.[29] For a couple of years, the neighborhood boiled with violence, bombings, and arson, and when Mayor Martin Kennelly stood up to a community group, noting the need for police protection of new Black residents, Marciniak strongly supported him.[30]

While *Work's* editor, Marciniak advocated for fair housing but considered a proposed ordinance ill-timed in the 1950s. Were he a Chicago alderman, he wrote, "I'd certainly support it." However, he believed such an ordinance was premature since private citizens had done too little to tear down the fences of segregation. Marciniak explained that "Nobody is exposing the dirty work done by Negro and white real estate operators alike, who connive, cheat, blackmail, and lie to prevent peaceful integration." He continued:

> Many (people) of good will who hate the sin of segregation are attracted to a law against racial bias in housing because it passes the buck to the government. Enacting such a law absolves them of a personal responsibility for crowded tenements, rat-infested buildings, and slum fires—which the Negro ghetto perpetuates.

He concluded: "Without a gigantic, whole-hearted drive by real estate men, money lenders, property owners, pastors and civic leaders, the ring of all-white suburbs will grow, and the Chicago center will become more solidly Negro."[31] His approach to this moral issue was like the one he espoused on the economic front: a radical social and legal reconstruction of the system that fostered segregation.

THE CHICAGO COMMISSION ON HUMAN RELATIONS AND MARCINIAK'S AGENDA

In 1945, Mayor Edward J. Kelly created the Committee on Race Relations because he wanted to avoid a major riot such as the one Detroit had experienced two years earlier. His successor, Martin Kennelly, converted the entity into the Chicago Commission on Human Relations (CCHR) and gave it a small staff overseen by mayoral appointees. The Commission's primary task had been to respond to incidences of racial conflict, but it did not deal with under-lying causes. In 1948, the CCHR presented the thirty-one-year-old Marciniak its Award in Human Relations, citing his work as editor of *Work* for demonstrating "how religious groups may advance the principles of Christian behavior and the universal brotherhood without racial discrimina-tion" and consistently gave "practical direction to democratic sentiments and faiths."[32] Ed was constantly involved with race relations through the 1950s in his roles as *Work's* editor and as a labor activist and a civic leader.

When the CCHR's' executive director died in 1960, Marciniak sought the position. That May, he wrote to the commission's president, Ely M. Aaron, and stated his desire to be directly involved in a government policy-making role and his confidence that he could provide both direction and leadership in meeting the "problems that the city and its people face."[33] Accompanying his letter was a lengthy list of references that included elected officials, educators, and labor and civic leaders. Within two weeks, Mayor Daley appointed Edward Marciniak to the directorship. While there is no written explanation for the appointment, Ed's record on race and his familiarity with union leaders, news-paper reporters, and business leaders certainly gave him strong credentials. Clearly of importance was the behind-the-scenes recommendation of Raymond Simon, a friend of applicant Marciniak. The two shared common connec-tions through Catholic social groups and Loyola University. Simon, the son of a precinct captain in Daley's neighbor-hood, had caught the Mayor's eye for talent. Simon served Daley, first as his administrative assistant and then as the city's chief legal officer.[34]

Marciniak was thus working for Chicago's most powerful political leader and the mayor who presided over the rebirth of the city's central business district. For his tight control over the levers of power, Daley had earned the name "Boss," which Chicago writer Mike Royko later used as the title of his book on Daley.

Daley's ability to hire and terminate the appointment of 40,000 patronage workers helped ensure his own reelection and that of his party's candidates. In almost all cases, loyalty was expected, and disloyalty punished. Marciniak never commented publicly on the expectations of the mayor for fealty nor the pressures he may have felt from aldermen and political operatives. He never directly criticized Daley after his death in 1976; rather, on a few occasions he defended the mayor's record on issues of race and public housing. His relationship with Daley appeared to have been based upon the mutuality of benefit for both men.

At the time Marciniak assumed the CCHR post, expectations on the part of Blacks had increased throughout the nation because of the growing civil rights movement. Genuine progress was made, but the tensions remained strong as Black people pressed for more access to public accommodations, quality education, and voting rights. The boycotts and demonstrations in the South would soon enough come to Chicago. The major challenges for the new director of CCHR would be to prevent further racial discrimination and help change those structures that fostered it. The most critical issue was fair housing, which became *the* agenda of the Chicago Freedom Movement led by Reverend Martin Luther King, Jr., and would draw national attention to the city.

In his first annual report, delivered at the CCHR's Fifteenth Annual Awards Luncheon in December 1960, Marciniak made clear his intention to change the Commission. He explained that CCHR had developed new techniques for dealing with "massive" racial tensions by using the public resources of numerous city agencies and by "taking the fullest advantage of the private resources of religious, welfare, and community organizations." The new director pointed out that the Commission had established orderly procedures for "adjusting" complaints against persons because of race, religion, and national origin, whether in employment, accommodations, housing, schools, or hospitals." Additionally, the Commission had re-examined its policies, programs, and procedures "in order to secure the civil rights of all our citizens."[35] However, the commission appeared not to be charged with much more than policing the racial situation regarding housing, and it had been given little power.

PUBLIC SPACES

Keeping racial peace had been the main priority of the CCHR, and Marciniak's mettle would soon be assessed as he sought to ensure the civil rights of all Chicagoans. The city's recollection of the 1919 attack on a young black swimmer who had crossed an invisible line on the lakefront that led to the terrible race riot still lingered in the minds of many officials as well as residents. For this reason, early each year CCHR prepared a list for itself of potential trouble spots in public places during the summer.

On the list in 1961 was Rainbow Beach in the South Shore neighborhood. It was in a semi-isolated location and this feature, according to Marciniak, "helped to create the impression of a private beach." He explained that the CCHR knew that as Black people moved further south, Rainbow would become the closest beach for them. More important, he also knew that the previous summer, when three or four Black families a week tried to use the beach, they were taunted and molested by white teenagers. Ed attempted a proactive strategy by meeting with the Park District to ensure that all staff knew the law and their responsibilities, and with newspaper and religious and community organizations, particularly those dealing with teenagers. His strategy was "to get normal use of the beach by Negroes, so that we could avoid a wade-in which, as a public demonstration, would attract even more people and heighten the possibility of trouble."[36]

Nevertheless, a demonstration on July 8, called the "Wade-In for Freedom," led by the NAACP, attracted 3,000 whites to watch and heckle a total of ninety-seven demonstrators. Two hundred police prevented a violent incident by dispersing the crowd and arresting the unruliest whites who defied orders. The following week another confrontation took place at Rainbow Beach, resulting in the arrest of more white teens and young adults who planned to attack the 175 demonstrators when a bugle was sounded. Learning of the plot, the police found and preemptively confiscated the bugle before there was violence. Marciniak was responsible for coordinating the efforts to defuse the powder keg on the beach.[37] His approach was to bring together clergy from all faiths and civic leaders from the neighborhoods from which the young troublemakers had come. In particular, he worked with the South Shore Commission, the state and city youth commissions, the NAACP leaders, and youth workers from voluntary organizations. Rabbis, ministers, and priests, along with civic leaders walked the beach with a police task force of 200 officers. On Sundays there were more clergymen in full dress on Rainbow Beach, Ed recalled, "than on any beach I've ever seen or heard about." Marciniak credited the "vigorous and decisive" action on the part of the police and the personal representation by rabbis, ministers, and priests for breaking the back of the resistance. However, he admitted "we continued to have uneasy moments."[38]

In his annual report of December 1961, he told his audience that the Commission's pledge to "match a problem with the people able to solve it" was successful at Rainbow Beach and demonstrated the "city's determination to get respect for the law" and "symbolized the alert police action and assisted by the Commission's experience in such matters."[39] Continued watchfulness and planning, however, would become more critical as impatience with civil rights progress increased.

Marciniak was resolute in his commitment to end segregation and focused on making changes that could be secured immediately and build momentum. He first tackled issues that were on the Commission's agenda from prior years and advanced these while he set the stage to deal with discrimination in the housing market. Marciniak's initial attention was directed toward ending discrimination in health care and medical education.[40] The city's healthcare was as segregated as its neighborhoods, if not more so, and with deadly consequences.

HEALTHCARE

Ambulances in Chicago often bypassed nearby all white hospitals and drove as far as ten miles to one of the two private hospitals where there were Black doctors on staff, or they went directly to Cook County Hospital. The city's medical schools had few Black students: only nineteen medical students in a pool of 2,000 were Black. Several nursing schools openly discriminated in admissions based upon an applicant's race and religion. North of Cermak Road (at 2200 south), there were 6.9 general hospital beds per 1,000. South of that line, where most Black people lived, there were only 2.8 beds per 1,000.[41] In 1956, the City Council had passed an ordinance prohibiting discrimination by hospitals, and the Archbishop of Chicago leaned heavily on the twenty-five Catholic hospitals to end discriminatory practices.[42] However, until Marciniak made it a priority, progress had been painfully slow.

On July 5, 1960, only days after assuming his post at the CCHR, Marciniak received a letter from his good friend, Dr. Arthur G. Falls, who wrote in his capacity as Chairman of The Committee to End Discrimination in Chicago Medical Institutions. Falls expressed the belief that the latter part of 1960 would be "a crucial period" in the organization's fight "to build a democratic pattern in the field of Medicine [sic] in Chicago," and looked forward to the continued cooperation of the Commission.[43] By December 1961, Marciniak was able to report that thirteen hospitals had added black physicians to their staff—raising the number of hospitals in the city with integrated staffs to twenty-five. He achieved results by cajoling relentlessly. Using his relationships with religious and civic leaders, the CCHR director pressed private hospitals to change admission and staffing practices. When a complaint was filed, the CCHR investigated and tried to "adjust" the matter. If a second case was filed, Marciniak had the Corporation Counsel direct the hospital's administrators to come to City Hall and put them on notice to end discrimination. With satisfaction, Marciniak explained, "In each case we arrived at an agreement whereby the hospital affirmed a clear-cut policy of giving equal care to nonwhite patients."[44]

By 1965, a radical change in care had been affected through a systematic analysis of the problems and targeted action. In a lengthy address to the Medical Section of the American Public Health Association, Marciniak outlined the approach taken and the outcomes.[45] There were two routes to hospital admissions, through the emergency room and by physician arrangement, and both had to be addressed. The city and state legislation must be made more rigorous and supported by increased policing. Hospitals located at the edge of predominantly white neighborhoods still resisted the admission of Black people. The emergency rooms were viewed as clinics, but beds were not available to Blacks, even those with employee-sponsored insurance. Further, white doctors who were on staff at these border territory hospitals and who had Black patients were strongly encouraged to limit their admissions.

In 1962, the City Council expanded the hospital ordinance to prohibit discrimination in the employment and appointment of physicians on account of race, color, creed, national origin, or ancestry, but it was not sufficient. To ensure compliance, the Chicago Board of Health with the assistance of Corporations Counsel and CCHR took charge of investigations and made sure those hospitals "lived up to the letter and the spirit of the laws."

Collaborating with the Cook County Physicians Association and the Chicago Medical Society, CCHR kept track of minority physicians who could be placed in all white hospitals.[46] Marciniak told the attendees that in 1960 the mayor had quietly appointed a committee of leading civic, medical, and hospital leaders to integrate hospital staffs "with full-time assistance from CCHR" and to execute day-to-day follow through. The committee board members contacted hospital administrators, chiefs of medical staffs, and hospital board members they knew who could pave the way for Black appointments. Marciniak noted that the "informal approach was ideally suited to penetrating the 'private club' atmosphere that dominated some hospitals and which characterized numerous hospital departments."[47]

Older Black doctors, "battle-scarred from earlier acts of discrimination against themselves or their patients," were reluctant to seek privileges where they had been rejected. Marciniak noted that it "would be hard to underestimate the importance of the committee's efforts to encourage Negro doctors to seek a hospital staff appointment away from Provident Hospital." They were, he realized, "trapped" by the self-fulfilling prophecy because they believed that they would be denied admission if they applied—so they did not apply. Younger Black physicians, especially residents who had completed their work in Chicago, were sought out as they were more likely to apply to hospitals with all white staffs.

The Mayor's Committee targeted private, not-for-profit hospitals. The Jewish hospitals and Catholic hospitals were the first to open to Black staff and eventually, according to Marciniak, the Protestant-connected hospitals, "joined the parade." The approach to each of the hospital groups was through the official power structure and unofficial networks with key people who sponsored the given hospitals. At the Catholic hospitals, the religious order sponsoring the hospital was contacted. At the Protestant-related hospitals contact was through the chief of medical staff or an influential staff member, and at Jewish hospitals board members or influential physicians proved to be keys. Hospitals on the near north and west sides were easier to integrate as many had low bed occupancy in obstetrics and pediatrics and were not "subject to the community pressures that feared 'inundation' by Negroes."[48]

Collaborating with medical schools was critical because their graduates were more open to seeking appointments. The Mayor's Committee, with the Commission providing staff and resources, launched a nation-wide campaign aimed at medical students and graduates to make them aware of opportunities in Chicago. Marciniak's office drafted reports on changing medical opportunities to professional, medical, and hospital journals, including *the Journal of the National Medical Association*, the deans of Meharry and Howard Medical Schools, counselors of Southern Negro colleges, and others. The CCHR circulated brochures such as "New Opportunities for Negroes in Medicine" published by the National Medical Fellowships for school counselors, the Chicago Urban League, and others who advised Blacks on careers.

During the first five years, the special committee made more than 900 personal contacts that produced real change.

In 1960, only fifteen non-governmental hospitals had a Black physician with admitting privileges. (The report excluded the non-discriminatory Provident, Louise Berg, and Ida Mae Scott Hospitals.) By 1965, thirty-seven hospitals had added Black doctors.[49] The number of Black physicians had previously declined as even the city's Black population increased dramatically. The number of Black doctors had increased from 215 in 1960 to 242.[50]

Marciniak was quick to acknowledge that a "major factor" in the progress was the result of an anti-trust suit that was filed by ten Black physicians, including Dr. Arthur Falls. They charged fifty-two hospital corporations with a conspiracy to deny or control admissions by Black doctors and their patients. The suit against these institutions, which had more than 75% of all the beds in the Chicago area, pointed out that Black doctors were unjustly deprived of a livelihood.[51] After a 1963 settlement provided an appeal mechanism for doctors denied appointment because of race and since then only one complaint had been filed. Marciniak recognized "the persistent efforts" of the Committee to End Racial Discrimination in Chicago Medical Institutions.[52]

Marciniak ended his address to public health gathering by laying out CCHR's future medical care priorities. First, CCHR sought a reservoir of doctors to equalize medical opportunities through sustained counseling programs aimed at bio-medical careers. Second, because there was overcrowding in the maternity wing at Cook County Hospital where most indigent maternity patients were normally assigned, the county had prevailed upon non-government hospitals to take these patients and receive public reimbursement. This program enabled "thousands of Negro women to receive maternity care in private hospitals" and promised a "major change in hospital services." Finally, CCHR asked the Cook County Board of Commissioners to appoint its own committee to work with the hospitals that ringed the city. "In a metropolitan area hospital needs and services crisscross political jurisdictions—making it absolutely necessary to have a single policy of hospital and medical integration for the entire metropolitan area," he concluded.[53] This regional approach was a precursor of Marciniak's approach to housing.

EMPLOYMENT

A third area of responsibility of CCHR was to investigate discrimination in hiring practices. Since 1945, Marciniak had led a fight for Illinois fair employment practices legislation on behalf of the Catholic Labor Alliance. As director of the CCHR, he continued his efforts. In 1960, Ed lamented that Illinois was the last major industrial state without such a law and reported that the city commission had succeeded in adjusting nearly 1,000 employment cases that year. But too often CCHR failed to rectify obvious cases of discrimination because the state lacked legislation. Where the city had power to collaborate with its purchasing agent and the corporation counsel, it was able to force city contractors to change discriminatory practices. He shared that in one case the purchasing agent "held up a substantial payment on a city contract until the company agreed to carry out the commission's recommendations."[54]

The following year Marciniak was pleased to report that Illinois lawmakers had finally passed the needed employment legislation; however, he explained that legal access would prove to be meaningless for many unless the applicants were qualified for the evolving job market. Even as the employment doors opened, he stated, applicants "must be prepared to walk through those doors qualified for the job available." Citing a recent state report he noted that 73% of unemployed Black people in Chicago had not completed high school. For this reason, he emphasized the necessity of addressing the job qualification shortcomings. Marciniak worked with the Mayor's Committee on New Residents to use neighborhood centers in Woodlawn, Uptown, and Lawndale to steer newcomers from the rural South, Appalachia, and Puerto Rico to the centers' adult job training program. Further he worked with the mayor to convene the major employers in manufacturing, transportation, utilities, banking, and commerce to press them to open training and employment opportunities. Ironically, just before the launch of the program Mayor Daley realized he had no Black staff person in his office. This prompted Marciniak to arrange to have a CCHR staff person join the mayor's circle, stationed in Raymond Simon's office.[55]

Solving the skill preparation problem also meant that the Commission had to take on the powerful trade unions for their "intolerable" discrimination. In 1962, there were unions that did not have a single Black apprentice, causing Marciniak to lament that it would be "easier for a Negro to get a Ph.D. and become a college professor than to qualify as an apprentice of a journeyman in one of these trades."[56] Chicago trade unions relied on the Board of Education for training funds and the use of the Washburne Trade School facilities to train thousands of apprentices annually. While

Marciniak did not have responsibility for the Board of Education program *per se*, he used his position to intervene to prevent discrimination in employment. Because of his earlier work at the Catholic Labor Alliance, Marciniak had influence with the trades, and he actively pressed unions to open their ranks to Black apprentices.

Three years later, in 1965, Ed expressed satisfaction that eight skilled trades had opened their ranks to admit Black apprentices for the first time. Moreover, Marciniak told the leaders of those unions that still excluded Black people to change their recruiting or lose the benefits of public funds and access to Washburne Trade School facilities. "There is no other reasonable alternative," he warned.[57] The following year, when the holdout unions still had no Black apprentices—because to avoid the issue some unions did not recruit any new apprentices to the program—CCHR demanded the Board of Education Oversight Committee force change. Marciniak implied that he had contacted the federal Department of Health, Education, and Welfare, which partially funded the school; and he warned that it was drafting new legislation to force an end to discrimination.[58]

The progress in the trades was gradual. The integration in the trade unions was "completed" in 1966 when the apprentice committee of the Local AFL-CIO Structural Iron Workers accepted its first Black apprentice to take training courses at Washburne. With this Chicago became the first major city in the nation to be open to Black people in all building trades. According to the CCHR's director of employment services, the commission worked directly with construction companies holding city contracts to have specific nondiscrimination clauses forcing the unions to initiate changes. The commission also worked with the Urban League, which had a big brother program for Black apprenticeship applicants.[59] Still, the pace of change was slow, especially in the more skilled and well-paying trades. Only 5% of the 2,000 apprentices enrolled at Washburne were Black, at a time when 25% of the city's population was Black.

ENDING THE DUAL HOUSING MARKET

Marciniak's efforts to end discrimination in public spaces, health care, and employment and training opportunities relied on the powers of government to legislate, shape policy, and police compliance. Additionally, he sought the help of his connections with religious, civic, and business leaders to eradicate systemic discrimination. Similarly, he tried to impact Chicago's segregated housing market; however, the challenge would be much greater because of prejudice and fear that underpinned the deeply rooted patterns of segregated housing in the city and suburbs.

Marciniak's first effort to deal with fair housing was to build a case for change, but he began very quietly. "Ed wanted to secure a Chicago fair housing ordinance, but he did not tell the mayor when he applied for the job," recalled his sister, Bernice Barta. He asked his sister and other friends to document the discrimination in housing they witnessed so he could give the mayor a report that would "convince him that he had to do something." They clipped ads from the city's major newspapers and called landlords and realtors to see if an apartment or house was vacant or still for sale. When assured that the property was available, they would advise the manager or realtor that they were calling on behalf of a Black friend. In most instances the property was promptly declared "no longer available."[60]

By the end of his first full year at CCHR, Marciniak began to take on the issue of open housing. His first step was to emphasize the successes of communities that broke the mold of "all white" or "all Negro" by demonstrating a third way: whites and Black people living together. He pointed to the successful experiences in urban renewal rental projects such as Lake Meadows, Prairie Shores, and Hyde Park, and developments such as Marina City. However, he insisted that there was need for a metropolitan-wide solution to the patterns of segregated housing. Rather than preaching and brow beating, Marciniak realized that all the players who created the problem had to come to the table. "We cannot ignore the real estate industry," he said. "We must work with it instead of constantly working it over." He reached out to the leaders who might be willing to remove the barriers of religion and race which prohibited free movement of families.

Initially, Marciniak sought to dismantle the walls of prejudice that ripped the city apart by convening more than a hundred real estate brokers, builders, and lenders to meet in small groups to discuss a report the Commission had prepared: "Housing in Chicago for Non-whites." Marciniak realized that not just brokers and lenders, but appraisers, architects, builders, contractors, and developers "must recognize that there is no substitute for leadership in human relations." He compared the *de facto* separations in Chicago to those of the Berlin Wall, which Communists had recently erected. That wall divided friends, families, churches, and neighbors and isolated them. In Chicago, Marciniak claimed, "there are those who built walls out of prejudice, ignorance, fear, and their own refusal to accept all of God's children as their brothers and sisters." He appealed for leadership on the part of those who could convince the "uncommitted majority" that freedom was a precious gift of God meant to be shared by all. [61]

Steadfastly, Marciniak advanced his efforts to secure a fair housing ordinance and was ultimately successful in 1963. In March 1961, the Commission and the Department of Planning prepared a study of fair housing legislation nationwide as it applied to private housing and/or real estate operations. Shortly after presenting the study, the City Council passed a resolution urging the Illinois General Assembly to enact a fair housing practices law to prohibit discrimination in the transfer, sale, rental, or leasing of housing containing more than five units. The legislation failed to pass when fifty-one legislators abstained. As civil unrest grew and anxiety grew in white neighborhoods, Mayor Daley directed the Planning Department and CCHR to undertake another study. Armed with the report, Daley pressed the city council to pass a law that would apply only to the city. The mayor twisted arms and granted favors to secure the votes of council members who feared retaliation by their constituents.[62] The CCHR was charged to oversee the implementation of the law to ensure it was followed. In his 1963 address to the annual CCHR awards luncheon, Marciniak declared that the ordinance was one of several steps that must be taken to protect the rights of people to shop for housing as they did for a car or furniture; that is "without fear of racial, ethnic or religious barriers."[63]

The CCHR also conducted training sessions designed to persuade brokers that the freedom of housing choice was "morally right, legally sound, and businesslike." Since the passage of the Chicago ordinance, other cities in the state passed similar legislation and numerous suburbs set up neighborhood human relations councils, often initiated by local interfaith leadership. While there was a growing number of move-ins to all white suburban developments, the actual number remained small in proportion to the substantial number of Blacks entering the middle class with too few housing choices. Marciniak reiterated his position that only a single housing market throughout the metropolitan region could end the dual housing market. Only a single market would end the power of panic peddlers to exploit both buyers and sellers.[64]

In 1964, civil rights activists began to place greater emphasis on direct actions including boycotts, demonstrations, political action, and mass picketing. The passage of federal Civil Rights Act in February seemed to make the American dream possible and increased expectations on the part of those committed to social justice. "The nation's movement for human rights is no longer on tiptoe. It is on the march," Marciniak exclaimed. However, Marciniak was also somber. He cited a Black teen's summation of the problem: "I've won the right to eat in the drive-in, but I can't afford the hamburger."[65] Education, he believed, must be upgraded, equal access to jobs needed to be assured, and people had to have access to better housing.[66]

Marciniak acknowledged that the pace of change was too slow considering the emerging rhetoric and expectations as enunciated by Malcolm X and other civil rights leaders.

The tensions among those seeking an end to discrimination were becoming frayed over the best course of action to secure the goal. As the tensions were mounting, Marciniak took the opportunity to reflect on his concerns when he wrote reviews of Whitney Young, Jr.'s *To Be Equal* and Nat Hentoff's *The New Equality*. Young was the Executive Director of the National Urban League and Hentoff was a vocal champion of the civil rights movement. Young proposed a ten-point plan to improve social and economic opportunities and called for Black participation in decision making, stressing that a voice for all parties was essential. Hentoff's book discussed the radicalization of the civil rights movement and called for the acquisition of power, particularly political power. Hentoff's call troubled Marciniak:

> A race-conscious civil rights movement (as opposed to a rights-conscious one) would give priority to the race struggle, to racial triumphs. It would tend to isolate Negroes from the mainstream of American life and place their political strategy outside the present two-party system.

> Will this happen? In great part, it depends upon whether the American people will endorse and implement Whitney Young's proposed national effort for interracial justice. If this happens, Negroes and other minorities will ignore proposals like Hentoff's and move forward into partnership with the rest of America.[67]

On occasion, Marciniak was challenged by his own friends and staff for not being more forthright in dealing with racism. A letter from his friend, Bud Herschel, on December 15, 1963, claimed that "Daley was damn lucky to get thru last summer without a big, raw, escalating riot. I am tempted to say you did a good job of covering up and glossing over." Herschel, a Hyde Park resident and justice activist, also wrote that the "fine pronouncements" of Cardinal Albert G. Meyer were not backed up by real action.[68] In fact, Herschel had written to Meyer criticizing Chicago archdiocesan clergy for not taking stronger action in support of racial justice. When Cardinal Meyer did not respond, Herschel stood in front of Holy Name Cathedral on New Year's Day 1964 and handed out copies of his letter to Meyer. Chicago police arrested him for violating an ordinance against distribution of handbills and littering; however, the city's attorney dropped the charges on January 13.[69]

Five days after the case dismissal, Marciniak responded to Herschel, emphasizing that Chicago was not as liberal as Hyde Park, and that the challenge was to figure out how to persuade the great mass of Chicagoans, as well as suburbanites, that discrimination in housing was a "moral problem." Ed optimistically noted the development of religious leadership at the National Conference on Religion and Race[70] and wrote:

> For the first time, we could find sizeable numbers of religious leaders to damn un-Godly practices. For the first time, political leaders, other than those of Hyde Park or in predominantly Negro-occupied neighborhoods, had some support when they took the right position on race. Don't underestimate the size of the problem. In December I discussed with an interfaith

delegation of religious leaders the problem of the generals getting way ahead of the privates. Right now, in the city and suburbs this is a real problem. The solution is not to have the religious leaders become more moderate; the key is to figure out how to get these ideas and ideals across, how we develop lay leadership with commitment in Deerfield and Morgan Park, and every place else.[71]

In September 1965, the Commission faced growing racial challenges. It sought to keep the peace through liaisons with community organizations and through communication, persuasion, and mediation when conflicts arose. This course was regarded as insufficient by two senior CCHR staffers, who sent Marciniak a memo questioning his lack of directness in handling conflicts. They expressed dissatisfaction with the Commission's defensive posture and "continuing failure, in will and execution, to establish meaningful communication and mutual respect between the Commission and the local civil rights movement and a lack of attention to the problems of the more deprived and oppressed of the Negro population." They saw an "undue concentration" of staff attention to the question of racial violence and asked: "Should not a Commission such as our own reserve its primary anxieties and efforts for problems of racial injustice?" Also, they pointedly asked what the Commission's attitude was to be in relation to the Southern Christian Leadership Council's establishing a Chicago office under Dr. King's direction. The writers concluded: "To many [staffers], it appeared that the Commission was drifting away from the real moral and political thrust of the civil rights revolution."[72] (I could find no evidence that Marciniak responded to the memo.)

The Commission would face its greatest challenge in the summer of 1966. The Coordinating Council of Community Organizations (CCCO) had been established three years earlier with parents seeking to improve education and to oust a Chicago's superintendent of education whose policies sustained segregated schools. As recounted in Alan B. Anderson and George W. Pickering's *Confronting the Color Line: The Broken Promise of the Civil Rights Movement in Chicago*, the CCCO, led by Al Raby, asked Dr. Martin Luther King, Jr. to come to Chicago in 1965 to help eradicate slums, poverty, and discrimination. King had been looking for an opportunity to bring attention to racial discrimination in the North, and he accepted CCCO's invitation and partnered with it in the formation of the Chicago Freedom Movement. [73]

In July 1965, Dr. King came to Chicago as part of his People-to-People tour. Mayor Daley was wary of the possible trouble King's presence might cause his leadership and his organization. With the mayor's blessing, Marciniak went to the airport, intending to welcome Dr. King to the city without causing a stir. Marciniak arranged for his car to be driven on to the tarmac so he could board the aircraft unseen and briefly and quietly greet the civil rights leader before he deplaned and entered the terminal where Al Raby and the reporters awaited him. As historian James R. Ralph, Jr. recounts, Marciniak wanted to "shorten the distance between civil rights demands and city policy."[74]

In the course of his 1966 campaign, Dr. King moved into a North Lawndale apartment on the West Side to draw attention to housing conditions for Blacks. Tensions heightened as King shifted his focus away from slum housing to fair housing. Throughout July, his Chicago Freedom Movement conducted marches, picnics in the park, prayer vigils, and other actions, including testing real estate brokers for discriminatory practices on the Southwest Side. As Dr. King led a march through Marquette Park on August 5, 1966, openly hostile white protestors attacked the civil rights group and injured him, prompting the civil rights leader to say: "I have never seen such hostility and hatred anywhere in my life, even in Selma." The news photos and video showed all the ugliness of racism. Other Chicago Freedom Movement marches in blue-collar, white, ethnic neighborhoods on the Northwest Side, as well as the Southwest Side, continued to require large police presences and put pressure on the city. The marches dramatically exposed the deep divide between races in the Chicago. The Movement had made its point, but marches could not achieve the goal of a housing market free of discrimination.[75]

Even as the Northwest and Southwest Sides were in turmoil, Marciniak's home was also on edge. His daughters recalled "Dad got death threats and we acquired an unlisted number at the new house…and, on occasions police guards." And on Sunday afternoons, their mother would hustle the four girls outside or upstairs "as dozens of reporters would converge in the living room for one of Dad's press conferences." Marciniak became the face of the city's efforts to keep the peace and address discrimination appearing on local and national news programs.[76]

The City of Chicago and some of its civic and religious leaders sought calm and urged a move from the streets to the conference table, from confrontation to discussion. A series of meetings was set to address the problems that had prompted the marches. The participants sought a clear and overwhelming set of actions that would make a powerful statement about the injustices that Black people endured and an action plan designed to bring a decisive victory for the Chicago Freedom Movement. Others, however, resisted the call for change and vocally threatened reaction if concessions were made to the civil rights groups. At the center, but clearly in the camp of the Chicago Freedom Movement, were many people who knew that the wrongs of the past must be redressed if the city were to avoid more violence and move forward.

The Chicago Commission on Human Relations met on August 9, in a special noon session in its offices at 211 West Wacker Drive, to develop a plan to bring together the contending sides of the conflict with the aim of reestablishing calm and moving toward a lasting solution to end the dual housing market. As Marciniak had often stated, a just solution required the commitment of the civic, religious, and business leaders of Chicago, as well as its government. The CCHR realized it was imperative to bring people from each of the groups together. CCHR determined to present a plan to the mayor immediately. The minutes of that meeting read as follows:

> The commission unanimously agreed that some effort should be made to set up a meeting with the mayor, civil rights leaders, the Chicago Real Estate Board, and other interested organizations and citizens to discuss the problems and try to make some recommendations for the solution of the problem.[77]

At 2:30 that afternoon, Marciniak and several Commission members went to City Hall to meet with Mayor Daley and develop a plan to get the head of the Chicago Real Estate Board to convene a meeting of business, civic, financial, and religious and civil rights leaders to discuss fair housing practices and to take the "issues off the streets" and bring them "to the conference table." Unsurprisingly, the real estate interests balked.

The Chicago Conference on Religion and Race, of which Marciniak was a founding member but no longer an officer, assumed responsibility for the "Summit" conference, and convened seventy top business, union, civic, religious, and civil rights leaders to meet on August 17. Among the participants were Dr King, Mayor Daley, Archbishop John Cody, and Episcopal Bishop James Montgomery. Chairing the meeting was Benjamin W. Heineman, President of the Chicago North Western Railway, who had recently chaired the White House Conference on Civil Rights for President Lyndon Johnson. The meeting began with an eleven-point plan by the CCHR which, according to Marciniak, "was not to be defensive."[78] The realtors and the leaders of the Chicago Freedom Movement were clearly at loggerheads, and it appeared that new marches would continue as the groups tried to work out a solution. The meeting ended with no resolution. On August 19, in a surprise move, Mayor Daley secured an injunction restricting the size of marches, arguing that the police protection needed to keep the peace at large marches was creating safety problems citywide.[79]

The Chicago Freedom Movement leaders were angry with the mayor's tactics, but they knew that marches alone would not solve the problem of the dual housing market and realized that they needed to obtain substantive and specific agreements that might come from the meetings. What eventually evolved was a multi-point program laid out in a report submitted by a subcommittee composed of civic leaders, realtors, members of the Chicago Commission on Human Relations including Marciniak, and civil rights leaders. On August 26, the full Summit Committee adopted the report which framed the housing discrimination problem in a metropolitan context and laid out steps for government agencies, churches, corporations, and lenders to conduct the program. Among the most action-oriented proposals was the formation of a program charged to create a fair housing policy for the entire Chicago metropolitan area and the creation of fair housing centers.[80]

As the leaders were drafting the report, Alderman Leon Despres, who was the only city council member to chastise Daley for the injunction,[81] wrote a scathing letter to Marciniak. He opined that Marciniak had undertaken the job as director knowing full well that to get it and hold the position "you would have to follow the Party Chairman's policies, but you believed they [members of the Cook County Democratic Party] would allow you leeway to advance human relations goals. In the marginal matters, your work has been impeccable." Despres proceeded to berate Marciniak telling him that he had been "required to support housing segregation policy at variance with human relations goals.... As you have trod the primrose path, the concessions which started as slight ones have grown monstrous." He pointed out that Marciniak had aided in keeping public housing in the mayor's neighborhood all white and had debilitated the Fair Housing ordinance and was "now fighting the civil rights movement." Instead of helping the mayor rise to extraordinary greatness by embracing a one-Chicago housing policy, "there has come from you no affirmative word of advice but reams of defense of the existing arrangements." Despres concluded his harsh critique of Marciniak:

> Knowing that if you were not in your job someone else would be, you may think you are doing more good than someone else. Perhaps you think you can do more good under party-imposed restrictions than outside.

> I think you have been seduced into doing harm you did not intend to do when you undertook the job. All of us reserve our special disappointments for those in whom we had special hopes.[82]

Marciniak, then consumed by the summit negotiations, did not reply to Despres until September 12. His response, written on personal stationary, was lengthy and particular to the points the alderman had raised, and gives insight to the differences Ed saw between what he called "insiders" and "outsiders." He was quick to acknowledge that God would be his judge to the charge of possible "public turpitude." His response sought to examine why Despres' judgment of the situation was at such variance with his. He issued a preliminary caveat: "I am presuming that you still give me credit for having a passionate aversion to racial discrimination and segregation." If that presumption were not accorded, Marciniak explained, his letter would not be understood.

First, he noted that public policy is influenced from the "outside" in one way and from the "inside" in a different way. Marciniak staunchly believed that he had influenced policy against segregation in housing through enforcement, through the development of Fair Housing Ordinance, and use of the CCHR apparatus to adjust complaints of discrimination. However, he did not believe that his role was to stand on a public platform, as that was the role of the outsider.

Next, he tried to deal with the alderman's apparent assumption that the CCCHR had power beyond its reach as a government agency. The open metropolis Marciniak sought was only to be brought about by breaching the "white wall" of segregation in the suburbs, he wrote. The city had no power to dictate beyond its borders and to ignore this fact was to mislead the public. Furthermore, he emphasized that "both the public *and* private sectors have to play a role." To argue that government alone can end racial concentrations is "witless folly." Moreover, he declared, if the private sector could resolve the matter, it would be to abandon the responsibility of public leadership. Explicitly, he added that Despres' own Hyde Park neighborhood demonstrated that public leadership and private sector action were essential to secure integration.

The solution to segregation, Ed continued, necessitated that white families continue to reside in a community after a Black family moved into it. Government, Marciniak stated, could encourage whites to stay but could not require that action, for the responsibility belonged to the private sectors. And he noted, as he often had in the past, "Without an open-housing market throughout the metropolitan area and without Black shoppers scattering throughout this metropolis, the pressure on single communities will only contribute to the historic succession of blocks from all-white to all-Negro."

Marciniak called Despres' charge that he had been required to speak on behalf of segregation "preposterous." He pointed out that the alderman had ignored his testimony in writings and at meetings and speeches throughout the city. Marciniak concluded, "With a twinkle in my eye, may I say, Len, that you should do your own homework first." He also challenged Despres' assertions on points about the Chicago Housing Authority's actions and wondered if his friend had been "victimized by a conspiratorial view of current history."

Most troubling for Marciniak was the alderman's labeling his work at the Commission over the past six years as "marginal." They had divergent views on social and political change:

> A goal is achieved by specific measures. There is no hydrogen bomb which government has, which can wipe out segregation or slums. It has to be accomplished, step by step, big step and small step, steady, pioneering, and courageous. What you dismiss as marginal will, I believe, in the long run, be regarded as a steady elaboration of a policy and a program. You can argue it should have been done faster and better. You can argue that other things should have been done. That's reasonable criticism and men in public office should be able to take it.

Marciniak next listed seven steps toward the goal of an open housing market that had already been taken: City support for a state-wide fair housing ordinance, passage of the city's own fair housing ordinance, the "Summit conference" plan, tens of thousands of rental units in all white areas "opened by the Fair Housing Ordinance, support of community organizations supporting integration, and opening of skilled and white-collar jobs on a non-discriminatory basis.

Marciniak finished his lengthy letter with an invitation that was typical of a negotiator seeking to ensure progress: "...it seems darn silly of us to be writing letters when we could be having lunch. How about it?"[83] There is no record that the lunch ever took place.[84]

CONCLUSION

The challenges of the job had worn Marciniak down and prompted him to resign in April 1967. In his letter of resignation, Ed disclosed that he had fallen ill the previous September and was advised by his doctor that the only remedy was to step away from his work. "Since I do not seem to be able to pace myself in the job to prevent ill health," Marciniak wrote the commissions' chair, "the only alternative is to seek new scenery."[85] At the Mayor's request he stayed on until that autumn.

In his first book, *Tomorrow's Christian*, written shortly after leaving the CCHR, Marciniak reflected on the limited success of the effort to end residential segregation. "Despite laws, court decisions, and educational campaigns, racial segregation persists and all-Negro neighborhoods in the cities and suburbs continue to spread." He contended that part of the failure of the civil rights activists was their inability to enlist the support and participation of the *insiders*, the real estate and mortgage brokers themselves, "in the organized strategy to remodel the social institutions which perpetuate racial segregation in urban neighborhoods."[86] He believed that the work of the insiders in these professions would be not only to see that housing opportunities for Blacks would be more scattered but also to see that once blacks had moved on to a block that whites should continue buy homes on that block.[87]

Even though he held tight to his conviction that moral imperatives of ensuring justice for all was everyone's moral obligation, Marciniak understood that mounting the pulpit was of limited value if the speaker did not respect and interact with those whom he hoped to convince.

More than two decades later, when he wrote a review of William J. Grimshaw's book, *Bitter Fruit: Black Politics and the Chicago Machine, 1931- 1991*, Marciniak suggested that reformers who glorify their progressive movements and attack party regulars too often fail to see that their own shortcomings were not helping their causes. Marciniak believed that the author distorted political reality saying, "Most political truth lies somewhere in between." He concluded that successful politicians "display a zeal for inclusion; they are skilled at the art of accommodation. For both lakefront reformers and party regulars, politics is a bittersweet enterprise."[88]

Edward Marciniak's eyes were on the same prize that Al Raby and Dr. King sought, and he worked in concert with those who pursued that goal. His early, sharp voice seemed to change after he joined public service. Assessing

Marciniak's endeavor to secure racial justice is not simple because of the language of the day and the intense passions for the civil rights cause. While Ed was criticized for his measured actions at the Chicago Commission on Human Relations, his method was purposeful—to ensure that meaningful changes could be made. His approach was to find ways to eradicate old perspectives and break down barriers to resistance by engaging with groups to make meaningful and concrete changes. He did not temper his passion, but he did temper his words while in public service, for he believed that lasting integration could not be brought about only by forceful protest—it had to be "lubricated with persuasion."[89] He knew that pursuing noble principles might, in the end, leave nothing to integrate. His goal was a metropolitan open housing market, an integrated Chicago surrounded by municipalities that were also integrated.

One of the most significant outcomes of the Summit agreement of August 26, 1966, was the creation of the Leadership Council for Metropolitan Open Communities (LCMOC) in December 1966. For forty years, the LCMOC was a nationally recognized housing organization that fought racial segregation and for fair housing through a mix of training, testing for racial steering, litigation, advocacy, policy research, and direct service in Chicago and its suburbs. Through its work and collaborating housing centers throughout the Chicago region, integration took place in communities that once practiced racial segregation.[90]

Most accounts of the open housing movement in Chicago are presented from the perspective of the rights activists, who had the moral high ground. Recognition of the role of the committed insiders adds nuance and greater understanding to the history of the drive to end segregation. Once an outsider himself, Marciniak chose to be an insider. He hoped that by being a problem solver he could respond to the advocates in the trenches and compliment their efforts to achieve common goals. Creating and implementing programs and policies as well as formulating and enacting legislation were, to him, essential to realizing moral goals. In my opinion, Ed Marciniak must be measured for what he accomplished, not solely by what others expected or said of him.

NOTES

1 Cited by Rita and Charles Strubbe, "Target Human Dignity," *St. Anthony Messenger*, June 1964.

2 *Chicago Tribune*, September 27, 1990. Daley cited by Rev. Raymond Baumhart in a pamphlet introducing Marciniak at the time he was awarded an honorary doctorate at Loyola University, 1983, Marciniak Papers, Shelf 3, Position 3; Shelf 2, Position 2; and Elinor Richey Soderberg to Marciniak, October 2, 1963, Marciniak Papers, Shelf 3, Position1; ; *Challenging the Daley Machine: A Chicago Alderman's Memoir*, (Northwestern University Press, Evanston, Illinois, 2005) p. 148; and Despres to Marciniak, May 30, 1960, Marciniak Papers, Shelf 2, Position 2.

3 *Richard J. Daley: Politics, Race, and the Governing of Chicago*, (Northern Illinois University Press, DeKalb, Illinois, 1995), p. viii.

4 *U.S. Census Reports, 1920-1950*.

5 Ibid.

6 Arthur G. Falls, *Reminiscences*, cited in Robert Loerzel, "Blood in the Streets," *Chicago Magazine*, August 23, 2019, http:// August 2019, http://www.chicagomag.com/Chicago-Magazine/August-2019/1919-Race-Riot/.

7 Edward Marciniak, *Tomorrow's Christian*, p. 145.

8 Edward Marciniak, "The Racial Attitudes of Students in the Catholic Colleges of the Chicago Area," pp. 98-101. Marciniak frequented Friendship House which fostered interracial experiences as did his sister while a student at Saint Xavier College. Author's interview with Bernice Barta, October 26, 2011.

9 Steven Avella Interview with Marciniak, February 15, 1988. The audio tape is in the Interview Files of the Archdiocese of Chicago Archives..

10 Steven Avella Interview with Cantwell and Marciniak, 1983, p. 21.

11 Ibid., pp. 14-17.

12 Avella Interview with Marciniak, 1988.

13 Edward Marciniak, Draft, "Catholic Approach to Racism," n. d., Marciniak Papers, Shelf 1, Position 2.

14 Cited in Rita and Charles Strubbe, June 1964.

15 Marciniak to Thomas Haggerty, Feast of the Immaculate Conception [December 8], 1946, Marciniak Papers, Shelf 1, Position 1. It is not clear that his letter made a difference at the time; however, Loyola did stand up for Black players on its team when in 1963, during the Civil Rights movement, it refused to adhere to the unwritten rule of college basketball to have only two black players start. That year Loyola started four black players in its NCAA championship year.

16 "Should Illinois Enact the Proposed Fair Employment Practices Law?" Transcript from 'Midwest Forum of the Air" Radio Station WIND, March 2, 1947, Marciniak Papers Shelf 1, Position 1.

17 "Catholics and Race Relations," *Work*, October 1946. The article was an address by the progressive bishop of Grand Rapids, Francis J. Haas, given to the Catholic Interracial Council of Detroit on September 8, 1946. He had the Catholic Labor Alliance sponsor Rev John LaFarge, S.J., the foremost expert on race relations and the person who influenced his own research, give a public lecture on "Catholics and Race Relations." See: "America' Editor to Talk on Interracial Problem," *Work*, January 1947.

18 "State Street Color Line Dented—Just a Little," *Work*, October 1950.

19 "Impossible? This Store Proves It Isn't," Work, January 1951.

20 "Should Illinois Enact the Proposed Fair Employment Practices Law?" Radio Station WIND, Marciniak Papers Shelf 1, Position 1.

21 *Volini Family*, p. 127

22 *Work*, August 1946. The map was provided courtesy of *The Chicago Defender*, the newspaper serving the city's Black communities. For a detailed account of conflicts in communities

adjacent to the ghetto, see Arnold R. Hirsch, pp. 1-99. Lorraine Hansberry's drama, *Raisin in the Sun*, 50's, portrays well the limits on employment and housing opportunities for residents of the Black Belt. See also: Isabel Wilkerson, *The Warmth of Other Suns: The Epic Story of America's Great Migration* (Vintage Books, New York, New York, 2010).

23   "Restricting Property," July 1947.

24   "Racial Covenants Losing Ground" Ibid, February 1948. Daniel M. Cantwell authored the article. See also, "Homeowners End Race Ban in Community," *Chicago Tribune*, January 24, 1948.

25   "'The Law' Watches' as the Law Is Broken," and "This Project Flopped," December 1946. Also accompanying these accounts was story about the peaceful integration of a similar project on the far Northwest Side's Sauganash Homes, where 13 Black families lived in a "well-integrated community" of 179 families. See also Ibid, "This Project Worked." Marciniak was a member of the Chicago Council Against Racial and Religious Discrimination.

26   May 1952.

27   "Ignores Pressure, Welcomes Negroes," September 1947.

28   "They Once Fought, Now they Act Like Good Neighbors," January 1951. See also: "Who says Negroes, Whites Can't Live Side by Side," Ibid., January 1950.

29   The paper praised Bishop William Cousins at St. Columbanus Parish and Rev. William Ford of the Evangelical and Reformed Church for speaking out while others remained silent. "Wanted Some Good Neighbors," September 1949.

30   When a delegation of white homeowners from Park Manor visited City Hall and told the mayor that there would be no need for police protection if the Blacks had not moved into their neighborhood. Kennelly responded that "'There is no such thing as a white community in Chicago.'" *Chicago Tribune*, cited in "No White, No Negros, But American, Ibid., September 1950. For details about conflicts, see Hirsch, pp. 68-99.

31   Undated draft of column for *Work*, Marciniak Papers, Shelf 2, Position 2.

32 Quoted in a Chicago Tribute notice, Ibid., February 1949.

33 Marciniak to Ely M. Aaron, Chair, Chicago Commission of Human Relations, May 13, 1960, Marciniak Papers, Shelf 2, Position 2.

34 Author interview with Raymond F. Simon and Mary Simon, July 23, 2015, South Beloit, IL, and Steven Avella interview with Cantwell and Marciniak, p. 8.

35 Copy of Speech, December 2, 1960, Marciniak Papers, Shelf 2, Position 2.

36 Dan Herr, "The Chicago Dynamo," p.70.

37 *Chicago Tribune*, July 9 and 13, 1961; and Marciniak, Sixteenth Annual Awards Luncheon, Shelf 2, Position 2.

38 Cited in Ibid., p. 71. A photo of Marciniak walking Rainbow Beach is in Herr, "Chicago Dynamo," p. 12.

39 Marciniak, Sixteenth Annual Awards Luncheon, Shelf 2, Position 2.

40 As early as 1947, Marciniak had commented on segregated Catholic hospitals and had expressed confidence in Cardinal Stritch's promise to community leaders that "administrative policies were being worked out so that Catholic hospitals would give equal opportunity in employment, training, and service to all qualified individuals regardless of race." Edward Marciniak, "… in Chicago," *Opportunity: Journal of Negro Life*, (Summer 1947). Copy of the article in the Marciniak Papers, Shelf 2, Position 3. *Opportunity* was a publication of the Urban League.

41 Arthur Falls, M.D., a Black physician, civil rights activist, and friend of Marciniak's from their Catholic Worker days, highlighted the extent of discrimination in hiring and care in letter to the editor of the *Chicago Tribune*. Falls, along with Quentin D. Young, M.D. and three other doctors urged support of pending state legislation (Senate Bills 529 and 530) that would impact licensure and remove tax exempt status of hospitals that discriminated in admissions. In June 1953, *Work* took up the issue of unequal treatment in an article entitled "Race Discrimination in Hospitals."

42 Avella, pp. 277-281.

43 Falls to Marciniak, July 1, 1960, Marciniak Papers, Position 2, Shelf 2.

44 Marciniak, draft of address to Sixteenth Annual Awards Luncheon, CCHR, December 8, 1961; and Avella; Marciniak, "Physicians, Hospitals, and the Negro Patient," unpublished report, circa 1963, Marciniak Papers, Shelf 2 Position 2; Marciniak, "Statement to the Citizens Advisory Committee Appointed by Mr. Seymour Simon, President, Cook County Board of Commissioners, May 2, 1963", Marciniak Papers, Shelf 2, Position 2.

45 "Address by Edward Marciniak at a luncheon Meeting of the Medical Section of the American Public Health Association, Chicago, Illinois, October 19, 1965" Marciniak Papers, Shelf 2, Position 1.

46 Ibid.

47 Ibid.

48 Ibid.

49 CCHR," Negro Physicians and Medical Students Affiliated with Chicago Hospitals and Medical Schools as of October 23, 1965," https://www.nlm.nih.gov/exhibition/forallthepeople/img/1230.pdf, retrieved May 24, 2022. The CCHR made annual reports which listed the names of all Black physicians, their specialization, and the hospital where they were affiliated.

50 Ibid., pp. 9-11. See also, Lincoln Rice, *Healing the Racial Divide: A Catholic Framework Inspired* by *Dr. Arthur Falls*, (Pickwick Publications, Eugene, Oregon, 2014) pp. 82-84.

51 Rice. p. 83. The plaintiffs believed that the restrictions were the cause in the absolute decline in Black doctors serving the Chicago area from 1950 to 1960.

52 Marciniak, address to the American Public Health Association.

53 Ibid., p 13.

54 Marciniak Address to the Fifteen Awards Luncheon, Marciniak Papers, Shelf 2, Position 2.

55 *Chicago Tribune*, January 1, 1965. Avella interview with Marciniak; and Author interview with the Simons.

56 Marciniak, Address to Sixteenth Annual Awards Luncheon, Marciniak Papers, Shelf 2, Position 2.

57 Marciniak, address to Nineteenth Annual Awards Luncheon, Marciniak Papers, Shelf 2, Position 2.

58 "Minutes of the Washburne Trade School Committee Meeting, January 1965," cited in the Hearings before the Special Subcommittee on Education and Labor House of Representatives, 89th Congress, Washington, D.C. July 27 and 28, 1965. The unions representing the pipefitters, sheet metal workers, structural iron workers, and foundry and pattern workers were the hold outs.

59 "Integration of the Building Trades Reported," *Chicago Daily News*, September 14, 1966. The clipping of the article was reproduced and circulated by the CCHR. Marciniak Papers, Shelf 2, Position 2.

60 Author's interview with Bernice Barta.

61 Marciniak, Sixteenth Annual Awards Luncheon. Marciniak Papers, Shelf 2, Position 2.

62 Author interview with Simon. Among those who were who were "convinced" to vote for the ordinance was Vito Marzullo of the West Side 25th Ward where he ruled for thirty years. Ray Simon recalled that he met the alderman just as he came from his meeting, and he was "steaming and cursing the mayor, but he went along."

63 "Report to the Mayor and City Council of Chicago on the Present Status and Effectiveness of Existing Fair Housing Practices legislation in the United States as of April 1, 1963, and Marciniak, draft of address, Eighteenth Annual Awards Luncheon, December 6, 1963, Marciniak Papers, Shelf 2, Position 2; Marciniak "Politics and Race in Chicago: Revised or Revisited?", *Chicago Books in Review*, Winter, 1995-1996. See also, James R. Ralph, Jr., *Northern Protest: Martin Luther King, Jr., Chicago, and the Civil Rights Movement* (Harvard University Press, Cambridge, Massachusetts, 1993), p. 82.

64 Marciniak, draft of Address to Nineteenth Annual Awards Luncheon of CCHR, December 2, 1964, Marciniak Papers, Shelf 2, Position 2.

65 Ibid.

66 For the account of the civil rights struggles in the North during this period, see Thomas J. Sugrue, *Sweet Land of Liberty: The Forgotten Struggle for Civil Rights in the North* (Random House, New York, New York, 2008).

67 Marciniak, draft of Book Review, 1964, Marciniak Papers, Shelf 2, Position 2.

68 Bud Herschel to Marciniak, Marciniak Papers, Shelf 2, Position 2.

69 The details of the incident are included in a court case that Herschel filed against the city demanding $125,000 in damages because he was deprived of his "rights, privileges and immunities secured by the Constitution of the United States, and particularly the First, Sixth, and Fourteenth Amendments." The matter was heard by the Court of Appeals in the Seventh Circuit, Austin Herschel **v.** Frank J. Dyra and Orlando W. Wilson, 365 F.2d 17 (7th Cir. 1966), http// http://openjurist.org/365/f2d/17/herschel-v-j-dyra-w and "Court Rules Pamphleteer within Rights," *Chicago Tribune*, July 16, 1966.

70 The Conference was held in Chicago in1963 to celebrate the100th Anniversary of the Emancipation Proclamation. The theme of the conference was "Race: A Challenge to Religion." Among those speaking at the conference were Dr. Martin Luther King; Jr.; Sargent Shriver, Peace Corp Director, and past Chair of the Catholic Interracial Council; Rabbi Abraham J. Heschel; and Cardinal Meyer and Msgr. John J Egan of the Archdiocese of Chicago.

71 Marciniak to Herschel, Second Sunday after Epiphany [January 19, 1964], Marciniak Papers, Shelf 2, Position 2.

72 Hal Freeman and Dan Overmyer to Marciniak, September 10, Marciniak Papers, Shelf 2, Position 2.

73 (University of Georgia Press, Athens, Georgia,1986), pp. 90-167. As early as 1961, Marciniak had shared the Mayor's confidence that the city could "remove every slum dwelling by 1971." "Human Relations in a Changing City," draft of a speech given at the University of Chicago's conference, "Renewing

Chicago in the 60's," April 20, 1961, Marciniak Papers, Shelf 2, Position 2.

74 Ralph, p. 85.

75 Cited in Anderson and Pickering, p. 228. For a detailed account of the Chicago Freedom Movement's strategy and initiatives see Ralph, *Northern Protest*, pp. 92-153; Anderson and Pickering, pp. 168-236; and David J. Garrow, *Bearing the Cross: Martin Luther King, Jr., and the Southern Christian Leadership Conference* (New York, Quill, 1986), pp. 431-526

76 Volini Family History, p. 134.

77 Cited in the minutes of the Chicago Human Relations Commission, October 13, 1966, Marciniak Papers, Shelf 2, Position 2.

78 Cited in Ralph, p. 153, and *Chicago Tribune*, August 19, 1966.

79 Marciniak's files do not indicate he had a direct role in the injunction filing. He did believe, however, the marches in all white neighborhoods contiguous to the black belt were misguided because they created the impression that Blacks sought to move into only these neighborhoods. See Marciniak interview, "Eyes on the Prize II," October 24, 1988, Washington University Libraries, Film and Media Archive, Henry Hampton Collection, http://digital.wustl.edu/e/eii/eiiweb/mar5427.0303.103edmarciniak.html. See also the *New York Times* editorial, "A Time Out for Action," August 18, 1966, which called for a pause in the marching because they posed a "risk of major violence." See also: Anderson and Pickering, pp. 237-255.

80 "A Metropolitan Fair Housing Program," *Human Relations News of Chicago*, September 1966; Ralph, pp.162-171; and Anderson and Pickering, pp. 255-267; and Garrow, pp..519-525.

81 Despres called it "divisive as it gave city support to one group against another." Remarks of Alderman Leon M. Despres in the Chicago City Council, August 25, 1966, cited in Ralph, p. 165.

82 Despres to Marciniak, August 22, 1966, Marciniak Papers, Shelf 2, Position 2. It is noteworthy that Despres had sent Marciniak a congratulatory note when he took the CCHR post. He wrote:

"You have every right to feel gratified at being chosen to head the work of the Commission on Human Relations. Although the work will be hard, you will find it congenial and interesting, and you will do an outstanding job. We are fortunate to have you doing it." Despres to Marciniak, May 30, 1960, Marciniak Papers, Shelf 2, Position 2.

83 Marciniak to Despres, September 12, 1966, Marciniak Papers, Shelf 2 Position 2.

84 The relationship between them worsened in 1987. During Despres' presentation on a panel discussing race and politics in Chicago at the American Historical Association's 1986 annual meeting, he referred to the white candidates as "racists" and referenced one as having "the instincts of Hitler." Marciniak confidentially reported Despres' "inflammatory rhetoric" to CONDUCT, a nonprofit watch dog group trying to ensure fair campaign practices in the 1987 mayoral election. As Despres' comments were made at private meeting, CONDUCT issued a confidential letter that noted his rhetoric was of the kind that "exacerbates group fears and passions and undermines civil debate." Despres never forgave Marciniak for his role in that matter. Marciniak to John McDermott, Chair, CONDUCT, December 30, 1986, and McDermott to Despres, January 21, 1987, Marciniak Papers, Shelf 4, Position 3; and Despres, p. 95.

85 Marciniak to Ely Aaron, April 17, 1967, Marciniak Papers, Shelf 2, Position 2. Earlier, in confidential correspondence with his close friend Monsignor George Higgins, Director of the Social Action Department, United States Catholic Conference, Marciniak told of his plans to leave his post but had not discussed this with the Mayor or the Commission as he did not want to "muddle the mayoral election waters." He explained that the decision was "strictly personal." He made it clear that he wanted and needed time to reflect and write, both activities he considered "essential to a human existence." Marciniak to Higgins, March 10, 1967, Marciniak Papers, Shelf 2, Position 2.

86 P. 93.

87 Ibid., pp. 93-96.

88 Marciniak, "Black Politics Chicago-style, Bears 'Bitter Fruit,'" *Chicago Tribune*, October 4, 1992.

89 Cited in Anderson and Pickering, p.135. The words are Philip Hauser's, Professor of sociology and noted demographer on the faculty at the University of Chicago addressed to Al Raby of CCCO regarding the integration of the Chicago Public Schools. Hauser was a friend of Marciniak's and served on one of the Chicago Commission on Human Rights' advisory committees on housing.

90 Poverty and Race Research Action Council, "Farewell to the Leadership Council," (May-June 2006) https://www.prrac.org/farewell-to-the-leadership-council/ retrieved October 3, 2022.

Chapter 6

Organizing Neighborhood Renewal and Livable Cities

Anybody can build housing.
Who will build Community?

EDWARD MARCINIAK[1]

"I am an urban man. I love cities," Edward Marciniak once explained to a reporter. "I analyze cities socially, not economically."

Marciniak conceived of cities as organic social entities that grew and changed through stages of youthful development, maturation, and renewal. He was an urban optimist, unlike many sociologists who devote their attention to the dynamics of social chaos and deviance. He did not hold in high regard such sociologists who made a name for themselves ferreting out faults and recording decay.

"Building inspectors." he called them for wringing their hands and filing reports that argued that cities were doomed. He acknowledged some building inspectors were

263

honorable, but they needed to make way for the "work and social vision of the architect who will dream, plan, and help build a community in which all God's children can live and work in peace."[2]

In a guest address to the weekly television service of the ecumenical Chicago Sunday Evening Club in 1989, Ed made clear his identity: "I am an urban planner.... I help to revitalize inner city neighborhoods." However, he prefaced that identification about his workaday mission trying to reform oppressive and unjust social institutions and shape public policy. He led with a discussion of a Christian work ethic, which he viewed to be a "social ethic" animated by an "aching desire to make social institutions more human, more just, more compassionate." Continuing, he noted, "Such a work ethic carries Christians into society's mainstream, into often turbulent waters.... Its destiny is not to Christianize society but civilize it, to humanize it."[3]

Ever the journalist/scholar/activist, Marciniak asked tough questions to get at the heart of problems but did not stop there; identifying problems for him was the first step toward removing barriers. People needed to be free to step forward to pick up the ball and advance it. His motivation had not changed since he had first read *The Catholic Worker*. He still relied on the Chicago Inter-Student Catholic Action (CISCA) framework, "observe, judge, act," to remove the barriers to opportunities and to create social and economic benefits. His networking and organizational skills facilitated him in his new roles as Deputy Commissioner of the Chicago Department of Development and Planning and as President of the Institute of Urban Life, plus his leadership positions in numerous organizations dedicated to urban life.

HOUSING ADVOCATE
AND PLANNER

Having exhausted himself after eight years, in what he described the "the hottest seat in Chicago next to the mayor's."[4] Marciniak had submitted his resignation as the director of the Chicago Commission on Human Relations (CCHR) in April 1967. Marciniak had counted on a smooth exit because he assumed his close associate Samuel Nolan, a Black Chicago Police Department sergeant who headed the human relations unit and worked with CCHR, would take the reigns as acting director. Mayor Richard J. Daley, however, tapped Nolan to be the city's first Black Deputy Superintendent, thereby nixing Marciniak's quick departure.[5] At the mayor's request, Ed dutifully stayed on to direct the agency through another tense summer when racial conflicts were again heightening. While continuing in his post, Marciniak huddled with Daley on receiving a new position with the city government. He expressed interest in a position in the city's development and planning office because he believed social planning needed to go side by side with physical planning.[6]

On October 18, 1967, after the pressures of summer unrest passed, the Mayor's Office issued a press release announcing Marciniak's new post. In the release Daley noted: "Marciniak, with his extensive background and experience, will be concerned with drawing to the planning process city-wide and neighborhood organizations and agencies, businesses, churches, unions, schools, and other groups concerned with human needs. In furthering development and implementation of the city's Comprehensive Plan, attention must be given to family and social environment[and] to education, training, employment, and income…. In short, to the total person, to the total environment, all of the family needs."[7] Marciniak would now report to Lewis Hill, who was a wily and trusted adviser to Mayor Daley and was Chicago's Commissioner of Departments of Urban Renewal and Commissioner of Development and Planning.

The responsibilities seemed a perfect fit for the new deputy. Marciniak understood that the poor were in constant search of quality affordable housing, the economic resources necessary for family stability, and the safety to build communal relationships. His experiences and classes in sociology had excited his interest in urban affairs and the impact policy had on neighborhoods. Further, he had become acutely aware of how policies affected neighborhoods, especially, slum clearance, urban renewal, and community conservation both as editor of *Work* and as director of the CCHR.[8]

One of Marciniak's first tasks was to help prepare the city's application for the Department of Housing and Urban Development's (HUD) Model Cities program. Model Cities was the centerpiece of President Lyndon Johnson's War on Poverty. It was intended to provide programs to stabilize and improve disadvantaged communities without the waste of earlier poverty programs and urban renewal projects. The programs of Model Cities were to be the joint product of local city and county agencies, non-profits, business leaders, and neighborhood resident councils. Mayor Daley secured a commitment for four Model Cities programs, one more than any other city in the country, to meet the special needs of: Lawndale, Near South, Uptown, and Woodlawn. Together these four areas were home to more than a quarter of Chicago's population, who resided in less than one-eighth of the city's footprint. The program would receive grants of $38 million in 1969 and $58 million in 1970.[9]

Chicago's application to the federal Department of Housing and Urban Development (HUD) included fifty-seven programs outlined in a 2300 page document weighing eight and one-half pounds and had to be reviewed by each of the four local councils prior to Chicago City Council's review. However, community groups and leaders who weren't recruited by the mayor's staff to serve on the councils became antagonists and, as a reporter wrote, a simple exchange of paperwork for federal money was "as deceptive as an iceberg, nine-tenths of which is not visible above the water." [10]

Much of Marciniak's work was done behind closed doors with the staff; seldom did he play a public role. Frequently he was in the audience, speaking quietly with community leaders, many of whom had been recommend by him to serve on the advisory council.[11] However, there was one notable incident recorded by the *Chicago Tribune* that highlighted some of the Lawndale community's distrust of Model Cities. Aware of that distrust, Marciniak spoke directly to community members about the need for involvement and the benefits of disagreements:

> Frank discussions during meetings of residents' councils have given me hope for model cities. But even if communities chaff [sic] at required city hall approval, one cannot by-pass the political process, nor can things be done without a government. This is an inescapable process.

Solutions to a community's ills are available in that community as in government. Nobody has a monopoly on action in the program. Involvement and change are not an easy task. We have to disagree; but then we have to move. Starting something like this is more difficult because of long neglect. But we must cut thru the flak to get money to move ahead.

Ed explained to residents that historical suspicions need to be replaced by maximum citizen participation and acknowledged that change might be necessary to achieve program goals and that "we always need to hear how we are doing."[12]

Marciniak's moderating statements were dismissed by Warner Saunders, the young Black executive of the Lawndale Better Boys Foundation. Saunders believed that Lawndale was a "political pawn" and that the community's residents had voted for a city administration that depended on their ignorance and apathy to keep them in the slums. He called for a moratorium on Model Cities plans until there was maximum citizens participation. Marciniak must have been distressed to hear Saunders say: "The best program to ever hit this area was the big fire last April that got rid of about half of the community's rot and a lot of its rats." His anger apparent, Saunders stated that residents "want to do things themselves" rather than deal with "institutionalized racism" in schools, public housing, and employment.[13]

Marciniak's effectiveness was in his connections with religious and community leaders with whom he worked behind the scenes. According to Thomas A. Volini, the deputy commissioner's young aide and brother-in-law, Ed "was a practical man in his role in helping to shape the Model Cities program. He was like an *outsider* to the agency." In meetings he often led a conversation in Socratic style, "questioning not staking out positions—though the 'right' position on a topic was always clear in the framing of the question. One of his roles was to translate the positions of the faith and business leaders into action plans and, in turn, to school the leaders in the characteristics of the action projects that were devised."

Volini noted that Marciniak unsuccessfully advanced his views on social services in public housing projects, though "his influence was heavily felt" in the development of fourteen Maternal and Infant Medical Centers. Other areas of impact, according to Volini were on programs supporting family life and early childhood education through enhanced Head Start funding.[14]

In fact, however, Model Cities was soon given over to the discretion of the city mayor under President Richard Nixon's administration, and then abandoned after a brief time and with little lasting impact.[15]

One of Marciniak's special projects stemmed from atten-dance at the Conference on National Unity in November 1970 that was funded by the Ford Foundation. Follow-up groups gathered to address the divisive effects of polariza-tion along racial and ethnic interests, including competition for residential space, with special concern for panic peddling and moderate-income housing; competition for jobs; edu-cational quality; law, order, and justice; media treatment of racial and ethnic groups. The group hoped to be a leavening agent that would foster livable cities through thoughtful intergroup discussion.[16] Marciniak headed one such group in Chicago called INTERCOM which was composed of influential Black and ethnic leaders. The initiative did not survive when the Ford Foundation cut aid to the project, and it failed to attract local support even though the need to address multi-racial and multi-ethnic issues to stabilize neighborhoods was critical.[17]

Marciniak grew restless in his role at the city and devoted a great deal of time to writing his first book on the role of Christians in the world and numerous articles on religious issues to be discussed in a following chapter. As early as December 1965, he had shared with a friend his closely held thoughts about leaving his position with the city. He had shared these intentions only with his wife to this point. He wrote about the reasons, "many of them with the nature of the job" and his desire to return to the typewriter and "defrost" his fingers:

> I am full of ideas accumulated though[sic.] this experience, which I've been unable to put down on paper in an organized fashion. My experiences have involved not only race, but the formulation of policy for urban renewal, city planning, the war against poverty and a dozen other municipal programs.
>
> One book I have in my system is on the social problems of the metropolis. I can do this without repeating all of the clichés dealing with inner city needs and the suburbs, etc. I've had a remarkable vantage point to view the human problems from the side where decisions have been made after twenty years on the outside demanding decisions.[18]

1969 was a year of great personal worry and stress for the Marciniak's. Virginia was diagnosed with colon cancer and hospitalized over a period of several months in 1969. Because of his concern about his spouse, Marciniak relied on the help of relatives to care for his four daughters, the oldest in high school and the other three in grade school. Christina, who was then in the eighth grade, remembers that her dad hired an "older" woman to come to the house on school days when he wasn't around, and over the summer the four sisters moved to various aunts' houses in the Chicago area or to East Troy, Wisconsin, where Ed's parents had a cottage.

Christina's June graduation was memorable because an aunt bought her a special graduation dress at Saks Fifth Avenue and her mother got released from the University of Chicago Hospital to attend the ceremony, but just for that day. Cancer was not discussed by the family; the girls were told that their mother had "tummy trouble." They only learned of the true source of her illness when Virginia disclosed it in 1985 after she developed breast cancer. Ed did not allude to Virginia's sickness and hospitalization in his correspondence during this time. A rare exception was in 1970 when he declined a friend's request for a membership contribution writing: "Virginia and I are still reeling from the medical and hospital expenses of last year when she spent nearly three months in the hospital."[19]

His time in the planning department became a personal challenge. He later told an interviewer, "I got buried in '71 and '72." Isolated and without outright political clout, his influence seemed to decline, and he did not take to warming the bench.[20] In late 1972, Marciniak, with the help of friends, secured a position with the Institute of Urban Life at Loyola University of Chicago, where he would be able to pursue his interests in urban affairs, housing, and much more while being an outside advocate. Mayor Daley and Commissioner Lewis Hill feted Marciniak at a farewell party at the Bismarck Hotel. A photo of the event captured the three of them under a hand lettered banner that appropriately recorded Marciniak's intent: "Write On!" Once again, Ed would be free to pursue ideas, teach, challenge the consciences of the powerful, and critique flawed public policy. The Institute would be his home base for nearly two decades and provided a platform for his varied interests and causes.

THE INSTITUTE OF URBAN LIFE

The Institute of Urban Life (IUL) was created in 1960 by Msgr. John Egan and John Ducey, both of whom shared an interest in the emerging problems of the city and a concern for the role of the Catholic Church responding to them. Ducey, a real estate expert, joined with Egan, who directed the Archdiocese of Chicago's Office of Urban Affairs to create a program to infuse a strong ethical dimension into an urban studies program that would blend economics, sociology, and city planning. The two men negotiated financing and an affiliate relationship with Loyola University Chicago and incorporated as a non-profit organization. Ducey secured consulting contracts to pay for his salary and a few researchers who also taught classes in the university's newly created Graduate Program in Urban Studies. The consulting arm flourished in the mid-1960s, but Ducey resigned because of health problems. Loyola's graduate program continued.[21]

Marciniak arranged with Loyola's President, Rev. Raymond Baumhart, SJ, for a loan to the Institute of Urban Life (IUL) and became its president. He shared an office with Michael E. Schlitz, who served as director of the Loyola graduate program and an assistant to IUL. Dark and dim, the office was in the rear room on the first floor of a three flat at 14 East Chestnut Street that featured an imposing limestone carved entrance. Loyola rented the space from George Dunne, Chairman of the Cook County Board, who resided in the floors above. Marciniak set up shop with his most important assets: two sixteen-inch file cabinets crammed with contact cards, a phone, telephone directories of fifteen major cities, personal and research files dating from his college days, and his trusty manual typewriter.

At home, Ed received five newspapers every day, and daily mail delivery to his office brought a plethora of magazines, journals, and some out of town newspapers. Added to these were neighborhood papers and church bulletins that Marciniak picked up when he visited places or received from friends. He did not hoard the papers, however. When he found items of interest, he used his long metal ruler rather than scissors to "clip" articles for his files or to send to associates locally and nationally. The clippings were always accompanied with a brief typed or hand-written note. This was one more of his strategies to maintain contact with his diverse network of collaborators and to provoke their responses.[22]

The freedom that Marciniak had sought came at a price; he had to raise his own salary and a portion of his assistant's.

He funded the IUL budget through consulting and research contracts he secured from his wide network of business and political people and from foundations. The contracts enabled him to cobble together enough revenue to have the freedom to write about and advocate for the issues he believed in. Over the years he would gather support from the Chicago Community Trust, The YMCA, the Field Foundation of Illinois, the Ford Foundation, and other entities of note. [23]

Marciniak set out to build a program to provide technical assistance to grass-roots groups and institutions that would benefit from IUL's research skills and from his network of talented experts. The latter donated their time to help struggling communities.[24] The first year's annual report listed twenty-seven individuals who provided direct help. Marciniak targeted impoverished communities to ensure aid would be personal, "not long distance," so that the people in the neighborhoods had time to articulate their problems and weigh alternatives. The Institute's activities ranged from aiding a block club to get a fire-gutted building demolished, finding a site for a half-way house for women just released from county jail, and securing a drugstore operator to replace a neighborhood's last pharmacy. His assistance also included consultation with a nonprofit day-labor agency fighting predatory for-profit agencies and with a consortium of churches seeking to acquire urban renewal land to build moderate income housing. Additionally, he helped groups secure financial assistance and access to private entities to provide medical services, childcare, and more. In many ways Ed served as an alderman for the marginalized.[25]

Keeping inter-city community needs high on the agenda of the city's civic and business leaders was also a priority.

Marciniak made the case by addressing in 1973 two conferences sponsored by the Economic Development Administration of the U.S. Department of Commerce and three meetings of the Chicago Association of Commerce and Industry, as well speaking at seminars and luncheons hosted by area universities. These kinds of activities were all part of his agenda for the Institute.[26] Three areas of specific concern occupied his greatest attention: community-based planning, poverty, and housing for the working poor and poor.

COMMUNITY-BASED SOLUTIONS

Marciniak's experiences with urban renewal programs of the 1950s and 1960s caused him to search for holistic solutions to end community disinvestment and abandonment. In his view, the wholesale demolition and relocation of people was a "dead-end." Even with the requirements of community concurrence on projects, neighborhoods were too often the pawns of city planners and real estate interests who seized upon subsidies for acquisition, infrastructure, and cash flows guaranteed by government assisted rents. While Marciniak was convinced government help was necessary to rebuild cities, he believed that broad-based community involvement was essential to their revitalization. In fact, he believed that cities were on the cusp of revitalization from the core out. It was imperative for neighborhoods to survive and continue their critical role.

When Marciniak gave the commencement speech to 2,000 Loyola graduates who crowded the Chicago Stadium in 1973, he acknowledged that those attendees could not have missed the evidence of old age and decay on their way to the venue. There were acres of vacant land covered by broken concrete, busted glass, and garbage, along with skid row taverns and "urban clutter" at its worst. He continued, stating that although downtown was showing signs of new life, for more than thirty years Chicago's neighborhoods had suffered disinvestment and abandonment. He urged the graduates of the urban Jesuit institution to meet the challenge of rebuilding the city through its neighborhoods. Only if the neighborhoods were revitalized would the city be strong and cease bleeding its population to the ever-growing suburban fringes. "These neighborhoods," he emphasized, "gave support to families moving up the economic and social ladder and supplied the political and social cement which held the city together. They took the hodgepodge of nationalities, races, languages, and cultures, the rich and the poor, the skilled and the poorly educated and blended them into a lively livable Chicago." He concluded with a call to the new graduates to help the city refashion itself in ways so that cultural pluralism and diversity survived in neighborhoods and defended against the divisive actions by separatists of whatever color.[27]

From his IUL post, Marciniak tried to be both a catalyst and agent of the change he expected from the graduates. He did this by assistance with community planning both in old neighborhoods near the urban core, as well as in his own community of Edgewater. His first major engagement was in the area immediately north and west of the central business district. Fittingly, it was the community whose graduates he had addressed at Wells High School in 1945. Back then, he challenged the students to fight to better their community and nation. At the request of the Ford Foundation, he wrote *Reviving an Inner-City Community: The Drama of Urban Change in Chicago's East Humboldt Park*, telling the story of one community's efforts to revitalize itself and retain its values. While this book, the first of four he would write on urban issues, was historical and factual, he noted that the "report does not pretend to be disinterested." Ever the teacher, he hoped the East Humboldt Park's case study would be a lesson for other communities as they grappled with the dilemmas involved in revitalization.[28]

The community of East Humboldt Park had been created by the stroke of a city planner's pen when defining part of a study area for the development plan for the revitalization of Chicago's central business district. The area's one square mile was home to a diverse population of 20,000 Poles, Mexicans, Puerto Ricans, Italians, Black people, and others. At one time its tenements had a population density exceeding all other Chicago neighborhoods and was the heart of Chicago's Polonia (Polish community). Within its triangular boundaries, were seven Catholic churches and those of other denominations. These churches served thousands of immigrants, who got their start in this port of entry. Many families stayed for its rich diversity and proximity to jobs. It was, as Marciniak noted, one of hundreds of neighborhoods in the nation's urban centers "facing the stress of economic and social crosscurrents that energize or enervate twentieth century metropolis" requiring residents "to assert themselves to fashion a future for their neighborhood."[29] To do anything less would lead to the neighborhood's slow death through deterioration and out-migration.

The organic nature of the community was earlier threatened by city hall's planners, who had slated an expressway to run through Saint Stanislaus Kostka Church, the mother Church of Chicago's Polonia. The community loudly and vehemently resisted the demolition of its anchor institution and successfully forced the reengineering of the Kennedy Expressway, creating an illogical bend in the road to skirt the church. The community did accept a well-intentioned urban renewal housing project, which soon became an island of lower income people. Thereafter, the community grew more skeptical of city hall and its planners. Residents joined with the confrontational organizing efforts of the Northwest Community Organization, which relied on Saul Alinsky's tactics of non-negotiable demands, demonstrations, and other direct actions.

In 1973, the city provided most communities proximate to the central business district an opportunity to plan their own upgrades as well as a subsidy for each area to hire its own planner to create a revitalization plan. With the grant and matching funds raised locally, the East Humboldt Park community did a national search for a planner. The winner of its selection process was the National Center for Urban Ethnic Affairs (NCEUA), which was recognized for its sensitivity to urban ethnic institutions. NCEUA assigned Marcy Kaptur, a young planner with impeccable credentials and neighborhood planning experiences based in maximum community engagement.[30] (Kaptur later became a long-term U.S. Congresswoman from the Toledo, Ohio, area.)

Marciniak believed that a neighborhood was a "state of mind as well as a designated piece of urban terrain." He zealously supported Kaptur's intensive community involvement process. She focused on the importance of place and community, using the lens of cultural pluralism which tried to frame issues in terms of ethnic and racial culture for individual rights and the universal claim of social justice. This was consistent with the positions that Marciniak had taken at the CCHR, his INTERCOM efforts, and his own experience living in diverse communities.[31]

After surveying residents and hosting group meetings, the community laid out its goals, plans, and tactics in its *Program of improvement: 1977-1980*. Its guidelines included community upgrades through repair of older buildings and construction of new homes and apartments on vacant lots without driving up prices and forcing current residents to leave the neighborhood. The goal was to protect its working class residents, who relied on location for access to nearby jobs and to retain diversity.[32] The steps to achieve this were conventional: enhancing landscaping in public areas, mitigating noise and pollution from the expressway, repairing sidewalks, using vacant land for parks, and protecting interior streets from industrial traffic.

Marciniak praised the Humboldt Park *Program for Improvement* as an alternate strategy for inner-city neighborhoods and noted that the upwardly mobile poor did not need to be replaced by an established middle class. He praised the strategy because it did not assume that deterioration was inevitable just because "a neighborhood is old, undergoing racial and ethnic change, mainly occupied by low-income households, or the victim of earlier mistakes in planning." He knew that healthy neighborhoods, with nourishment and strong institutions, could continually renew themselves through intentional acts of improvements that preserved a sense of identity and pride of place and welcomed newcomers. The best solution to urban blight was not a big project of "renewal" that changed the neighborhood and scarred its state of mind. Instead, he emphasized that smaller projects that were mindful of place and culture, flexible in outlook, and reliant on consensus built community stability.[33]

While the plan for Humbolt Park was a major step toward creating community confidence, Marciniak opined it was the first of many more uncertain steps that the community would have to take to end the typical pattern of inner city disinvestment. It was an up-hill fight as the bankers and planners and investors were waiting for the community to get worse so they could "reclaim" the land through demolition and housing developments for new people who would pay higher prices. To be successful, Ed insisted, the community would have to regain its attractiveness for current residents as well as develop an affirmative marketing program to attract newcomers.

Marciniak concluded the book urging communities to plan and create subsidiary corporations to become the developer and co-developer of neighborhood projects that the marketplace would not undertake. This was a natural progression he and other community development advocates had come to see as necessary to community conservation. Community organizations served as full-time protectors against those entities and forces that sought to change the status quo. But that defensive mindset was not enough. According to Marciniak, "It is easier to distrust than trust, simpler to put together a confrontation than a partnership. Collective bargaining needed to replace collective battling." Community development required sharing power with those private institutions and public officials who could help; putting aside the "fireworks of confrontation" for telephone calls [and] conferences; and the use of ordinary channels of influence, such as politics and friendship."[34]

The book was Marciniak's effort to teach community groups a lesson on progressing from combat to revitalization. He also wanted to educate bankers and public officials. In Chicago, he was in constant contact with those who could help build bridges. For example, he reached out to the CEO of the Jewel Tea Company, the city's largest grocer, and provided him with data demonstrating how Jewel had abandoned the poorer neighborhoods. This friendship and reasoned appeal secured a commitment for a desperately needed new store on intersecting bus routes in Lawndale.[35] Similarly, he appealed to his friend, Congressman Daniel Rostenkowski, who chaired the House Ways and Means Committee to sponsor tax legislation that would increase incentives for business to donate to not-for profits agencies, thereby filling the gap for government reductions in human services.[36]

In 1976, Marciniak was enlisted to take on a national leadership role as the Board Chairman of the National Center for Urban Ethnic Affairs (NCUEA). Msgr. Geno Baroni had created the Center seven years earlier to assist working class and ethnic groups trying to revitalize their neighborhoods. Marciniak and Baroni shared common perspectives on Catholic action, cultural pluralism, and community development and networking connections.[37] When Baroni was nominated by President James Carter to be Undersecretary of the Department of Housing and Urban Development, Marciniak was urged to take the role of Board Chairman by the Ford Foundation, which was a major NCUEA funder. He did so with no compensation from 1976 to 1984 to help set the national agenda for community development, including vital legislation on redlining and community investment. The only benefit Ed accrued was NCUEA's publication of three of his books on community revitalization.[38]

Marciniak's concern about the future of urban neighborhoods centered on the "tension between priority to be given to place or person, to software *vs* hardware."[39] This tension was in his own neighborhood of Lakewood-Balmoral in the Edgewater Community. His reflections on its revitalization in his second book was highlighted in *Reversing Urban Decline: The Winthrop-Kenmore Corridor in the Edgewater and Uptown Communities.* The community struggled with the destabilizing effects of employers abandoning the community and from certain public policy decisions. Both changed the nature of the area's resident population. For too long, the planners looked at infrastructure, land use and zoning, and drew colored lines on maps that collided with the emotional sentiments and social networks that create community bonds through a kaleidoscopic web of churches, public park and library committees, scout troops, garden clubs, and other place-based associations.[40]

Marciniak recounted the challenges faced by the families and individuals who shared twelve contiguous blocks as they tried to enliven their neighborhood and to leaven those adjoining neighborhoods that eventually comprised the much larger Edgewater community area. In his lexicon, a *neighborhood* was the area with close primary contacts and a *community* was a larger area of shared institutions and a shopping district, an area such as a Chicago police district or ward. In 1962, Ed had moved his family from the two-flat in

Albany Park to 1341 West Catalpa Street in St. Ita's Parish. The community was ethnically and racially diverse and filled with families and singles who appreciated diversity and the liveliness of urban living. This community, nonetheless, faced an uncertain future at the hands of government policy (for example, the deinstitutionalization of state mental facilities resulting in the "flooding" of Uptown and the eastern portion of Edgewater with poor and troubled individuals). Testifying to the community's dicey prospects was Marciniak's own need to borrow $25,000 from his father to buy the home. The neighborhood was redlined and written off by lenders. His family and others could not get mortgage guarantees.[41]

The book's account of the neighborhood's hard choices highlighted the limits of planning and the lack of power of even a self-conscious neighborhood had to energize urban revitalization. Marciniak does not tell the story in the first person. However, Virginia and he hosted many of the early discussions in their living room, where Ed often sat on the floor as the conversations and brainstorming led to concrete strategies and action. The group's decisions to organize, pester politicians, turn up the heat on slum lords, organize a neighborhood watch, and much more began to turn the tide.

Concluding the book, Marciniak warned community groups not to expect a great deal from the planners, "the theologians of public policy,"[42] who propose parkways and cul-de-sacs and who change zoning and set building density. These actions might help, he wrote, but they were secondary to the real work of the community. He offered practical approaches to curb blight and spur improvements. Among the twelve actions he recommended were: a clean sweep of political candidates and their cronies who profited from flop houses and "roach hotels" and took "gifts" for ignoring building code violations; mobilizing the electorate to rid the neighborhood of liquor stores and taverns that were magnets for trouble; a community escort service to accompany witnesses to criminal court appearances; active encouragement of investment in older buildings; and a marketing program to recruit urban pioneers[43] Among the many changes that ensured continued successes was the 1978 election of Alderman Marion Kennedy Volini, Marciniak's sister-in-law and a community activist, who was one of the original organizers of Lakewood-Balmoral. From 1978 to 1987, she served as alderman of the 48th Ward and got the city to designate Edgewater a "community area" so that its development and planning would receive special status apart from Uptown. Marciniak provided organizing assistance in addition to strategic and moral support.[44]

Marciniak's was proud that he had never donated funds for party politics, but he did support individual candidates. Prior to supporting Volini, he had supported Sargent Shriver's bid for the presidential nomination in 1976 and served on the National Committee to Elect Shriver, raising funds from his Chicago network. That same year he gladly contributed to Daniel Patrick Moynihan's New York Senate bid, telling his long-time friend that he would give more but had four girls going to school. His greatest enthusiasm was evident in his encouragement and support of Marcy Kaptur's run for the U.S. House in 1982. Marciniak had stayed in touch with her after she left Chicago to serve in the Carter administration and thereafter as a graduate student at Harvard University. Marciniak was one of the first persons to raise funds for her campaign by hosting an event for her in his office at 14 E. Chestnut. Also, among the list of candidates he supported was former city hall attorney, Marvin E. Aspen. When Aspen sought reelection to the Circuit Court of Cook County in 1974, Marciniak served on his committee and assisted in the development of his campaign literature.[45]

POVERTY

Ed Marciniak's understanding of poverty's causes deepened while he was assisting community organizations later in life, but his concerns began much earlier and continued to receive his thoughtful consideration. From the time he was a child at the family grocery store pondering about income disparity and families surviving on his father's store credit, he was conscious of poverty. His concern was further sharpened by the radical messages of *The Catholic Worker* about voluntary poverty and care for the marginalized and his contact with Dorothy Day. These experiences, informed by religious convictions, led him to not just want to understand the causes of poverty but to do something concrete about it as a Catholic Worker, union organizer, and journalist. His actions were buttressed by his graduate studies, voracious reading, contributing to and editing sociology journals, and reflecting on the Gospels and encyclicals as a Catholic layman.

The immensity and persistence of poverty's impact on individuals and society became clearer to Marciniak during his time on the staff of the City of Chicago. While working on the Model Cities' application for the four target areas, for example, Ed met with community leaders and sought first-hand ideas to weaken the grip of poverty in Chicago. Poverty was on display for anyone who would venture out of the confines of their comfort zone to see how others lived, and Marciniak did just that. His long-time assistant at the Institute of Urban Life at the time, Kathryn Hills, explained that when Marciniak was writing about the Chicago Housing Authority he would frequently arrive at the office and say things like: "Let's get in the car and go to Cabrini-Green." Realistically, he chose mornings when all was ordinarily quiet. The two of them would hop out of Ed's modest sedan and talk to people, or he would decide to cruise the area noting: "There are liquor stores all around here but let's see how far people have to walk from this project to get a loaf of bread, medicine, and other essentials." As he drove the near north area, he was ever alert to the ruinous effects of poverty and puzzled over their causes and remedies.

From probing the causes of both poverty and discrimination, Marciniak developed a framework for analysis that was one of his most important career contributions: a comprehensive approach to analyzing poverty and the identification of strategic passageways out of poverty.[46] Marciniak best crystallized his views on poverty in an article titled: "The Case for a Non-Economic Definition of Poverty" published in *Social Thought* in 1985. He had earlier authored papers and given addresses that dealt with poverty. However, this article best conveys his overall perspective on it.[47]

Marciniak first laid out the evolving nature of poverty, noting "in every age, society defines poverty in its own ways." Biblical scholars and social philosophers might see poverty in the hallow and gaunt faces of the starving and others might see it in the blank, vacant eyes of the wealthy who had nothing inside. Social workers, economists, and politicians also had their own points of view.

Marciniak recounted Herbert Hoover's optimistic words to Republican conventioneers in 1928 that America was near the "final triumph" over poverty. Soon the Depression came, and his successor, Franklin Roosevelt, faced the daunting task of caring for the "ill-housed, ill-clothed, and ill-nourished." The architects of the New Deal regarded poverty as income deficiency and set out to address low wages, unemployment, employment uncertainty, and the lack of financial credit through programs that included social security, a minimum wage, unemployment compensation, and farm credit. Marciniak continued his narrative about President Johnson's War on Poverty, sharing Johnson's Secretary of Health, Education and Welfare's words, "I believe that we can eliminate poverty in the Seventies" as well as Ed's friend Sargent Shriver's words to Congress that America should have the "courage and vision to demand that poverty itself be ended."[48]

Johnson's initiatives did not end poverty. By 1982, in fact, the rate of people living in poverty had increased to one in seven Americans. Marciniak believed that it was now time for a reassessment, and for Ed the necessary first step to solving a problem was always to define it precisely. He cited French author George Bernanos: "The worst, the most corrupting of lies are problems poorly stated."[49] Marciniak observed that there were three types of poverty and that each required different treatment. He identified 1) mainstream poverty, 2) case poverty, and 3) social poverty. Only with such an approach that considered all three types of poverty could America hope to develop strategies to end it.

The *mainstream poor* were in the "purgatory of jobless-
ness" due to recession and depression, and these people,
economists believed, would—with or without help—return
to employment or higher wages with the prospect of
upward mobility. The *case poor* were the traditional poor
who suffered mental or physical disabilities that precluded
employment and forced them to rely on begging or assistance from government, family, or charitable agencies. Their
mobility was blocked by their handicaps. Society dealt with
these two groups through New Deal's programs, charitable
institutions, and social service agencies.

America's challenge, according to Marciniak, was the
growth in *social poverty*, a non-economic poverty. This was, he
stated: "a new urban condition, a concentration of dead-end
poverty radically different from anything previously known."
Social poverty is not merely income deficiency. Rather it is
an overwhelming social disorder, with social disorganiza-
tion that entwines with the lives of those in similar straits.
The "new poor" lived in high rise public housing or slums
cut off from "sturdy social institutions, self-help groups, and
community based services" as well as those helpless patients
"evacuated" from state mental health institutions, detoxifica-
tion programs, and rehab centers. Also, among the concentration of the new poor were families abandoned by fathers,
the increasing population of teenage unwed mothers, and
juvenile dropouts who were functionally illiterate and hard
to employ. This new group did not respond to traditional
social services or income strategies; they were snared in a
web of pathologies that made it difficult if not impossible to
break away from the daily experiences of "needless violence,
gang extortion, the quick fix, helplessness, prostitution,

and the rip off." Most of these hard-core poor, Ed feared, would remain victims without new strategies to address the challenges. These hard-core poor, he explained, were "held back because of limited access to private resources.... To lift themselves out of social poverty, the poor require multiple passageways to the private sector."[50]

The past and current anti-poverty approaches were not adequate, Marciniak argued, because they were not community-based. He offered three strategies at the onset: 1) strengthening neighborhood support systems, 2) reducing alienation, and 3) reducing government dependency. As a child growing up, Ed had witnessed the power of strong self-help organizations from churches, fraternal societies, and settlement houses, and local support systems from self-help groups to bridge the gap in a minor emergency or time of crisis. Most of those institutions and societies fled the inner city and those that remained had meager budgets and minimal staffing, leaving poor people bereft of their help.

Marciniak also noted the sturdy PTAs in poor, dense communities made little progress. He felt their situation existed not because there were no leaders but because the principals and teachers in the school system were migratory and never got to know interested parents. "The high turn-over rate and weak institutions," he concluded, "undermine the support that struggling, broken families desperately need to break out of the hellish circle of poverty."[51]

Social poverty isolated its victims from the rest of society in massive housing projects and terrible slums. Here, Marciniak observed, connections to the outside world were absent and role models to stir the imagination of the young and the grapevine for jobs leads were sparse indeed. The neighborhood had been "forsaken by doctors, pharmacists, tailors, bakers, dentists, lawyers." Compounding the alienation was the fact that the teachers, truant officers, counselors, and even the ministers and precinct captains lived outside of the community and were unavailable when a problem arose. [52]

Marciniak's third strategy on social poverty was to lessen dependence on government. He believed that the new poor were being held back because government interventions created a new dependency. For example, a poor person in public housing soon was trapped by dependency on public aid, public medical clinics and a county hospital, state job services, and government-funded job training. Despite government intentions to help the poor, it had a deleterious effect in that it sealed the passageways to the private sector—the chance to live beyond a neighborhood of wall-to-wall poverty absent private networks. He offered counsel and this caution to planners and policy makers:

In assessing the effectiveness of any government funded welfare program, two questions always arise. Does it increase dependency while decreasing poverty? Does it retract or extend the recipients' range of choices beyond government.? Near total reliance upon government has all the earmarks of nineteenth-century dependency on the company-owned town and its company store.[53]

Marciniak concluded his article not with economic or social theory but with moral reflections, noting that a

Christian response to the expanding pool of social poverty had implications for professional and paraprofessionals in social service agencies, public and private schools, and community-based organizations. People were wrong to shrug off their duty to the poor by citing Mathew's Gospel (26:12): "The poor you will always have with you."

Responding to the poor, Marciniak believed, was "certainly a religious imperative, no matter one's faith," for the phrase should be understood as "that the poor you will always be with." That understanding, he concluded, "together with a passion for justice, keeps faith with the Christian social tradition."[54]

PUBLIC HOUSING'S TIRELESS CRITIC

Building bridges out of poverty consumed Marciniak, for he knew full well the dysfunction and crises of those who were confined to severely disadvantaged communities, especially public housing. He had opposed high rise public housing as early as 1950, and more than ever after he left city government, Ed persisted in his criticism of the Chicago Housing Authority's mismanagement and maintenance. He became more vigorous, more relentless, and sharper in his call for radical action, and not just as a critic. Along with others, he proposed new bridges that would open doors for people trapped in these severely disadvantaged communities. Among the steps he urged were a phased but total eradication of public housing high rises, the development of mixed-income public housing throughout the metropolitan area, and the development and management of the low income housing by not-for-profit community development corporations. He supported these proposals with research and direct action. He knew that anyone could build housing, but he believed that building community took even greater skill and commitment.

The history of the Chicago Housing Authority, as D. Brad Hunt recounts in *Blueprint for Disaster: The Unraveling of Chicago Public Housing,* is a tragic tale of good intentions destroyed by willful segregation of poor and Black tenants, the ouster of the working class residents, and malfeasance in administration and maintenance. The creation of high rise public housing, especially for larger families, led to ever increasing social deterioration and dysfunction. In the 1960s, public interest lawyers and social activists challenged the CHA's site location policies that isolated the poor in existing ghettos by acquiescence to aldermanic veto over public housing in their respective wards. Alexander Polikoff, a corporate attorney, joined with the ACLU to sue the CHA and HUD on behalf of tenants on the CHA waiting list in 1966. The fifty year battle that followed the filing of the case, *Gautreaux v The Chicago Housing Authority,* impacted both Chicago's and the nation's housing policy.[55]

In February 1969, the federal Judge Richard B. Austin, who initially presided over the case, found that the CHA violated the Fourteenth Amendment's equal protection clause by intentionally discriminating in both site and tenant selection and found the CHA complicit in the use of the aldermanic veto to "confine public housing to all-Negro or immediately adjacent changing areas." The judge left correcting the past discrimination to further negotiation between Polikoff and the CHA.[56]

Raymond Simon, Chicago's corporation counsel, sought Marciniak's advice on the CHA's strategy to persuade Judge Austin to issue an order with broad guidelines. Simon wanted to measure the CHA's future performance through periodic reviews. Marciniak agreed with the strategy but urged the CHA to press for flexibility in its interpretation of percentages as "new approaches" may be discovered and developed if CHA moved diligently and expeditiously. Further he urged that the CHA bargain with HUD for a commitment of funds to build or acquire 20,000 units to honor a negotiated settlement. Marciniak supported Polikoff's idea to use quotas for the few present CHA projects that were predominantly white, because it offered hope "that the final order will not produce an all-Negro public housing complex throughout Chicago." Again, he urged flexibility on the number of units and project heights but advised: "Small, scattered projects, in large numbers, offer the CHA the best way out of the present dilemma." As he often did when trying to prod action, Marciniak asked Simon a question. "Are DDP and DUR (Department of Development and Planning and Department of Urban Renewal) far enough along with planning and vacant site locations so that CHA will not be delayed in starting construction in volume large enough to meet the shortage of housing for large, low-income families?"[57]

The 1966 Summit Agreement that Marciniak helped the City of Chicago negotiate with Marin Luther King's Southern Christian Leadership Conference (SCLC) created a framework for middle class Black people to buy homes wherever they chose with the city responsible for the enforcement. The Polikoff team sought to secure the same rights for the poor who had no choice but the CHA. This put the CHA under pressure to advance new policies under Judge Austin's watch and Polikoff's persistent advocacy. Part of the Polikoff proposal would include vouchers prospective tenants could use in privately owned buildings as well as in CHA properties.

In 1979, the court ordered the CHA to reverse its concentration of poor families in all-Black high rises by moving them to scattered site housing in racially integrated neighborhoods. This was the very thing that Marciniak had long advocated. Soon he would be given an opportunity to assist in this effort. Judge Marvin Aspen was appointed to the U.S. Court for the Northern District of Illinois in 1979 and was selected to preside over the Gautreaux case in mid-1981.[58] In January 1984, Judge Aspen approved the CHA's plan to acquire seventy-two buildings with more than 400 apartments, half in white areas and half in areas at least thirty percent Black. Significantly, he appointed an advisory committee to be chaired by Edward Marciniak and Nancy Jefferson, a Black West Side community leader who served as Vice Chair.[59] The judge did not give the committee veto power over CHA acquisitions; however, he wanted candid assessment of progress.

In November, the committee gave Aspen its first report with seven recommendations urging the CHA to stop putting units in neighborhoods with large numbers of subsidized housing. The report charged that the CHA put an excessive number of units in Uptown, which already had more than 5,000 units with government subsidies. It recommended that the CHA put units "in communities with little or no public housing." It also recommended that the

CHA only acquire vacant buildings or vacant lots on which to build new units. The committee noted that CHA created hardships for low and moderate income tenants by forcing them to move out of the buildings it acquired, explaining the intent of the Gautreaux decision was not to mandate the eviction of such tenants to make room for other low income households.[60]

The following July of 1985, the advisory committee gave Judge Aspen an update which warned that the CHA's failure to effectively manage its properties, especially the hundreds of boarded-up properties, could "trigger a new round of community confrontations." Again, it pressed the CHA staff to take seriously the rule that fifty percent of the tenants of a scattered housing site come from the local communities. This was especially important to ease community tensions. The committee also repeated its call to end to the "inhumane displacement of families" by the CHA upon acquisition of buildings. This was especially tragic as these buildings lay vacant for years and diminished housing supply for those who needed it. The authors noted that while race remained an issue in some communities, community negativism and hostility was aggravated by CHA practices.[61]

The CHA advisory Committee submitted its final findings after eighteen months of work. One of its goals was to help the CHA improve relations with the communities resistant to the CHA's scattered-site developments; however, it determined:

> By its delays and incompetence, the CHA played into the hands of the opponents of scattered site housing. They can now point to the disastrous experience of

neighborhoods which, having approved of public housing as a neighborhood improvement, soon found themselves fighting unoccupied, slum-like properties owned by a government body. Today several hundred CHA-owned units, neighborhood eyesores, are scattered across the city.

What distressed the committee was that both the CHA and HUD attorneys played a numbers game, acquiring units to satisfy court directives, but then only "displayed passing concern about the quality of the CHA's management of properties purchased." The Committee also noted that despite improved CHA community relations efforts, they fell "far short of what is needed to promote and implement what has become an even more unpopular public housing program than it was in late 1970s." The report concluded that the burden for the mismanagement of the "plagued" scattered-site program was not insurmountable as the concept of scattered site public housing "is a sound and humane program, even more so if the suburbs are included. The program should be continued."[62]

The press continued to put CHA management under the gun and inspired media investigative reports on malfeasance.[63] Marciniak was pleased at the news coverage and sent Judge Aspen news clippings on the CHA scattered site program, adding, "Nancy Jefferson and I have disbanded the advisory committee you appointed. When you have an easy assignment, please don't hesitate to call upon me." Aspen reiterated his deep appreciation of the work of the Advisory Committee and continued, "It was not for naught, since you were able to achieve a public and media awareness of the failures of the CHA rehabilitation program." Aspen demonstrated his appreciation and regard for Marciniak's help and friendship nine years later by inviting him to his installation ceremony as Chief Judge of the United States Court of the Northern District of Illinois.[64]

Marciniak's "crusade" was to humanize the CHA's treatment of residents. As noted previously, Marciniak had advocated for special initiatives for the CHA residents in the Cabrini-Green housing projects. While at IUL, he put together the Chicago Alliance for Collaborative Effort (CACE), a consortium of business, not-for-profit, and government leaders to implement his strategy to provide individualized services at Cabrini Green.[65] In the process, he became increasingly critical of the CHA. In 1986, he completed his third book, *Reclaiming the Inner City: Chicago's Near North Revitalization Confronts Cabrini-Green*,[66] in which he traced the history of the Lower North Side from port of entry for new immigrants to slums and then the creation of the Cabrini Green housing project which became an island for the poor and powerless. Now, rather than private slum lords, the City of Chicago had *become* the slum lord, with twenty-three high rises with nearly 3,000 apartments. Ed realized that the hard-core poverty in the high rises had superseded the "up and out" philosophy that saw public housing as a temporary residence. The projects had become a social hospital without supportive services. The management policy was "one of benign neglect," which invited drug users, muggers, prowlers, purse snatchers, and rapists to run the dark hallways and squat in vacant apartments. Amidst this chaos, Marciniak recorded the comment of a resident who asked: "Which is the greater danger? Being mugged by a streetwise thug or by the system?"[67]

Reversing Decline, outlined steps that the CHA needed to take make the projects livable. But its longer term goal was demolition of the high rises. Marciniak knew high rise public housing was on a collision course with the future of the city and was certain that the high-rise projects must be recycled or torn down as they blocked the billions of dollars of development that would be available near Michigan Avenue's Magnificent Mile to the east, from the resurgent Lincoln Park to the immediate north, and from the ever-expanding Near North Side.

Similarly, the CHA's Abbott, Horner, and Addams projects on the West Side and the Raymond Hilliard and Robert Taylor Homes on the South Side faced similar pressures.[68] Marciniak believed: "The future of Chicago does not depend on the activity along its suburban edges. The urban frontier of the 1990s lies in the inner city.... Here twentieth-century pioneers struggle to reclaim the inner city as they rout the urban pessimist."[69]

The following year, he wrote his friend that "I think we are making some progress in persuading the establishments in City Hall to take a second look." In 1988, Mayor Harold Washington's Advisory Council on the CHA submitted a report that criticized the administration of the CHA and called for razing 8,000 units over ten years. Marciniak was not on the advisory committee; however, when asked to comment on the report he told a reporter that public housing residents should be relocated throughout the metropolitan area and added: "People have blinders when they think we can solve the challenge of providing safe, sanitary, decent housing in the city itself."[70]

Besides his new book, Marciniak wrote numerous opinion columns in the city's dailies and in national journals, trying to keep up the pressure. Certainly, he was not alone; however, he offered solutions with his critiques. He tried to educate government officials, community residents, and business leaders not simply on the flaws of the high-rise projects but on the importance of education, social services, employment training, and more. Success required the end to the isolation of the poor, he insisted. In 1993, he challenged the CHA's proposal to use one billion dollars in federal funding to rehab the CHA's "high-rise hell." He asked, "Why then make a second gigantic mistake by prolonging their presence among us for another generation—or even longer? Is there no other alternative?" His answer was:

> Yes. The CHA can use these scarce HUD dollars instead to stimulate and fund new construction and rehabilitation of low-rise housing for thousands of low-and moderate-income families as it starts to dismantle these conglomerations of ungodly poverty.

Ed had just chaired the City Club of Chicago's study committee that wrote "A New Day for the CHA," a proposal to eliminate vacant high rises one building at a time "while multiplying other and better housing options for CHA families—in the city and suburbs."[71]

In late 1997, Mayor Richard M. Daley announced plans to remake the Lower North Side and by the following June unveiled plans for a billion dollar redevelopment that included the demolition of 1,300 units and construction of low-rise subsidized housing and mixed income housing over the next ten years. "We're setting out to prove that a struggling public housing development can be transformed and made a part of a healthy, mixed-income community," he explained. One thing that was absent was support from the leaders from Cabrini-Green, who were anxious about losing their housing and relationships.[72]

Marciniak was quick to support Mayor Daley in a Chicago *Sun-Times* commentary, "Big Risk, Big Payoff." He noted that the residents of Cabrini would be the major beneficiaries and downplayed the media penchant for highlighting voices of opposition and countered that "thousands of CHA dwellers are ready to leave tomorrow." Already thousands had departed when given the chance in the past decade, he pointed out. Marciniak emphasized the importance for the CHA needed to partner with not-for-profit institutions and that the plan had to increase other federally subsidized housing so as not to "upset a balance of income and purchasing power needed for a mixed-income community to succeed." Further he stressed the need for both HUD and the CHA to "determine the major purpose of government owned housing for lower-income households with children."

Hoping to prod his readers, especially public officials, Ed posed questions to spur awareness and involvement. Was public housing a way station for families temporarily or a permanent situation for a family? Was it housing of last resort? Was it housing to shelter the physically disabled, recovering alcoholics? Was it housing for teenage unwed mothers, the homeless, those difficult to employ? "Any future for public housing rests upon an unequivocal answer to these questions," he emphasized.

The last point was vitally connected to Marciniak's perceptions of community building in seriously disadvantaged communities. Key to protecting the rights and dignity of the poor, he maintained, was the opportunity to help them be part of viable communities. By 1996, the Leadership Council for Metropolitan Open Communities had assisted more than 5,000 families to find housing through the voucher program. Only five percent of the children of voucher families dropped out of school and fifty-four percent went on to college. Furthermore, seventy-five percent of the parents found jobs and were soon gainfully employed. Marciniak had supported scattered site housing throughout all of Chicago because he believed, as he wrote in a *Commonweal* article: "Residential mobility made a difference."[73]

ATRIUM VILLAGE

To end segregated housing required a sustained effort to integrate communities both racially and economically. In *Reversing Urban Decline*, his last book, Marciniak urged communities to form not-for profit community development entities to build both housing *and* community. In his 1988 publication, *Non-Profits with Hard Hats: Building Affordable Housing*, he had provided case studies with valuable lessons. In her preface to that book, U.S. Representative Marcy Kaptur praised Marciniak for providing examples of how housing initiatives became "the turning points in diverting neighborhoods away from precipitous decline." Atrium Village was one of those cases, and Marciniak, had been an important supporter and adviser from its inceptions.[74]

In 1968, a group of leaders from five churches on the Lower North Side formed the Chicago-Orleans Housing Corporation (COHC) dedicated to building a racially integrated, mixed income housing development in the "No-Man's Land" east of Cabrini-Green. They hoped to build a "bridging community" that would connect people of different income levels and races. In his first year at the Institute of Urban Life, Marciniak had helped the group secure seven acres of vacant land from the Department of Urban Renewal. The group carefully selected a seasoned development team and partnered with the general contractor to build a 307-unit development at the corner of Wells and Division Streets. Its architect designed the project around an atrium to provide defensible, secure space as well as a locus for resident communication. When completed in 1978, the $10.7 million project with a 205-unit, mid-rise elevator building and 102 larger garden units, apartments at the Atrium were leased to both low-income voucher holders from the CHA and to market rate renters. Key to its success was a stringent applicant review and a race-and-income-based quota policy. The quota was a financing requirement by both HUD and the Illinois Housing Development Authority.[75]

Ironically, in 1987 this successful development, which had achieved COHC's goals to improve the housing and living environment in an economically and racially integrated area, was threatened by the U.S. Department of Justice's Civil Rights Division for its use of quotas. Marciniak was asked to testify in the case both for his role as an adviser to COCH and his expertise in housing and race relations. In a deposition for the case, *Charlena Edwards v. Atrium Village, et. al.*, Marciniak noted his lengthy list of credentials, including testimony before the U.S. Civil Rights Commission and work for the federal courts. He proceeded to explain that he had given advice to the defendants on the best ways of achieving racial integration and testified, "I believed racial balance was necessary to avoid racial tipping."[76] He recounted that in the first weeks at Atrium Village, the first 600 applicants were from Cabrini-Green. He opined that, if first-come, first-served had been used, Atrium Village would have been unlikely to attract market-rate-income white and Black tenants. If the racial tipping process began, it would have been "exceedingly difficult, if not impossible to reverse it."[77]

Marciniak had seen the impact of public perception in Chicago's neighborhoods. Specifically, he pointed to HUD's failed experiments to affirmatively market the Academy Square development near the West Side medical district. Despite strong housing demand and despite HUD's affirmative marketing, takers were few. He emphasized that if Cabrini-Green remained as it was it would be difficult to attract whites without the use of racial quotas. He focused on Atrium Village's positive impact as a "buffer" between Cabrini-Green and its neighbors and pointed to additional development of a series of market-rate and partially subsidized properties it had spurred along LaSalle Street. Should the Atrium Village complex become segregated either way, he believed, "the continued revitalization of the Chicago-Orleans neighborhood will be significantly impaired."[78]

Marciniak believed in racial and economic integration and sought to foster positive experiences that would birth more positive experiences. He knew that the absence of racial integration resulted from prejudice, market manipulation by government agency policies, and realtor deceitfulness. In the conclusion of his Atrium Village case study, Marciniak observed that "necessity and idealism converged" as COHC sought to "demonstrate to the city how the poor and prosperous could live together in harmony and community." He supported quotas, not because he believed in them *per se* but because he regarded them to be "necessary to effectively bridge between two worlds in close physical proximity, but whose social distance is vast."[79]

The city did revive from the core outward as Ed Marciniak had predicted. However, Chicago's inadequate efforts to eliminate racial segregation and social poverty moved the problems to other communities rather than solved them. Recent racial conflicts in the nation's cities, as well as the careful work of sociologists and housing experts,[80] have renewed awareness of the issues that Marciniak addressed. However, the challenges of removing barriers and impediments to community development remain, even with the continued demolition of ill-conceived housing projects. The opportunities are still, as Marciniak might have said, "tantalizing" for optimistic, resolute, and inventive solutions to rebuilding local communities, the building blocks of livable cities.

NOTES

1   Edward Marciniak citing a local pastor in, *Reclaiming the Inner City*, National Center for Urban Ethnic Affairs, Washington, D.C., 1986) p. 126.

2   Cited in "His Kind of Town," *Loyola Magazine* (Fall, 1981), pp. 6-7.

3   Draft of an address to the Chicago Sunday Evening Club, January 15, 1989. Marciniak Papers, Shelf 8, Position 3.

4   "His Kind of Town" p. 6

5   Marciniak to Ely Aaron, June 19, 1967, and Peter Fitzpatrick to Marciniak, August 9, 1967, Marciniak Papers, Shelf 2, Position 2.

6   Marciniak to Ely Aaron, April 17, 1967, and Marciniak to Earl Neil, October 16, 1967, Marciniak Papers, Shelf 2, Position 2. In a letter to Earl Neal, the mayor's press secretary, Marciniak noted that "social planning" strikes "sour notes in some places." He did mention his present salary was $23,500 and that the commissioner could furnish the new salary figure. Ultimately the title was set as Deputy Commissioner for Community Resources and Services in the Department of Development and Planning. Aaron, who had served on the Commission for twenty years and the past six as Chair, praised the three directors he had worked with as directors "Thomas E. Wright, Francis W. McPeak, and presently Edward Marciniak, as "Brilliant men, all of them—each different in his approach toward problems, but all with unswerving faith in equality." Aaron to Richard J Daley, May 24, 1967, Marciniak Papers, Shelf 2, Position 2.

7   Press Release, City of Chicago Office of the Mayor, October 18, 1967, Marciniak Papers, Shelf 2, Position 2. Marciniak's successor at CCHR was also announced; James Burns was promoted from his deputy director post.

8   Illinois House Resolution HR1043, http://ilga.gov//legislation/fulltext.asp?DocName+09300HR1043.

9   *Chicago Tribune*, "Model Cities Head Outlines Chicago Plan," August 2, 1968.

10 "Chicago's Model City Plan Looks Promising," Ibid., March 9, 1969.

11 Ibid.

12 "Distrust Poses Threat to New Poverty Program," March 16, 1969.

13 Ibid. Warner Saunders became an award winning Chicago television journalist.

14 Thomas Volini to author, July 9, 2020. Marciniak sustained his commitment to children through his service on the Illinois Humane Society for Children (now the Bright Promises Foundation) that was one of the nations' earliest advocates for children and juvenile courts and social services. In 1982, Marciniak was elected president and served on the board for more than two decades. The Society's programs for underprivilege children and legal assistance were for children living in North Lawndale and Cabrini-Green housing were Ed's special concerns. See: Loyola University Press Release, December 30, 1982. Marciniak Papers, Shelf 4, Position 1.

15 D. Bradford Hunt, "Model Cities", Encyclopedia of Chicago. p. 538, and "Model Cities Program," http://encyclopedia.federalism.org/index.php?title=Model_Cities_Program retrieved July 16, 2020.

16 Marciniak to Lewis Hill, November 10, 1970, and Marciniak notes, "What should Be the Form and Function of the Follow-Up Group to Result from the November 4-6, 1970, Leadership Conference?", Shelf 6, Position 1.

17 Victor Weingarten to Marciniak, November 9, 1970; and Charles Davis to Marciniak, Dec 1, 1970. Marciniak Papers, Shelf 6, Position 1. Marciniak reported to Intercom's steering committee that he got the impression from a Sears Foundation contact that the money would not be forthcoming because it "had gotten 'burned' by the Black Strategy Center dissension and was proceeding very cautiously." Marciniak Memo, February 10, 1971, and Charles Davis to Marciniak, February 17, 1971, and Marciniak to Weingarten, Marciniak Papers, Shelf 6, Position 1.

18 Marciniak to Ed, December 13, 1965. Marciniak Papers, Shelf 2, Position 2. This letter appears to have been written to Edward T. Gargan, a friend and respected historian who had been a professor at Loyola prior to going to University of Wisconsin.

19 Christina Marciniak to author, July 30, 2021, and Marciniak to Eleanor Peterson, November 17, 1970, Marciniak Papers, Shelf 2, Position 2.

20 Avella Interview with Cantwell and Marciniak, p. 4.

21 "A Memorandum on the Early History of the Graduate Program in Urban Studies and the Institute of Urban Life: 1960," Marciniak Papers, Shelf 5, Position 1. The report appears to have been written in 1979 and relied upon the Graduate Program in Urban Studies archives.

22 Interviews and correspondence with William Droel, Kathyrn Hills, Mary Schiltz, and Andrew Rodriquez. His box of contacts bulged with 3-by-5" index cards that had the phone numbers, both home and office, of thousands of persons he had met and sustained contact with. It was a reporter's dream. According one associate, Marciniak laughingly claimed to even have the phone number for the pope. However, it is certain that he did have the office number and, most often, the private and home number of senators; congressmen; aldermen; mayors; labor, business, and non-profit leaders; religious leaders; and scholars and journalists. Equally important, he had the phone numbers of their assistants, who would get him to the person he needed to reach.

23 See "Institute of Urban Life: A Report for 1973" and "Russell Barta Interview with Ed Marciniak," (1975) The annual reports of the Institute for Urban Life 1973-1993 are in the Marciniak Papers, Shelf 5, Position 1.

24 "A Report for 1973," p. 10. Twenty-seven "associates" were listed as supplementary staff who volunteered time and talent to inner city institutions receiving assistance from the Institute. Many of these were friends from Marciniak's work in Catholic action and from community development and planning days.

25 Ibid., p. 1-8. Not only was the response technical and financial. He even helped to find and secure tons of steel scraps for a welding class's job training program. Supporting his help to groups was fee-driven research IUL did to ensure inner- city services. For example, IUL analyzed the U.S. Census Bureau data and found it had undercounted Chicago's population by 135,000 thus enabling the city to secure tens of millions of dollars to pay for services in economically depressed areas. Similarly, it aided the city's Department of Public Aid analyze its caseload records and found unremunerated services. Additionally, its research helped community groups in Uptown and Edgewater with data collection on the "saturation" of shelter-care facilities in their neighborhoods. This would lead to active lobbying to change government approvals for such shelters. Further, Marciniak directed a report on the representation of minorities, Poles, Italians, Latinos, and Black people, entitled "Executives Suites of Chicago's Largest Corporations" and the publication of the "Directory of Community Organizations in Chicago." Draft, April 19, 1973, Marciniak Papers, Shelf 6. Position 1. Marciniak's special labor of love was a directory of community not- for-profits which IUL published annually for twenty years to encourage networking among organizations.

26 "A Report for 1973," Marciniak Papers, Shelf 6, Position 1.

27 "Has Chicago a Future?", Shelf 3, Position 3. The address was published as a pamphlet.

28 (Loyola University, 1977) p. 7.

29 Ibid.

30 Marciniak, *Reviving*, p. 33-34. Msgr. Geno Baroni was the featured speaker at a national conference of ethnic groups on Chicago's Northwest side fighting red lining by banks, the F.H.A, and blockbusters. Reporting on the conference, the *New York Times* noted: "Baroni's gospel is that ethnic cohesiveness is a legitimate and powerful force that should be mobilized to preserve neighborhoods. If working-class ethnics have their own turf, Baroni argues they can make common cause with their

Black neighbors. "Ethic Renewal," May 6, 1976. NCUEA was led by Msgr. Geno Baroni who had previously spoken at NCO conference and would soon become an undersecretary for the Department of Housing and Urban Development.

31 "Reviving," pp. 40 and 49. Baroni and the NCUEA forged social legislation and schooled planners who became national leaders: U.S. Senator Barbara Mikulski (MD, D) and U.S. Rep. Marcy Kaptur (OH, D).

32 Ibid., pp. 51-54.

33 Marciniak, *Reviving*, pp 54-58.

34 Ibid., pp. 58-59.

35 Perkins to Marciniak, July 5, 1974; Marciniak to Donald S. Perkins, July 10, 1974; and Marciniak to Richard Dube, December 18, 1974. Marciniak Papers, Shelf 4, Position 2.

36 Marciniak to Rostenkowski, August 6, 1981, and Rostenkowski to Marciniak, August 24, 1981. Marciniak's "Dear Danny" letter was followed by the Congressman's letter which noted: "I share your concern, Ed, and am gratified to be able to report to you that the Congress has adopted your suggestion with respect to tax incentives for charitable giving." Marciniak Papers, Shelf 4, Position 1.

37 In May 1976, Baroni, Marciniak, and other ethnic American leaders attended the White House conference on and ethnic affairs and had a ceremonial meeting with President Gerald Ford in the Rose Garden. Attendee list from the Presidential Daily Log, https://www.fordlibrarymuseum.gov/library/document/0036/pdd760505.pdf , retrieved May 27, 2022.

38 Marciniak to Don Perkins, December 31, 1984, and Susan V. Berrsford, January 21, 1985. Marciniak Papers, Shelf 5, Position 1.

39 Marciniak to Julienne Bolker Minas, March 20, 1978, Marciniak Papers, Shelf 5, Position 1..

40 Marciniak, *Reversing Urban Decline,* (National Center for Urban Ethnic Affairs, Chicago, Illinois, 1981)

41 *Volini Family History*, p. 122.

42 Marciniak used this phrase of his close, lifelong friend Charles P. Livermore, who served as a deputy director of the Chicago Department of Planning and Development. Ibid., p. 73.

43 "Reversing," pp 79-103.

44 Chicago *Tribune*, May 21, 2018.

45 Marciniak Correspondence, Marciniak Papers, Shelf 4, Position 1

46 Interview with Kathryn Hills, July 21, 2020.

47 Marciniak Lecture: "Social Justice in Public Housing in Chicago," 1984; draft of a book review of Michael Harrington, *The New American Poverty*, September 1984 for *Commonweal*; and "Forms of Poverty," text of his address on March 28, 1985, at the Seventieth Anniversary of the Loyola University School of Social Work, found in *Origins*, (April 18, 1985) pp. 726-729, in the Marciniak Papers, Shelf 3, Position 3. His review of Harrington's book was positive, but he pointed out that the author had given scant attention to the new forms that had developed in the past twenty years, including: the "feminization of social misery and the simultaneous violent crimes conspicuously evident in the Black community; the deinstitutionalization of the mentally ill, and the growing underclass made up of long-term welfare recipients, drifters, addicts, and hustlers of the underground economy."

48 Cited in "Non-Economic Definition of Poverty," pp. 50 and 51.

49 In providing the reference for the Bernanos quote, Marciniak cited Daniel Patrick Moynihan's article in the *American Scholar* (August *1969*). This was a quote often used or paraphrased in Moynihan's writings. Marciniak was a friend of Moynihan's and had contacted him for assistance when he was searching for an academic position. Ibid., p. 57.

50 "Non-Economic Definition of Poverty," pp. 52-54. Marciniak sometimes used the term "severely disadvantaged" communities. The term "severely disadvantaged" was used by the Ford Foundation's vice-president for national affairs to describe the underclass who did not respond to the traditional social service and

income strategies.

51 Ibid., p. 55. Marciniak was devoted to Catholic education as path to success. He supported St. Joseph's Catholic School in the shadows o the Cabrini Green, organizing a program for scholarships and a tutoring program to help the young.

52 Ibid., p. 55-56

53 Ibid., p. 56.

54 Ibid., p. 57.

55 (University of Chicago Press, Chicago, Illinois, 2009), pp 239-127, and "53-Year-Old Discrimination Case Settled," *Chicago Tribune*, January 24, 2019.

56 Gautreaux v. Chicago Housing Authority, 296 F. Supp. 907 (N.D. Ill. 1969), https://law.justia.com/cases/federal/district-courts/FSupp/296/907/1982538/

57 Marciniak to Simon, Marciniak Papers, Shelf 3, Position 3.

58 For a timeline on this case and summary of issues see: "Case: Gautreaux v Chicago Housing Authority," Civil Rights Clearing House Clearinghouse https://clearinghouse.net/case/11085/?select_docket=55976.

59 "CHA told to Scatter Sites Better," *Chicago* Tribune, November 20, 1984.

60 Edward Marciniak and Nancy Jefferson "CHA Advisory Committee appointed by Judge Marvin E. Aspen: Final Report.," Section 4. Other recommendations included completion of construction or rehab and code compliance prior to releasing units for occupancy. Further it called for buildings already in the CHA stockpile be rehabbed and completed before work was to begin on additional sites since too many were unusable but would meet the court's acquisition deadline. Finally, it urged CHA cooperation with community groups for recruitment and selection of tenants from the local community. The author is grateful to William Droel, who served as a member of the committee, for this report.

61 *Ibid.*, Section 3.

62 Ibid., Section 2.

63   See: "Investments Rot While CHA Sits "CHA, *Chicago Tribune*, February 18, 1986, and "Target for 1986: No more Shabby Shells," Ibid., February 20, 1986.

64   Marciniak to Aspen, April 3, 1986; Aspen to Marciniak, April 9, 1986, Marciniak Papers, AAC, Position 4, Shelf 2; and Aspen to Marciniak June 21, 1995, Shelf 4, Position 3. Before he retired in 2019, Aspen was able to bring the Gautreaux case to a settlement. "53-year-old discrimination case settled," Chicago *Tribune*, January 24, 2019.

65   Andrew Rodriquez Interview with author, August 3, 2020, and IUL Annual Report, 1973.

66   (Washington. D.C.: National Center for Urban Ethnic Affairs, 1986)

67   Ibid., pp. 66-67,

68   Ibid., pp. 152-158. See also, Marciniak, "How to Undo Housing Mistakes," an op-ed that summarized the challenges and steps forward to claim Cabrini Green. *Chicago, Tribune*, February 20, 1986.

69   Ibid., p.159.

70   Marciniak to Livermore, September 18, (n.d.) Marciniak Papers, AAC, Shelf 4, Position 2. And "Mayor's Panel Urges Razing CHA High-Rises," Chicago *Tribune*, July 5, 1988.

71   "Why Perpetuate Chicago's High-Rise Hell?" *Chicago Tribune*, November 26, 1993.

72   "Daley's Cabrini Dream: Rehab Plan Fails to Win over Residents," *Chicago Tribune*, June 28, 1996.

73   "More Than a Roof: Promising Moves in Public Housing," (June 1, 1996), p. 12.

74   Christine Kuehn Kelly, Donald C. Kelly, Ed Marciniak, (Washington, D.C. 1988), pp. 7-8.

75   *Hard Hats*, pp. 51-62.

76   *Tipping* is a term often applied to racial housing patterns. A *tipping point* refers to the situation at which people will leave a neighborhood because they are uncomfortable with the percentage of persons unlike themselves for economic, social, or racial

reasons. The idea was first used to explain segregation by economist Thomas Schelling.

77 Affidavit of Ed Marciniak in *Charlena Edwards v. Atrium Village, et al*, April 1, 1987, Marciniak Papers, Shelf 5, Position 3.

78 The same position was reiterated in the Atrium attorney's plea to the Edwin Meese, Attorney General of the United States, which asked that the Civil Rights Division drop its planned challenge to the defendant's quota. Michael Shakman, COCH's attorney, noted that it had dropped quotas as the rental was stable; however, it sought the right to reinstate them if it should be necessary to maintain racial balance in the future. See: Shakman to Meese, July 20, 1987 (copy) Marciniak Papers, Shelf 5, Position 3. The Department of Justice ignored this plea, arguing the quota "'no matter how well-intentioned, constitutes discrimination—plain and simple.'" Cited in "Justice Department Sues Atrium Village, Cites Bias to Black people," *Chicago Tribune*, July 24, 1987. Three years later the case was settled with a consent decree, with Atrium Village promising not to fill vacancies based on race without first seeking permission of the DOJ. "Integrated Complex, US Settle", *Chicago Tribune*, February 23, 1990.

79 *Hard Hats*, pp.64-65.

80 See such as Matthew Desmond, *Evicted: Poverty and Profit in the American City*, Crown Publishers (New York, 1916), and William Julius Wilson, *More Than Just Race: Being Black and Poor in the Inner City*, W.W. Norton (New York, 2009).

Chapter 7

Defining the Role
of the Laity

The noblest function of the Christian in the world
is not to protest human wretchedness
but also to alleviate it.

Edward Marciniak[1]

As a young man, Ed Marciniak defined his intentions when he wrote his mentor about his decision to leave Quigley Seminary. He intended to be an "agitator" for Christ's sake through a life of social action as a student feeding the homeless, as a teacher and journalist, as an organizer of movements for economic justice and integration, as a public official wrestling with structures of discrimination, and as an urban planner helping to build communities.

His role as an agitator, however, was equally, pronounced in his relationship with the Catholic Church. He was intensely devoted to his faith. He often proclaimed the scriptures at Mass in his own Saint Ita's Parish, from the same pulpit from which Dorothy Day had inspired him years earlier. Like Day, Ed's religion was essential to all that he did, and like her he sometimes found the institutional Church to be out of sync with what Christians are called to do. This tension would grow through his life. He wrote *Church* with an upper case "C," plainly meaning the formal Catholic Church as differentiated from the church catholic with a lower case "c." For Marciniak the church was all Christians fighting the battles to improve the world in the spirit of the Sermon on the Mount.

⌒

Illustrative of this tension was his experience in his own parish in 1977. Marciniak had received a letter requesting a contribution for the archdiocese's program that connected prosperous parishes with poor parishes in the inner city. The pastor of St. Ita's, Rev. Richard J. Feller, advised the parishioners of the archdiocese's "twinning" program and noted that after consultation with parishioners, the parish would share with St. Vincent de Paul Parish, located four miles south in the Lincoln Park neighborhood.

On Ash Wednesday, Marciniak penned a blunt and fiery letter to Feller to explain why he would not be contributing to St. Ita's twinning program. He noted that Feller's claim to have selected the parish after "consultation" with parishioners was not born out by his own check with at least a dozen active parishioners. He further told the pastor, "None of them was consulted, nor did they know anyone who had been." He labeled the selection a "Feller project," or perhaps the chancery office's choice. He concluded his critique by

saying that it "could be a St. Ita project only by doing violence to the English language and God's holy truth."[2]

The letter writer was not finished. Marciniak was disturbed that Feller had invoked the name of the late Bishop
Michael Dempsey, who had lovingly cultivated the program
in Chicago. Marciniak noted that he and Dempsey were
"good friends and had spent many an hour reflecting on how
parishes might be twinned in a truly Christian way." Dempsey,
he noted, painstakingly labored to ensure the paired parishes
involved included person-to-person and family-to-family
exchanges. He explained to Feller that the program was not
intended primarily to connect a financially stable parish with a
needy one but to build personal bridges between parishioners
of both parishes. The "foremost" purpose of the program, he
wrote, was to join the parishes in sharing concerns and talents
and that money should be a lesser concern. Feller's approach
stamped the program not as a sharing program but "just
another collection." "What a tragedy!" Marciniak exclaimed.

Considering the nature of St. Ita's approach to the
sharing program, Marciniak concluded: "Since we have not
been allowed to share as a parish community at St. Ita's, my
financial 'share' will go to an inner-city parish on Chicago's
west side." Significantly he copied Msgr. Francis Brackin, the
archdiocesan vicar general in charge of administration, who
also resided at St. Ita's, as well as the pastor of St. Vincent
de Paul Parish.[3]

This letter to Fr. Feller was reminiscent in its directness to the
telegram that Marciniak and his fellow Catholic Workers had

sent to Bishop Bernard Sheil over his apparent support for a union-busting newspaper nearly forty years earlier. The 1939 missive "humbly" petitioned for a congruency and an assurance of consistency in the Church's message to the workers.

The Feller letter, however, marked a strained relationship between a parishioner and his pastor and much more. It revealed Marciniak's growing frustration with the manifestations of creeping clericalism that he was witnessing in the American church after the Second Vatican Council that had ended in 1965. He believed the Church, was called to inspire and support the church, the laity, to carry the gospel into the world every day. Marciniak keenly felt a call to refocus Christians on their mission to live the gospel in their daily lives. With his old Smith Corona typewriter, reasoned arguments, direct style, and bevy of like-minded friends, Marciniak sustained the ecclesiastical mission on behalf of the laity he had first undertaken as a collegian.

CLERGY AND LAITY

Chicago was the center of lay activism and social reform in the 1930s through the 1950s, with a cadre of Catholic clergy that encouraged and supported lay people to exercise their initiative in the world. Seeing and meeting a need had been Marciniak's *modus operandi*, in establishing St. Joseph's House of Hospitality, the Catholic Labor Alliance and co-founding numerous other and entities supporting justice and reform such as the Catholic Interracial Council, and National Catholic Social Action Conference.

Reflecting on Dorothy Day's influence, Ed explained that she never shuffled to the rectory or chancery office to seek approbation for some project but rather "she had asked us to find our true Christian identity by identifying with the suffering, the abandoned, the alienated and the young of heart—whatever their age." Day appealed to the individual's personal responsibility, Marciniak recalled: "She reminded us that the initiative was ours, as was the yoke of responsibility. We too were the Church. And to wait and do nothing was to be nothing."[4] He would not wait.

Marciniak believed the church's social teaching was to answer the question "How would Christ act," whether Christ were banker, baker, or a bartender. It was to provide the meaning of the Gospel in every person's working life, neighborhood, family, and government. In a widely circulated pamphlet published in 1959 by four Catholic social action organizations titled "Catholic Doctrine and the Layman," Marciniak laid out his understanding of a lay person's Christian duty. He contended that the Ten Commandments were not to be used as a mere yardstick to escape mortal sin. The essence of Catholic social doctrine, he maintained, was found in the Sermon on the Mount and in encyclicals such as *On the Condition of Labor, Reconstructing the Social Order*, and *The Mystical Body of Christ*.

Catholic social principles were not limited to the field of labor and economics but included family life, the conditions of migratory labor, hiring Black people for white-collar jobs, the impact of advertising on family values, and much more. The lay person should be "intoxicated" by social doctrine and find in it not only a vision of a just social order but a cause in their everyday work and family situations.[5]

The pamphlet provoked serious thought on the wider implications of Catholic social doctrine. Marciniak posed a series of questions that few others were asking. How can lawmakers defend private property while devising equitable tax systems to make it possible for the propertyless to own productive goods? What is the duty of stewardship in age of abundance? What is the importance of free trade? What is the impact of advertising, installment buying, and the "the march of monopoly upon the media of mass communication?" Marciniak believed that the answers to these questions were found, not in simple moralizing about the evils of money, but through painstaking professional competence. It was, he wrote, through their daily work that lay people served and praised God, very much as the architects who designed the great cathedrals glorified God through *their* skilled labor. Catholic social doctrine provided the tools a person needed to formulate ideas necessary to meet the moral challenges implicit in policy questions and in concrete economic and social situations. He understood that the core of social doctrine concerned social justice, with the goal of organizing "human talents and society's resources so that ungodly social practices will be replaced by a framework of justice." Marciniak emphasized: "Without the virtue of social justice, the layman is left with a mere handbook of 'dos and don'ts' about social policy, with no sense of how intelligent, God-loving (men and women) actually go about 'reconstructing the social order.'"

In his work with both the labor schools and his classes at Loyola University, Marciniak repeatedly emphasized that the principles in papal encyclicals were to be implemented by the laity in their own occupations, trades, or professions. It was not the duty of the priest to tell lay people how to implement the doctrines. It was laypeople whose mission it was to devote themselves to the task of "developing habits, policies, and laws and institutions that reflect[ed] the Christian spirit." For Marciniak, social doctrine was a starting place, a vantage point from which a layperson was to regard his or her vocation; and it was up to each layperson, not a pope or priest, to apply the general principles of those teachings.[6]

Marciniak had been influenced in his understanding of Catholic social action by Revs. Martin Carrabine, SJ and Daniel Lyons, SJ, who mentored him in college; the words and writings of Dorothy Day and other Catholic Workers; Catholic novelists such as Graham Greene; and the philosophy of Jacques Maritain, the influential French Thomist philosopher. Marciniak considered Maritain's book *Scholasticism and Politics* a crucial text for all Catholics, and it fundamentally shaped his conception of the role of the Catholic lay person. Maritain's influence is clear throughout Marciniak's thoughts and writings.

Based on a series of lectures Maritain delivered at the University of Chicago in 1940, *Scholasticism and Politics* developed a foundational "moral and political" philosophy to undergird the principles of democracy and a Christian civilization. Contrary to other leading social theories of the time, Maritain argued that neither Marxism, fascism, nor simple humanism were adequate to improve the world, and instead he proposed "love and holiness," as essential to a "supra rational" Christian humanism to transform the human condition.[7] Maritain's final chapter, "Catholic Action and Political Action," stressed that temporal actions under spiritual inspiration expand the kingdom of God.

Catholic action, Maritain insisted, happens when a person applies ethics to social, economic, and political life.

Specifically, the philosopher distinguished between the work of the lay person in the world and the Catholic Church as institution, with its clergy and lay employees. He argued that the duty of individual Christians-in-the-world was to influence politics and social systems in their own spheres of life. Direct interventions of the institutional Church leaders should be a thing of the past. When the individual Christian (or organization) engaged in a social or political action inspired by spiritual motives, he taught, *that* was Catholic action.[8] This distinction was central to Marciniak's conception of a lay Christian's vocation.

As he saw more priests and religious speaking for the Church in public forums, Marciniak emphasized this distinction. For Marciniak and his like-minded friends, the struggle over the use of a word was something important. Once young adults equate religion with the Church's employees, they lose interest. Without avenues for their participation, few youths invest much in a staff-driven organization. Marciniak was prophetic in fighting for the prophetic role of workaday laity out in the world. Those who didn't grasp his point, Ed felt, unwittingly gave ground to the passive culture of pay, pray, and obey.

In 1966, Marciniak's journal *New City*, featured two perspectives on the role of clergy and religious in social action, one by Msgr. John Egan, Director of the Archdiocese Office of Urban Affairs, and one by Marciniak. Egan guardedly approved of ecclesiastical institutions becoming directly involved in social action and argued that the Church must at times directly use its economic and social "power" to advance social justice. Marciniak, on the other hand, questioned this ecclesial approach to social justice and supported church (small c) involvement based on the idea of the lay Christians stewardship of secular power.

According to Egan, the Catholic Church had a self-interest in neighborhood stability and had a right to support community institutions in accord with its mission. He carefully distinguished between political and moral questions and noted that policies that "work public damage to public morality" or "redress a serious moral grievance" were acceptable grounds for the institutional Church's engagement in social action through its clergy and resources. In fact, the Chicago Archdiocese had financially supported initiatives by the noted community organizer Saul Alinsky and other activist groups. Egan argued that perhaps clergy should not lead people to a city hall protest but accompany them to city hall rather than stay at home.[9]

Marciniak disagreed with Egan on the priests' role in the Christian community. He considered the role of a congressman a fitting analogy. A member of Congress was elevated to serve their fellow citizens yet remained a citizen with obligations to obey the law, pay taxes and the like. His vocation of legislator was to make laws for all citizens, the legislator included. Marciniak regarded the priest as a man whose vocation was to serve God and his world and who would be judged by how well he used his priestly vocation. He continued:

> While the priest shares his vocation as a Christian with all the People of God, his special calling is to serve as the ordained minister in the Christian community. Since it is the layman who is primarily and directly responsible for serving the temporal community, the

vocation of priests is to help the layman carry out his Christian vocation.[10]

But how should the priest conduct his mission as a Christian without undercutting the layman's responsibilities? Pointedly, Marciniak stated: "As long as a priest sits in the driver seat of a community organization, for example, with the laymen in the backseat, his problem has not been solved." And he acerbically added, "The thrill of being behind the wheel is a temptation to be resisted not encouraged."[11] The priest's first place of responsibility was at the altar celebrating Mass and nourishing the people of God with the Gospel message to go into the world sharing the responsibility to shape government, corporations, community organizations, political parties, labor unions as well as family life. He cautioned that priests needed to re-examine their relationship to the world for "there is a danger by unthinkingly copying the layman's vocation [a priest] will usurp [the laity's] special responsibility for the temporal order." This would create a new modern clericalism, assigning priests a competency in secular affairs for which they displayed little talent. Marciniak's concern resulted from his encounters with both ministers and priests who had become increasingly aware of moral issues in the social order but often lacked an awareness of their own deficiencies in dealing with secular problems.[12]

Ideally, the priest was to be inspirational, not directive. The greatest challenge for the church, Marciniak believed, was not the "meandering of the minority, but the mass unconcern of the majority, priests and laymen alike." The community of Christians must be both invited and urged into service by the clergy, not led or forced by them. This jogging of the layman's awareness by the clergy demanded that they be men of Scripture who announced the good news of the Gospel every day of their lives. In short, Marciniak expected the clergy to be a "hairshirt" to make laymen uncomfortable in their smugness and remind them that God's abundant gifts were to be shared with others. Much as a cadre of informed priests who identified moral issues in the 1930's and 1940's and urged the laity to take direct action in labor and race relations, the priests of 1966 should help set an agenda for tomorrow's issues.[13] This article formed the genesis of a more comprehensive approach to the role of the laity in both church and society. Marciniak's deepening convictions about the laity's role took on even greater significance as the Second Vatican Council unfolded.

TOMORROW'S CHRISTIAN

Pope John XXIII had convened Vatican Council II in 1962 to bring new consideration to the Christian's place in the world. Marciniak was encouraged by the Council's statements as deliberated by more than 3,000 bishops, religious, and theologians from around the world. Among the Council's changes were a new direction in ecumenism; liturgical reform (most notably the use of the vernacular in liturgy rather than Latin); support for human rights, democracy, and freedom of religion; and a clear statement on the sinfulness of anti-Semitism.

Most of these reforms were consistent with Marciniak's own strong beliefs and support for democratic institutions and human rights, commitment to the centrality of liturgy, and ecumenical partnering with Protestants and Jews. These Vatican documents offered hopeful signs of change, especially *The Dogmatic Constitution on the Church* (*Lumen Gentium*) which declared that the laity is "the church in the world," and *The Church in the Modern World* (*Gaudium et Spes*) which declared that it is not "the church against the world [rather] the world together with the church."[14] Also, the intellectual leadership of Chicago's Cardinal Albert Meyer at the Vatican Council buttressed Marciniak's confidence in the renewal of Catholicism.

However, Marciniak saw clear danger signals in some popular interpretations after the Second Vatican Council. Particularly troubling was that the Catholic Church with a capital "C" brought into its bureaucracy many of the initiatives that had previously been developed by *lay* people as part of their mission as Christians in the world. *New City* regularly addressed these concerns. As editor, Marciniak occasionally submitted articles under his own name, but anonymously as well because of his high-profile position with the city government. After he left the director position at the Chicago Commission on Human Relations in 1967, however, he immediately turned to more extensive writing.

Marciniak's first book, *Tomorrow's Christian*, outlined his fundamental distinction between the laity and the role of the priest in much greater detail than his previous pieces on the subject. Although written in the third person, *Tomorrow's Christians* was highly personal. Marciniak's introduction noted that his chief concern "lies at the rubbing edge of contact between church and world, that no-man's-land of theology which religious scholars often tiptoe but seldom plow. There lies the territory of the ordinary Christian, the (laity)." The secular Christian, citizen of the church and the world," he continued, "becomes the (person) in the middle, the double agent who works for both and serves both integrating them in (his or her) life and person." Ed noted that theologians had long concocted theories regarding the institutional church and state, but most often they bypassed the secular Christian. Marciniak's stated intention was to outline strategies that would best strengthen the vocation of the "double agent.[15]

Throughout his book, Marciniak emphasized the term "secular Christian" as a better substitute for the term "(laypeople)." Similarly, he believed the term *church* had been clouded by fuzzy thinking and practice by priests and bishops. Increasingly, ordained clergy were implying that they were speaking on behalf of the whole Church when in fact they were expressing their own opinions. In truth, they were speaking *to* Christians rather than *for* them and usually were doing so without the benefit of consultation with the laity.

Marciniak did not want to laicize priests or clericalize laymen. Instead, priests would benefit from a better theology of Church and secular Christians needed "a more sensitive social conscience."[16] Not surprisingly he noted that the title *Tomorrow's Christian* was the publisher's choice rather than the one he believed more appropriate; his preferred title was: "*Some Secular Notes for an Introduction to a Theology of the Church.*" The author's hope was that his efforts would help the community of Christians prepare the next generation of believers to respond to their calling as "double agents"[17]

To make his case, Marciniak began with a caricature of the Church and laid out stereotypes of the institution that held people back from their real vocation. He argued that the lessons Catholics learned from parochial schools, the pulpit, and lived experience had negatively shaped the responses of adult Christians. For example, lay saints were presented as role models, but mostly for their work on behalf of the Church, "not for their work on behalf of the world." This caused laypeople to focus on the parish building and its functionaries rather than its role as a communal center to serve people. The bad habits of inner-directed piety, Ed contended, restricted Christians in their freedom to serve a new generation in a changed world where their grandchildren might be commuting to the moon.[18]

Marciniak laid out a map of where changes provided fertile ground for developing a genuine vocation for Christians in the world. Among the avenues for action were Christians' roles as employers, elected officials, union members, teachers, and voters—each of whom should choose the general principles for their own situation on the wisest and most just course of action. Marciniak believed that a priest or bishop could never know all of the rubbing points between the sacred and secular, and it was the lay individual who was called to apply the "relevant principles of the Christian's personal response to the Gospel in each situation."[19] Most troubling was "the presumptive role of Church officials who spoke for their members on temporal matters and directed their engagement with the world in person from backstage, undermining the unique authority of the secular Christian by implying moral superiority where none exists."[20]

Marciniak doubled down on his advice to the clergy to be more pastoral and educational rather than "dogmatic and censorious." He sought to clarify that a bishop's authority was of the Gospel. Bishops were to stand with the Christian community, "not above or outside it." One function of authority was "to provide a center for encounter" where the bishop and people of God listen and learn from each other.[21]

The separation of Church and state was an essential element of Marciniak's frame of reference, and he appreciated the theology of John Courtney Murray SJ, who had laid the groundwork for revisions in the Church's position on religious freedom. This enunciation of the separation of church and state helped shaped the presidential election of John F. Kennedy. In September 1960, the candidate muted the opposition of some Protestants when he explained his concept of the separation of church and state to a gathering of Baptist ministers in Texas. Kennedy declared his allegiance to the country, not the pope, in civil and political matters. The entire speech was included in the appendix of *Tomorrow's Christians*. Equally significant, Marciniak included the "Text Statement by Catholic Laymen on Separation of Church and State" which was signed by 166 leaders from throughout the nation and had been published in the *New York Times* on October 6, 1960. Marciniak had been one of the signatories, but he did not mention this in his book.[22]

Marciniak's critique of clergy using the Church's power to solve community problems became more pronounced and his examples sharper. When he was director of the human relations commission, Ed regularly collaborated with clergy and religious leaders, and he witnessed some of them had grown impatient with their congregations and dissatisfied with their internal or congregational role. "Inexperienced in secular seas," Marciniak observed, "many [clergy and religious] have dived into shallow waters or swam too far from shore and had to be rescued." He believed that the charge of the minister was to open the eyes and ears, to become the social conscience of believing Christians. When a priest marched in a picket line to protest discrimination, Marciniak contended, he was unintentionally publicizing "his failure to develop laypeople who hate racial discrimination as much as he does."[23]

Central to his thesis, which he called the "eye of the storm," was the need to distinguish between "insider" and "outsider." Moral theologians, he opined, failed to incorporate the genuine experience of secular Christians in their considerations. Marciniak contended that the priest had the tools of preaching, writing, and counselling to set a general path. However, rarely did the cleric have the insider's perspective to identify the best path to a solution. Clearly reflecting on his own experience, he said a protest alone "seldom on its own produces a solution." In fact, the daily jeremiads unaccompanied by a positive remedy had brought some urban ghettos almost to the point of explosion. The critical task of the savvy lay person, whom Marciniak called "the insider," was to address the question of how to solve such problems by marshaling talents, funds, and programs. The "insider-Christian" was a person of action who was responsible for solutions by shaping policy, custom, and law. Marciniak consistently argued that a theology of the lay person was needed to protect the secular Christian from "indigestible prescriptions and quack remedies apt to be found in the clerical pharmacy."[24]

Elaborating on his point, Marciniak explained that while the priest might emphasize wickedness in the finite world, the layman-insider better understood the finite in the wickedness. The real world of work had some situations wherein evil was clear; however, most of the world's issues required compromise between conscientious people who always lived with ambiguity and halfway solutions, selecting the lesser of two evils until a better choice was available. Once again, he returned to the phrase that he had used earlier in a letter to Alderman Despres, "there is no hydrogen bomb" on social policy.

Effecting change most often required the insider to locate the point of least resistance to change, the crack in the wall of opposition, and push through it with calculated steps to lessen the human misery and viciousness of racism.[25] In this situation, the amateur moralists—among whom Marciniak counted many clergy—took the craft out of politics, failing to realize personal virtue was only one element of leadership. "The noblest function of the Christian in the world," he wrote, "is not to protest human wretchedness but also to alleviate it." This phrasing echoed the words of Marciniak's friend Senator Eugene McCarthy that the role of a Christian politician was "not to judge society but save it."[26]

Marciniak hoped that the Catholic Church in the United States would be "the salt of the earth" deploying at that time its 60,000 priests, 165,000 religious sisters and brothers. along with thousands of laypeople now in its employ to new ministries of service to humanize the world. To do so the Church would have to be less defensive and open enough to listen, accept feedback, and demand accountability of all its personnel. In doing so, it would have to give elbow room for experimentation and special projects that reveal the ways in which the Creator was present among people. He counselled an embrace of diversity: "reformer and radical, conservative and traditionalist, and unconventional Christians—all whom have rights to full membership in the congregation of Christians."[27]

A closed community, Marciniak believed, ceased to be Catholic. To remove all doubt of his position, he provided practical examples. Several years earlier Marciniak had recommended to Archbishop Meyer an archdiocesan strategy to attract Black people to the priesthood with the understanding that these priests would be assigned to parishes throughout the diocese, not just to parishes with a predominance of Black congregants. In *Tomorrow's Christian*, he added detail suggesting the American Church allocate people and resources to recruit seminarians who represented minorities including Blacks, Mexican Americans, Puerto Ricans, and Asians. Fewer sermons on racial justice would be necessary, he contended, when priests were distributed randomly throughout the parishes without regard to race. His intention was to see that secular Christians would develop an "allergy" to racism and commit "to a life hunt to make Jim Crow as extinct as a dodo bird."[28]

In his concluding chapter Marciniak reflected on the mission of the Catholic Church in the new millennium. It would be essential for the Church to encourage secular Christians to reexamine ideas of the Church so they would "run with the world, not against it or from it." He believed that Catholics needed to be less doctrinaire, less organization-minded, and freer to realize their Christian mission to build bridges between disparate communities: "small villages and metropolis, urban and rural, Phi Betta Kappa and high school dropout, Black and white, comfortable rich and uncomfortable poor." He emphasized that protecting the rights of one group did not exclude protesting the wrongs done to another group.[29]

This litany of the elements of Ed's call to action was not just pious phraseology. While he never referred to his thirty years as a bridge builder, peacemaker, feeder of the hungry, and provider of shelter and hope, Marciniak's genuine conviction, urgency, and passion were palpable. He wanted his readers to be liberated from the stereotypes of waiting for clerical directions and be empowered by the gospel message to join in renewing God's handiwork. He "wanted the secular Christian to see the world not just with the problems to be confronted but the source of wonder and mystery." His final words were to the countless Christians who waited for cues that never came or blamed stodgy pastors, cautious prelates, or pastors and ministers chafing under restrictive collars: "A man of personal responsibility recites his personal act of contrition, shoulders his share of the burden, and then takes the initiative."[30]

Tomorrow's Christian achieved Marciniak's intention to provoke discussion.[31] Most of his reviewers began with a tribute to the author's years of leadership in Catholic social action efforts and were sympathetic to his lament about clericalism and impatience with priests who often tripped over their cassocks to participate in the public forum. However, many took issue with Marciniak's theologizing about the sacred and secular and charged him with a lack of clarity in distinguishing the role of the clergy from that of a secular Christian. Few reviewers disagreed with his intent to emphasize the priest's primary role to gather people around the altar and inspire them with the Gospel message. However, several reviewers, most often priests, faulted him for trying to silence the legitimate right of the cleric to speak personally on public issues.[32]

Among the defenders of priests' activism was Marciniak's friend John McDermott, who had previously served as Executive Director of the Catholic Interracial Council of Chicago. He pointed out that a "picketing priest" has congregants who are powerless. And added they do not need spiritual formation "as much as they need defense against the bloodsuckers of an oppressive social system." In McDermott's view, Marciniak's perspective reflected Ed's personal point of view and exhibited "a distressing middle-class blindness."[33]

Marciniak also came in for criticism as a political insider. Priests would not have to become prophets if people in city government, people like Marciniak, were to act on failures of justice quickly and effectively. Ed's severest critic was Msgr. Charles O. Rice of Pittsburgh, a labor activist and columnist for the *Pittsburgh Catholic*, who attacked Marciniak as a "tired old New Dealer." Marciniak had crossed swords with Rice over his extreme anti-communist position decades before, and now Rice struck back. The priest's column claimed that Marciniak had abandoned his social activist heritage to praise "experts" and to rise in Mayor Daley's bureaucratic "hierarchy" by opposing Dr. Martin Luther King's anti-racism demonstrations. Rice contended Marciniak had become a captive in his efforts to convert the wielders of power and "lost his freedom to confront social evils," giving Daley the chance to "bring about total segregation in public housing in Chicago without an outcry from the likes of Ed."[34]

The attack unsettled Marciniak and prompted him to draft a private response to Rice that was uncharacteristically brief: "For shame: you roast me on your Irish spit...and don't even mention the title of my book, *Tomorrow's Christian*. I hope you read it to find out for yourself whether or not I did say the things you attribute to me." Characteristically, Ed concluded with best wishes and signed off "Fraternally in Christ." Significantly, written in Marciniak's hand at the top of this sharp letter was: "Not Sent!" He must have realized there was no need to further irritate the contentious priest.[35] It is noteworthy that negative reviews were sometimes followed by positive opinion pieces by Marciniak friends including Bruce Rattenbury, board member of *New City*, and Emery J. Biro, a member of the Catholic Interracial Council.[36]

Lawrence J. Suffredin, Marciniak's friend and member of the Executive Board of the National Catholic Social Action Conference, responded to Rice's harsh column. Writing directly to Rice, Suffredin explained that he also had reviewed the book and, in reading the comments of other reviewers, noted that many had not taken it at face value. He explained: "Most either project their own prejudices into the book; or reflect on the author's life and search for the real reason he wrote." Suffredin told the Pittsburgh priest that he misunderstood Marciniak's genuine appreciation of religious who acted fearlessly for no gain and reiterated that Marciniak had seen activism often detour priests from their primary goal of inspiring lay people to participate in social action. He emphasized: "Ed, I am sure, would not question the right of citizens (religious or secular) to express a well-thought-out opinion on any social matter."

Suffredin labelled as "unfair" Rice's blanket statement about the work Marciniak had done for Mayor Daley in changing the attitudes of Chicagoans toward many social issues,"because you are unhappy with the speed in which he has been able to bring about lasting social justice."

"Anyone who has worked with Ed," Suffredin continued,"knows he is not a captive of Richard J. Daley or anyone else." Suffredin's patience had worn thin, and he admonished the priest: "Men like Ed Marciniak have had an impact on the social and political climate in Chicago—a much greater impact than your friend, Bishop [Bernard] Sheil, or any other cleric or religious has had…. It is very unfair of you to simplify Ed's book to "who's using whom?"[37]

Nearly twenty years later Marciniak told an interviewer that his book"turned out to be a dud as a seller."[38] However, the lack of sales never deterred him from sharing his perspective that the layperson's role was to complete God's creative work in the world and that the institutional Church's clergy and staff should be civil-servant-like aids who support the laity. As more dioceses"coopted" lay initiatives and made Catholic action an extension of the chancery office or rectory. Ed spoke often and firmly against what he saw as a new Catholic clericalism. In doing so he would foment discussion and ignite disagreement both among liberals and traditionalists.

POST-VATICAN II CATHOLIC ACTION

For American Catholics, the 1960s had been a time of profound change and uncertainty. Their identity as Americans was no longer in question since the election of one of their own to the presidency. Their social position had changed

thanks to a vibrant economy that supported upward mobility, greater education, and suburbanization for the children
and grandchildren of the immigrants. Many had developed
the confidence to question authority, even the directives of
their pastors and bishops. Also, some traditionalists were
distressed to see that their church had changed with priests
and nuns speaking out and marching for peace and civil
rights and English replacing Latin at Mass and in hymns.
For others, the changes had come too slowly on matters of
married priests, on developing substantive roles for women,
and on the topic of birth control. Whether the changes
were prompted by the Vatican II Council in Rome or by
the rigidity of bishops or sociological trends and political
events at home, Catholic religious practice declined. Traditional markers of such as attendance at Sunday services and
Catholics only marrying other Catholics declined, especially
among younger and more liberal Catholics.

By February 1970, the Catholic social action movement,
which had started five decades earlier with the Bishop's *Program of Reconstruction*, the far-sighted program directed by
Rev. John Ryan, had petered out. What should have been
the year to celebrate its golden anniversary was, Marciniak
noted, more of a wake, with the friends of Catholic social
action "torn between lighting the birthday cake or calling the
undertaker." At the end of the year, he addressed the situation in an article entitled "Catholic Social Action: Where
Do We Go from Here?" for the influential Jesuit magazine,
America.[39] The signs were clear as many social action organizations had "committed suicide" or merged with other
entities because of dwindling membership rolls. They
failed to attract young and enthusiastic members and left

the silver-haired remnants to turn out the lights. Marciniak made a case for change. Also, he hoped to elicit discussion.

Marciniak laid out the phases of the movement and the influences that had shaped the paradoxical successes of Catholic social action. In the first phase the movement had been based upon encyclicals and activists who laid the groundwork, and in the next phase it grew in the hands of priests and laypeople who had a knack of inviting men and women into their organizations. They operated outside of the strictly institutional structures and gave progressive bishops cover when things went badly yet freedom to take credit when things went well. The third phase, which Ed called "transitional," had begun in the 1960s with a new breed who made their mark taking on a broad array of social challenges such as poverty, peace, civil rights, religious liberty, political and religious reforms, and international development.[40] These movements, he contended, paved the way for the Vatican Council by creating an openness, ensuring local acceptance of reforms, and stirring bishops and vowed religious to give priority to social justice and freedom.[41]

An unintended consequence of the new activism, Marciniak believed, was that this changeover "dealt older social action a nearly fatal blow." The social action programs formerly lodged outside diocesan institutions were brought in-house, and they took with them many activists who became part of the Church apparatus. As he had in his book, he emphasized that the institutional style of the third phase was "out of tempo with the times and the best current pastoral theology." It gave scant room for ordinary Christians to direct their confrontation with the world's joys and sorrows. As he explained:

Ours is an age that demands "maximum feasible participation." How can a heavily institutionalized approach to social justice offer anything more than minimum opportunity to a handful who make up the staff and board of directors? The social involvement of a chancery office or a provincial may demonstrate personal courage and initiative. These virtues, however, do not satisfy the urgent need for involving the entire Christian community and the hunger for co-responsibility within the Church.[42]

What Marciniak found missing was a "common thrust" that exploited the "the total resources, personal and institutional of the Catholic Church in the United States," one that drew on the revitalized theology of Vatican II and could steer the attention of the whole church to national problems. Where there should have been excitement and dedication to causes, he saw a "pernicious anemia" afflicting Catholic social action. In his typical fashion, he asked questions to prod his readers: Where is a movement that is "both national and local, wholeheartedly ecumenical, and roomy enough not only for conservatives and liberals but especially for those radicals and innovating elites who have begun fashioning a style for tomorrow's Christian?" The roominess was especially important for the religious coalitions that would make youth feel welcomed rather than "elbowed out and denied a share of the action."[43]

The malaise at the grass roots level demanded strategies that could mobilize people and initiate a fourth phase. Marciniak laid out guidelines like the ones he had presented in his recent book. The first step required collegiality, a genuine co-responsibility in social action. Such co-responsibility celebrated the common consciousness of Christians, not one social action tactic, however effective it might be. Second, it needed a leadership that was less judgmental and reliant on hierarchical structures; one committed to creating a sense of urgency that "tantalizes the imagination and offers them [Christians] hope for the future." Also, he called for integration of action and reflection, a broad ecumenical approach, and a follow-up system to ensure accountability for actions.[44]

At the time, Marciniak submitted the article to *America*, he urged the editor to secure responders to sustain the discussion. Thus, Marciniak's article was accompanied by four responses from the field.[45] In sum, they each agreed with Marciniak's accounting of the evolution of Catholic social action and shared his belief that the role of the Church was to inspire and motivate, but they diverged on how to achieve the near utopian vision they ascribed to him. While Marciniak envisioned a movement that bridged the gap between "we" as the church and "them" as a Church institutional entity, one observer noted that he lapsed into a dualism typical of the very hierarchy he criticized.[46]

David J. O'Brien, a historian of American Catholic social reform, questioned Marciniak's reliance on "collegiality" to advance the agenda of Catholic social action. He noted that Marciniak's presumption that the Church could act effectively might have been overly optimistic, writing: "Surely a collegial approach ensures moderate action as a result, since differing views are blended and compromised into a reformist solution." In fact, O'Brien believed that Marciniak needed to take more seriously the national crisis that was reflected in the dissatisfaction with the state of Catholic social action. Acknowledging the benefit of the discussion Marciniak had begun, O'Brien called for a serious new way for American Christians to creatively confront the "evils of war, racism, militarism, and oppression which concern us all."[47]

Marciniak's reflections proved timely, as Pope Paul VI would soon issue *Octagesima Adveniens* ("A Call to Action"). This was an apostolic letter calling on all Christians to take up their work of renewing the temporal order. It encouraged a plurality of options as unique situations required. This included "innovating to make structures evolve, so as to adapt to the real needs of today."[48] In anticipation of the American bicentennial, the American Bishops sponsored a national series of hearings on social problems to be addressed, and to that end convened the Call to Action Conference in Detroit in 1976. At the Conference's conclusion, the diverse group of more than 1,300 delegates endorsed resolutions to advise the Church to "reevaluate" its positions on clerical celibacy, male-only clergy, homosexuality, birth control, and lay involvement in important decision making. The bishops promised to take the recommendations seriously but appeared to bury them, fearing that the ideas were too extreme for many Catholics.[49] In fact there were conservatives who saw the Call to Action recommendations as a form of apostasy, while some liberals believed that the American church was being held back from its social mission by both its own bureaucracy and numerous conservative bishops in the grasp of the Roman curia.

A CHICAGO DECLARATION OF CHRISTIAN CONCERN

Ed Marciniak was much less than enthusiastic about the Call to Action Conference, as it accentuated the focus by the delegates on Church-sponsored "social action" by pressing the agenda of liberal clergy and Church professionals. He regarded the conference as "navel gazing" and preoccupied with the workings of the institution when it should have been driven by the call to serve the physically and spiritually poor. Previously, he had signed declarations designed to advance such positions and energize the public on social issues. Now, he saw the value of a similar undertaking.[50]

With like-minded and trusted friends Russ Barta and Rev. Daniel Cantwell, Marciniak discussed developing a response to the malaise affecting the Christian community through a strategy of publishing a document that would refocus the discussions away from "churchy" issues. They drafted *A Chicago Declaration of Christian Concern* and gathered signatories, both lay persons and priests and religious who were respected in the Chicago Catholic community. Not only would they publish the document, but they would also circulate it as broadly as possible to promote a social action agenda that focused on the work and life of the laity.[51] On "*The Third Sunday of the Coming of the Lord, 1977*" (December 18), the thirty-seven signatories released their declaration.[52]

Marciniak later made clear the signers were not interested in "a skirmish with authority or in any hit-and-run manifestos. They had larger issues in mind, compelling ideas they hoped would catch the imagination's eye and would project a vision of Christianity they were eager to share with others."

A Chicago Declaration," he continued "sought to redirect the Church's strategic approach to social action and to urban ministry; to refocus attention on the secular role of the laity and to update the peace and justice agenda...and awaken the sleeping giant—the U.S. church of fifty million Catholics." They sought to create new priorities and, most critical, to accent the laity's everyday role in the workplace. [53]

The *Declaration* summarized the history of the Chicago Church's vital past when it nurtured a vision of lay Christians in society and priests whose ministry was primarily arousing the laity to accept their vocation in and to the world. The current focus of many Catholics on internal Churchy issues exhausted energies and seemed to the signatories be a desertion of the laity who spent their workaday time and energy in secular fields. A vision to sustain lay people "in the arena in which questions of justice and peace are really located" was essential if leaders were to be energized to reform systemic failures.

The signers explained: "We wait impatiently for a new prophecy, a new word that can once again stir the laity to see the grandeur of the Christian vision for (people) in society and move priests to galvanize lay persons in their secular-religious roles." Vatican II had emphasized that God calls the laity to exercise their proper function to "work for the sanctification of the world from within as a leaven."[54]

The document reiterated Marciniak's prior contention that many clergy had "acted as if the primary responsibility in the Church for ending wars and defending human rights rested with them as ordained ministers," thereby bypassing the laity. For this reason, the *Declaration* warned the present usurpation of the laity's roles by the clergy might cause a revival of clericalism, but this time on the left.[55] The post-Vatican II trend of the Church steadily depreciated the laity's roles in the world as businessmen, as public officials, and as factory workers and gave the impression it was only the activity of "outsiders" (i.e., bishops, clergy, vowed religious, and lay Church employees who were responsible for changing the system). This departed from mainstream Catholic social thought and practice regarding the role of the laity in advancing of social justice. The signers felt that if Church bureaucracy took over ministries of peace and justice it would inevitably lead to the disappearance of lay social action organizations.[56]

In conclusion, the signers declared:

[We] address these words of hope and in deep concern to the members of the Church throughout the nation as well as to members of the Church in Chicago. We invite them to associate themselves with this declaration. We prayerfully anticipate that our words and theirs will prompt a re-examination of present tendencies in the Church and that out of such a re-examination will emerge a new sense of direction, a new agenda.

In the last analysis, the Church speaks to and acts upon the world through her laity. Without a dynamic laity conscious of its personal ministry to the world, the Church, in effect does not speak or act. No amount of social action by priests and religious can ever be an adequate substitute for enhancing lay responsibility. The absence of lay initiative can only take us down the road to clericalism.

We are deeply concerned that so little energy is devoted to encouraging and arousing lay responsibility for the world. The Church must constantly be reformed, but we fear that the almost obsessive preoccupation with the Church's structures and processes has diverted attention from the essential question: reform for what purpose? It would be one of the great ironies of history if the era of Vatican II which opened the windows of the Church to the world were to close with a Church turned in upon itself.[57]

The response to the *Declaration* was electric and super-charged by Barta and Marciniak's strategy to circulate the document broadly. Barta noted that letters poured in from almost every state and from countries throughout the world, including Italy, England, Switzerland, Australia, and Japan. As the authors had intended, *A Chicago Declaration* was reprinted and discussed in newspapers and magazines as liberal as the *National Catholic Reporter* and as conservative as *Our Sunday Visitor*. *Commonweal* magazine reprinted the entire document and ran a symposium of four articles on *A Chicago Declaration*. Even Episcopalian, Lutheran, and Baptist journals pointed to the ecumenical significance of the issue of clerical agenda-setting. Four months after the document appeared it became necessary to establish a secretariat to keep up with the correspondence generated. Barta became the President of the National Center for the Laity (NCL) and operated it from his office at Mundelein College.[58]

In the succeeding two years, more than two million copies of the document had been printed and distributed, and it continued to be quoted and debated in newspapers and magazines. It was also translated into Spanish to reach the fastest growing segment of Catholicism in the United States. As the interest in *A Chicago Declaration* continued to grow, it became "a major reference point" in discussions of the laity and appeared to have achieved permanence in the public domain. From a variety of quarters there developed a call for a national meeting to discuss the issues raised and, as Barta noted, "to dramatize the need for a new agenda in the Church—one in which the top priority would be given to the Christian role of the laity in the worlds of business, politics, and various professions and occupations." In March 1979, the National Center of the Laity accepted an invitation from the University of Notre Dame to co-sponsor an event that brought together 125 lay leaders from a spectrum of occupations and professions and every region to discuss these issues.

The Conference's four major speakers were Edward Marciniak, followed by Michael Novak, a philosopher and journalist; John Coleman, SJ, a noted theologian; and Sargent Shriver, formerly President of Chicago's Catholic Interracial Council, first Director of the Peace Corp, and the Democratic vice-presidential candidate in 1972. Each speaker dealt with practical and theoretical issues raised by *A Chicago Declaration*. Marciniak and Shriver served as bookends of the conference, each suggesting practical implications of a lay spirituality that could support people in their daily transactions at work, in the neighborhood, and at home, as well as in the civic arena. No grand agenda or strategy was proclaimed by the conference attendees, but the challenge to get on with the work of creating initiatives to deal with specific and necessary problems facing the world was affirmed. There was an openness to multiple approaches to foster justice and peace in the world from the position of the "lay insider."[59]

In 1978, the National Center of the Laity created a newsletter, *Initiatives,* to keep people informed about the response to the document and address common questions about next steps and highlight undertakings. This was in keeping with Marciniak's vision. His aim was not to direct a strategy or an agenda but to let ideas and practices bubble up from Christians who sought to create their own responses to the Gospel. For Marciniak, providing "roominess" for new initiatives was always important, as he believed that one size never fit all. As when advocating for economic democracy in the 1950s, he argued for no one pat formula but rather applications of the spirit of the Gospels and encyclicals specific to people's talents and communities of interest. In terms of social action, this approach was paramount.[60]

After *A Chicago Declaration* was published, Marciniak authored numerous articles and gave frequent talks and interviews that reiterated the message of the document, even while maintaining a busy schedule at the Institute of Urban Life. Ed persisted in emphasizing the ordinary roles of both the clergy and the laity, but he seemed to be hampered by the imprecision of language and absence of a clear theology of the laity. The phrase he preferred, "secular Christian," confused people and he was forced to rely on the term "laity" that he had frequently criticized. One long-time friend and former editor of *Work* told him: "You are trapped by your vocabulary."[61] Marciniak was at his best giving examples and telling stories to illustrate what he meant.

In 1982, Marciniak criticized Rev. Anthony Barbaro's article in *Center Focus* that circumscribed the laity's role in peace and justice to only self-consciously identified Church networks. His impatience with Barbaro's "clerical contrivance reflecting a 'churchy' approach to peace and justice" was palpable as he noted that workers in trade unions, agriculture, hospitals, state and local government, the United Nations and corporations were often committed Christians who quietly advanced peace and justice by working from the "inside" to bring about social justice. Insiders were not to be regarded as adversaries to be criticized by clerical and lay Church ministers.[62]

Dennis Geaney OSA, a constant champion for greater roles for the laity and Marciniak's friend, rebuked him for being heavy-handed in his Barbaro critique. Geaney told Marciniak that his criticism reflected his worst side and advised him to give up his "soap box" and "sledgehammer," noting "you are clobbering people like myself [clergy]." Marciniak admitted his language had been "heavy-handed" but did not back off from his position.[63]

Later in 1982, Ed challenged the Presbyteral Senate of the Archdiocese of Chicago for its plan to provide the incoming new archbishop, Joseph Bernardin, with five goals for the next five years for the archdiocese. Marciniak was blunt about the body's "presumptuousness," telling the Senate's priest-president:

> You were establishing goals, not simply for priests and deacons, but for the Church in Chicago. Priorities and goals were being set for me, my brothers and sisters in Christ's Church. As a member of that community of faith…I now found myself not simply in the bleachers but outside the ballpark itself. I was being left out of

something important, something that could heal divisions and help re-unite the Church of Chicago.

Marciniak noted that the laity also had a vision of the Church in Chicago, and for the Senate to speak for the laity to the new archbishop without consultation was unacceptable. He concluded with the question:""Would it not be far better if we were all engaged together in begetting a common vision?" and signed his letter "One of your brothers in Christ"[64] As with many of Marciniak's letters, it was direct and unapologetically confrontational in the interest of protecting the laity's right to be full partners in the Church.

Through his writings, both published and unpublished, Marciniak continued to urge American Bishops to broaden their appeals for vocations beyond priestly and religious life and service in a specific Catholic ministry and to help educate the laity in their own vocations. Marciniak's, Barta's, and Cantwell's collaborators and allies, such as Msgr. George Higgins, helped to change the dialogue and focus of the approach of the U.S. bishops toward expanding their Synod positions to rely on broad consultation with the laity. Cardinal Joseph Bernardin especially appreciated Marciniak's contributions and connections and sought his advice on a variety of issues. In 1986, Bernardin asked Ed to help him develop of a formal response to a statement on the role of the laity in the Church and the world. When completed Bernardin sent him a private copy noting, "I trust that you will find your input represented in the report." Later that year, the cardinal placed Marciniak on the list of persons for the Bishops Committee on the Laity to assist the Synod delegates "gain a sense of the experiences, visions, and needs which make the life of Catholic laity in the U.S Church at this time."[65]

In October 1987, twenty years after the Vatican Council, Edward and Virginia Marciniak, Russ and Bernice Barta, and several other members of the NCL went to Rome to "lobby" the attendees to the World Synod on the Laity. Bernardin, one of four American prelates at the synod, had been pleased with the work of NCL and hosted a dinner to pave the way for its members in their encounters with bishops.[66] The Synod clarified the laity's role in the Church, but they did not succeed in reigniting the laity to action in the United States. The Synod documents were turned over to Pope John Paul II who drafted "The Vocation of the Mission of the Lay Faithful in the Church and the World," an exhortation that reinforced the message that the laity's role was to bring Gospel values into the home and workplace in the common good of society. However, in doing so, the pope broke little new ground. He cautioned against a too indiscriminate use of the word "ministry" and once again emphasized the distinct ministries of priests and laity.[67]

The initiatives envisioned by *A Chicago Declaration* required the action and energy of autonomous lay persons who had a sense of mission.[68] In the end, despite serious discussion and thoughtful reflection among many Christians, little seemed to change. In 1986, in the foreword to William Droel and Gregory Pierce's book *Confident and Competent: A Challenge for the Lay Church*, Msgr. Higgins emphasized that what was needed were the living examples of lay-initiated programs based on the principles of *A Chicago Declaration* and not to spend "too much time theorizing about the role of the laity or lamenting the failure of church leaders to take the lead." He added that it would be a mistake to rely on books and statements "to bring about the changes that are rightly called for. In short, the time has come for a new burst of lay-initiated action of the type (if I may say so chauvinistically) that made Chicago famous in the 1940s and 1950s."[69]

On the fifteenth anniversary of *A Chicago Declaration of Christian Concern*, *Commonweal* published a special issue on the laity. Marciniak was asked to comment on the *Declaration's* origins and consequences. He explained that it was meant to be "a gracious but uncompromising polemic on behalf of a cause, and its rhetoric[was] aimed to trouble theologians and officials of the church." He acknowledged it had encouraged rank-and-file to be more questioning of their bishops and pastors, but said that too many still waited for direction rather than taking up the initiative for the burden of renewing the face of the earth through their individual vocations. More than ever, Ed Marciniak still believed that individual Christians, even without marching orders from those above and amidst inherent ambiguity, need to take up his or her individual burden and "stride into the darkness...." He concluded reiterating his lifelong maxim: "To do nothing is to be nothing."[70]

NOTES

1 *Tomorrows Christian*, p. 110.

2 Marciniak to Feller, Marciniak Papers Shelf 4, Position 1.

3 *Ibid.*, While Marciniak was blunt in disagreeing with Feller's approach, he did respect him as a person, writing: "I pray frequently for the restoration of your good health." St. Vincent de Paul parish was in the regentrifying neighborhood of Lincoln Park and clearly was not the typical candidate for "twinning."

4 "In this Pagan: Land," *America*, November 11, 1972, p. 393. The article was a series of reflections by persons who knew Dorothy Day and reflected on her contributions.

5 The pamphlet was printed by The America Press on behalf of the Catholic Council on Working Life, Christian Family Movement, Young Christian Students, and Young Christian Workers. Marciniak Papers, Shelf 1, Position 2.

6 *Ibid.*, pp. 2-7, 9-10, and 17-18

7 *Scholasticism and Politics*, (1954 edition) | Open Library, pp. 7-16. The lectures were translated by Mortimer J. Adler, Marciniak's *Great Books* mentor.

8 Ibid., pp. 192-229.

9 "Power and the Church's Approach to Community, I. The People of God and Power," March 1966, pp. 7-9.

10 "Power and the Church's Approach to the community, II. The Priest and Power," p.11.

11 Ibid., p. 11. He carefully distinguished the role of stewardship noting that clergy and religious as heads of hospitals, school, and parishes need to be in the driver's seat.

12 Ibid., p. 12.

13 Ibid., pp. 11-12. In September, the magazine published eight letters by ministers and priests, both in response to the articles. One pointed out that Egan dealt with the Church's role in community action and Marciniak with the role of the priest in the community. "New City Readers answer Mr. Marciniak," September 1966, pp. 19-23.

14 *Gaudium et Spes Pastoral Constitution on the Church in the Modern World*, Second Vatican Council, 1965. https://www. cctwincities.org/wp-content/uploads/2015/10/Gaudium-et-Spes-Pastoral-Constitution-on-the-Church-in-the-Modern-World.pdf.

15 P. ix.

16 P. xi.

17 P. xii and xiv. Consistent with his wry humor, he dated his introduction: "May Day, 1968".

18 Ibid., pp. 1-16. When Loyola University's archivist approached Marciniak about initiating the process to have Martin Carrabine, S.J. canonized, Marciniak opposed it. His rationale was not to dismiss the saintliness and importance of Carrabine's life, but emphasized that it was time to canonize Christian lay people. Michael Grace, S. J. to Marciniak , August 4, 1986; and Marciniak to Grace, n.d. Marciniak Papers, Shelf 4, Position 2.

19 Ibid., pp. 17-25. The Catholic bishop of Oakland and Sacramento and religious groups signed a resolution of public opposition to California ballot issue on property taxes, Proposition 14, also was given as another example of overreach.

20 Ibid., p. 33. See pp. 33-45.

21 Ibid., p. 48.

22 See Appendix I and II. Kennedy's speech had been written by John Cogley who had edited *The Chicago Catholic Worker* with Marciniak. Marciniak signed as "executive director, Chicago Commission on Human Relations," although he had been invited to sign as "President of the Catholic Council on Working Life," a position he no longer held. Several of his Chicago friends signed the letter, including Patrick F. Crowley, president Catholic Council on Working Life, Jerome G Kerwin, Professor, University of Chicago, and Bob Senser, editor, *Work*. See Heinrich Rommen, Jerome Kerwin, Joseph O'Meara, Francis Wilson, George N. Schuster to Marciniak, September 26, 1960, Marciniak Papers, AAC, Shelf 2, Position 1.

23 Ibid., p. 62 and 77. Also see pp. 53-85.

24 Ibid., p. 90.

25 Ibid., pp. 103 and 107.

26 Ibid., p.110. Marciniak had published Eugene McCarthy's article in *Commonweal* in a pamphlet for several Catholic social action organizations more than a decade before.

27 Ibid., p. 119.

28 Ibid., pp. 148. In 1965, Marciniak had pressed Cardinal Meyer to appoint a Black person to be an auxiliary bishop in Chicago. He wrote on personal stationary as he was then director of the CCHR and felt "a personal responsibility to express my own attitude." Marciniak to Meyer, February 8,1965, and Meyer to Marciniak, February 11, 1965, Marciniak Papers, CAA, Shelf 2, Position 1.

29 Ibid., p. 146.

30 Ibid., p. 168.

31 Marciniak and Rev Daniel Cantwell did request people to review his book hoping to extend the discussion. See: Marciniak to William Brown, May 29, 1969, Shelf 3, Position 2; copies of Cantwell to Bishop John L. May, January 24, 1969; Sen. Eugene McCarthy to Cantwell, January 28, 1969; Rev. Andrew M. Greeley to Cantwell, January 31, 1969, AAC Position 3, Shelf 2.

32 See: Rev. Carl Lezak, "Tomorrows' Christian, , A Review," *Chicago Studies*, Fall, 1969 pp. 235-245; Rev. John T. Pawlikowski, "Letter to the Editors," National Catholic Reporter, June 28, 1969, Even Marciniak's friend and mentor Msgr. George Higgins' nationally syndicated column, "The Yardstick," which tried to temper the criticism of priests by indicating Marciniak's "severe criticism" of priests who have resorted to using institutional power, noting often times priests feel pressed by the laity to exercise that power in the community. NC Features, For Release Week of June 16, 1969, Marciniak Papers Shelf 3, Position 2.

33 John A. McDermott, *Commonweal*, September 19, 1969, p. 572.

34 Who's Using Whom?" *Pittsburgh Catholic*, June 6, 1969, https://thecatholicnewsarchive.org/?a=d&d=TPC19570606-01.1.1. Rice contended that nuns and priests who marched against *de facto segregation* at great peril "do more to change the world and the hearts of men by fearless activism than all the back-room liberals in the corridors of power. Old fashioned liberals became captive to LBJ, the evil war and the neglect of the destitute, whereas the 'clerics and their secular counterparts dumped the whole crowd and gave us a chance at salvation! Their work is far from finished and they have just begun to fight and that is more useful and pertinent than collaboration with hope of conversion. Old style liberals at all levels speak of their heroic effort to convert the wielders of power but the real question that has to be asked over and over again is: who is converting whom? and its more baleful corollary, who is using whom?" A similar point about insiders being coopted was made by others. See: James Cunningham, a community planner who Marciniak knew from his earlier work in Hyde Park and now was on Pittsburgh's Diocesan Synod Commission on Community Affairs. Cunningham, counselled his friend that "meaningful reform came from outside, not from inside the structure." In "Who is tomorrow's Christian," *Pittsburgh Catholic*, September 26, 1969, https://thecatholicnewsarchive.org/?a=d&d=TPC19690926-01&.

35 Marciniak to Rice, June 10, 1969, Marciniak Papers, Shelf 3, Position 2.

36 Bruce Rattenbury, "Unfair to Marciniak," National Catholic Reporter, May 28, 1969 and Emery J Biro, "Guest Dear Jim, Opinion: Its Unfair to Knock Ed's Insiders," https://thecatholicnewsarchive.org/?a=d&d=TPC19691121-01&e=————-en-20—1—txt-txIN————-.

37 Lawrence Suffredin, Jr., to Rice, June 24, 1969. Marciniak Papers, Shelf 3, Position 2.

38 Rosalie Riegle, Marciniak Interview, January 6, 1988, p. 2. Pflaum sold approximately 1700 copies and destroyed the unbound warehouse copies that remained in 1972. Marciniak wrote a friend that he was "quietly exploring the paperback

possibilities," but never followed up. Marciniak to John McHale, July 6, 1972, Marciniak Papers, Shelf 4, Position 1.

39   December 12, 1970. The article's title incorporated the title of Martin Luther King's last book, *Where Do We Go from Here: Chaos or Community*, which dealt with the challenges facing the civil rights movement.

40   Among these he listed Dag Hammarskjold, John Kennedy, Martin Luther King, Cesar Chavez, Thomas Merton, Daniel Berrigan, Saul Alinsky, and Michael Harrington.

41   Ibid., pp. 511-513.

42   Ibid., p. 513.

43   Ibid., p. 514.

44   Ibid., pp. 514- 516.

45   Marciniak to Donald R. Campion, S. J., Editor-in Chief, August 31, 1970. Marciniak Papers, Shelf 3, Position 2, and "Reactions from the Field," Ibid., pp. 517-519. Marciniak suggest four or five responders and listed nine individuals to contact. Only one recommendation was used: David O'Brien, author of *American Catholics and Social Reform: The New Deal Years*. The list of his recommendations demonstrated his concern for a diversity of reactors as well his connection to people in the field of sociology, history, social justice, and members of the American and Canadian Church's bureaucracy. Included were Daniel P. Moynihan, Msgr. George Higgins, and Revs. Donald Clark (Office of Black Catholics) and Charles Burns, S.V.D (Bishops' Urban Task Force).

46   Joseph P Fitzpatrick S.J. "A Sociologist Comments," Ibid., pp. 517-518. The author was a professor at Fordham University.

47   "As Seen by a Historian" Ibid., p. 518-519. *America* followed up with other responders two months later declaring: "judged by the letters, below, Mr. Marciniak's piece was a live shot into the field—and received distinguished notice." William E. Brown, a Catholic social actionist and friend of Marciniak's, called for practical and justifiable steps to set challenging goals and establish tough-minded programs. Brown believed it was not just a matter of strategy but was a moral issue. He emphasized

Marciniak's point that personal courage and persistence thrived in a "social setting," a community that was not inward looking and parochial but truly catholic and ecumenical. "'Where's the Action' in Catholic Social Action?" February 6, 1971, pp. 126 and 128.

48   The letter was written on May 14, 1971, to commemorate the eightieth anniversary Pope Leo XIII's *Rerum Novarum*. See paragraphs 48-52. *Octagesima Adveniens*, May 14, 1971, Pope Paul VI.

49   "Catholic Call to Action," *New York Times*, October 27, 1976. David J. O'Brien, *Public Catholicism*. 2nd ed. (New York, 1996), pp. 243-244.

50   For example, Marciniak had signed documents such "A Declaration of Economic Justice" in 1946 and through his career as a member of the American Newspaper Guild and as a founding member of the Americans for Democratic Action. See Chapters 2 and 3 above.

51   Author interview with William Droel, December 9, 2020.

52   "The Chicago Declaration of Christian Concern," in Russell Barta, ed., *Challenge to the Laity*, (Huntington, Indiana, *Our Sunday Visitor* 1980), pp. 19-17. "The Declaration," including the 37 signatories, is in Appendix 1.

53   Ed Marciniak, "On the Condition of the Laity," in Russell Barta, pp. 29-30.

54   "The Declaration," in Barta, pp. 19-21.

55   "The Declaration," p. 22.

56   Ibid., pp..22-23.

57   Ibid., pp. 24-25.

58   Barta, Introduction, "*Challenge to the Laity*, pp. 10-11.

59   For the four major speeches see: Barta, pp. 29-124.

60   William Droel, Interview. See *Initiatives*, March 2020.

61   Senser to Marciniak, December 10, 1985, Marciniak Papers, Shelf 4, Position 2. Marciniak was conversant in the theological reflections of the most prominent contemporary Catholic theologians in Europe and America but found them wanting. In

a series of an extended correspondence with the associate Editor of *America*, he labored to arrive at an adequate definition of the layman and lay spirituality but remained vexed after several interchanges. Marciniak to Rev. Thomas J Reese, SJ., November 26, 1979; Reese to Marciniak December 4, 1979; Marciniak to Reese, January 10, 1980; Reese to Marciniak, April 2, 1980; and Marciniak to Reese, June 9, 1980. Marciniak Papers, Shelf 8, Position 3.

62   Marciniak to Editor, *Center-Focus*, April 12, 1982; Marciniak Papers, Shelf 8, Position 1.

63   Dennis Geaney to Marciniak, April 22, 1982; and Marciniak to Larry Ragan, April 28, 1982, Shelf 8, Position 3.

64   Marciniak to Rev. Thomas I Healy, Feast of All Saints [November 1, 1982], Marciniak Papers, Shelf 4, Position 1. Marciniak's position was consistent and direct even with friends. When his friend from Catholic Labor Alliance days wrote to ask Ed about his "present" positions on Catholic issues including married priests, women priest, the priest shortage, vocations to the priesthood and convents, nuclear war and the spiritual formation of the laity, Ed responded: "Most of those are 'churchy' issues, which I try hard not to discuss because of the really important ones." With his response he enclosed "a bushel of things I've written recently." At this time he was writing the about the vocation of Christians in the workplace, the rights of workers to unionize at Catholic Institutions, approaches to addressing urban blight, and rebuilding neighborhoods. Art Sullivan to Marciniak, November 28, 1984 [actually, 1983] and Marciniak to Sullivan, August 8, 1984, Marciniak Papers, Shelf 4, Position 2.

65   Bernadin to Marciniak, March 27, 1986, and August 20, 1986, Marciniak Papers, Shelf 4, Position 2.

66   William Droel to author, February 12, 2021.

67   *Christifideles Laici*, http://www.vatican.va/content/john-paul-ii/en/apost_exhortations/documents/hf_jp-ii_exh_30121988_christifideles-laici.html. See also "Mission of Lay Catholics Defined," *Los Angeles Times*, January 31, 1989, https://www.

latimes.com/archives/la-xpm-1989-01-31-mn-1240-story. html

68   Marciniak gave lectures to encourage a more active role of the laity. Excerpts of a series of lectures he delivered in the Diocese of Savanah, Georgia. were recorded and accompanied by a study guide and reproduced. The tapes reiterated his positions on role of the laity. Ed Marciniak, *A Worldly Vocation*, ACTA Publications (Chicago, 1990).

69   "Foreword" in William L. Droel and Gregory F. Augustine Pierce, (Chicago, 1997), p.12. https://stcathofsiena.org/ documents/2020/1/Confident%20and%20Competent%20 -%20OCR%201-23-20.pdf. Droel and Pierce were Marciniak's associates. Droel has edited the NCL's newsletter, *Initiatives*, for over three decades and Pierce served as president of NCL for five years in the early 1980s. Also, see David J. O'Brien, "The American Laity: Memory, Meaning and Mission," *America*, March 7, 1987, pp. 187-193.

70   "Why We Wrote It," September 11, 1992, pp. 12-14.

Epilogue

W hen the testimonials and speeches at the All-City Salute for Ed Marciniak at the Bismarck Hotel in September 1990 ended, Ed and Virginia were surrounded by friends expressing affection and deep appreciation for their devotion to church, city, and social justice.

But what was meant to be a marvelous evening and a prelude to the next decade of work on the urban agenda and a time to relish the parental joys of watching their children succeed in their professions and roles as parents was not to be. Even as Virginia courageously smiled and hugged and greeted friends with her husband nearby, only a few knew how sick she was or could have guessed how little time remained for her. Within days, she would be in the hospital and succumb to her second battle with cancer. The words and letters of tribute they had just received would soon be followed by a husband's cry of absence for his cherished partner and lover.[1]

Many who attended the event at the Bismarck a short month before now came to the funeral service for Virginia at St. Ita's Church, where her rich voice had so often filled the nave. Subsequent letters of sympathy and compassion touchingly reflected on Virginia's generosity, artistry, and vital spirit. Beethoven's *Ode to Joy* had been selected by the family as the funeral recessional and was performed on the magnificent 4500 pipe organ of the church, but the music's beauty could not offer consolation. Ed Marciniak had lost his soul mate and his anchor, the one person with whom he had exchanged love letters and dreams and honored vows.

Marciniak maintained his post as the president of the Institute of Urban Life and eventually took an office at his sister-in-law's real estate office near his home in the Edgewater Beach neighborhood. He continued to write on poverty, housing, and justice; but he wrote less frequently. His evenings were often spent swimming in his lakefront apartment building's indoor pool and playing pinochle with a few close friends. He was, at best, in irregular attendance at events. As he aged, he weakened and his memory diminished, but his intention and interests remained unchanged. When Cardinal Francis George, OMI, heard that Marciniak was nearing death, he arranged to meet him for a pastoral visit.

This was a final challenge Marciniak wanted to meet. He called Bill Droel of the National Center for the Laity and told him they should put together talking points to advance the cause of lay leadership. Droel reminded his close friend and mentor that this was to be a pastoral visit, not an occasion for lobbying. Marciniak's zeal for the vocation of the laity never seemed to lessen.[2]

EPILOGUE

Edward Marciniak died of pneumonia at St. Joseph's
Hospital in Chicago on May 23, 2004. His funeral took
place at St. Joseph's Church, on the near north side, where
he had started a scholarship fund and a tutoring program
for the children of the nearby Cabrini Green housing projects. Marciniak would not witness the final demolition of
the high-rise project as he had demanded for years; but as
his friends, family, and dignitaries came to hear him eulo-
gized, they noted that there were already far fewer towers at
Cabrini Green to cast their menacing shadows.[3]

Larry Suffredin, a Cook County commissioner, and
Ed's friend of almost forty years told the congregation: "Ed
had an extreme sense that we have a duty to bring justice to
any circumstance that we find ourselves in. He combined
that with a phenomenal work ethic and faith in God's will
and grace to do these things."[4]

Christina Marciniak spoke on behalf of her sisters and
asked, "[What] did Dad teach us?" She noted that she had
learned their father's favored phrase whenever someone
pontificated around him: "Cut the baloney." She continued
with others: "Sing your song with gusto. Question the status
quo and figure out if you can make it better. Relish diversity. Look beyond appearances. Be self-reliant. Pick a cause
and be passionate about it." With pride she concluded, "He
managed to live the lives of ten men during his 86 years here,

and in doing so contributed so much that the lives of many others are better for it."[5]

For four decades, Ed Marciniak challenged allies and foes with forthrightness and an ever-present twinkle in his eye. He was guided by an ever-deepening conviction that each person was meant to employ his or her unique talents to work with others to improve society. He sought the common good, not partisan or ideological victories *per se*. At times, his dogged persistence to reach a solution rankled or confused liberals and conservatives alike when advocating for reforms and demanding accountability of those with economic, clerical, or political power.

~

More than fifty years ago, in 1969, Marciniak concluded his book *Tomorrow's Christian* with a firm challenge to everyone who seeks a more just and peaceful world. He noted that the cemeteries of this world are filled with countless Christians "who spent their lives waiting for cues that never came and summons that never were delivered, who bided their time looking for others to take the initiative and to bear the burden of responsibility. [Whereas] the man of personal responsibility recites his personal act of contrition, shoulders his share of the burden, and then takes the initiative."[6]

Ed Marciniak's words and his life are a call to action and an invitation for each of us that demand a personal commitment today. How will *we* respond to issues such as worker exploitation, racism, homelessness, healthcare and educational inequities, the climate crisis, and things we haven't even yet realized are issues?

NOTES

1 There was no correspondence in the Marciniak papers during the last three months of Virginia's struggle, indicating the seriousness of her condition. Clearly, they had both put on a brave front. Among her papers Marciniak found an untitled poem she had written about pain and sent it to *Commonweal*. Her words appeared October 23, 1992, two years after her death. Clipping from *Commonweal*, Vol 119, No. 18 in the Marciniak Papers, Shelf 7, Position 3.

2 Droel correspondence the author, August 4, 2021

3 The phased demolition of the project began in 1995 and the last buildings were razed in 2011.

4 Cited in *Chicago Tribune*, May 27, 2004.

5 Eulogy, May 27, 2004.

6 *Tomorrow's Christian*, p. 168.

Author's Note

I first met Ed Marciniak in 1977 on the tenth floor of Chicago's City Hall, in the reception area of the Department of Planning and Development where he had worked nine years earlier. Ed had come to meet a former friend and colleague, but it was my first visit to the storied building. I had come as an associate in the Archdiocese of Chicago's Office of Research and Planning to gather information about a proposed expressway project. I knew of Ed as "the guy" at Loyola's Institute of Urban Life, but little more. Over the next two decades, I encountered him in the course of my community planning and economic development roles, but I never got to know him well or his various roles in church and city.

When casting about for a topic for the Catholic Historical Association meeting slated for Chicago in 2012, I asked Ellen Skerrett to suggest topics that might fit a panel on Chicago Catholicism. She suggested a couple options. Ed Marciniak's work was one possible topic, and she pointed me to the Archdiocese of Chicago Archives where twenty-seven boxes of his uncatalogued papers were stored. I found enough material in his first two legal boxes of correspondence to set me on a journey to discover what was in the others and to learn about his ideas, motivations, accomplishments, and more.

~

Over the course of my research, I got to know Ed through his letters, reports, books, and incredible input in the periodicals *Chicago Catholic Worker, Work,* and *New City,* as well as from his articles in many other magazines and newspapers and scholarly journals. What I learned about this man, who peppered me with questions whenever I spoke with him, was eye-opening, partly because he never spoke about his accomplishments. As I did archival research and interviewed many people, I came to realize that his ideas and work had prepared the way for the work in which I engaged over my own career: to foster stable, integrated communities through various organizing, housing, and economic development entities, and as a faculty union member at Saint Xavier University in Chicago.

I was amazed to learn of Marciniak's critical role in helping to fight segregation in neighborhoods in Chicago, for example. Ed helped shape the outcomes of what is called the "Summit," a series of high-level negotiations between city leaders and Dr. Martin Luther King and other movement leaders held in August of 1966; one critical outcome was the creation of the Leadership Council for Metropolitan Open Communities (LCMOC).

Years later, as director of the Beverly Area Planning Association in the late 1980s, I turned to the Leadership Council for assistance. In partnership with LCMOC, the

Association challenged the destabilizing actions of realtors who practiced racial steering. We tested realtors by using matched pairs of qualified white and Black prospective buyers and filed suits in federal court against brokers identified for racial steering. Further, I identified with Ed's ideas of community-building with business and government as partners rather than enemies in determining the direction of housing and community development.

I also came to appreciate Marciniak's perspective on labor unions and negotiating when I co-chaired the faculty union at Saint Xavier University and twice served as its contract negotiator. His ideas about co-management and compromise were invaluable and his critique of Catholic institutions faced with unionization prophetic. Regrettably, his advice was too often unheeded by professional managers who sought to please bankers and donors at the expense of their founding mission as well as the welfare of their employees, students, and patients.

⌐‾

This book began as a series of papers presented at the American Catholic Historical Association and the Urban Studies Group of the Chicago Historical Museum in 2015. Portions of Chapter Two and Five were previously printed in articles I wrote that appeared in *American Catholic Studies* and *The Journal of Illinois State Historical Society*.

Writing is an individual undertaking, but it is only possible with the support of family and friends and the knowledge, insights, and generous assistance of fellow writers, editors, and other people who share their recollections.

I have had the benefit of individuals in both groups and, in some cases, scholars who personally knew Ed Marciniak and his work well.

I am grateful to Ellen Skerrett, the unofficial dean of Chicago Catholic Studies, for her suggestion that I consider writing about Ed Marciniak, for her sage comments on the early drafts of each chapter of this book, and for her enthusiastic support through its completion.

I was also incredibly fortunate to have met Bill Droel early in this process, who spent twenty-five years as Marciniak's friend and assistant. Bill is the long-time editor of *Initiatives*, the National Center for the Laity's indispensable newsletter. After my first presentation about Marciniak at the Chicago Marriott hotel, Bill stepped forward and offered resources including electronic copies of the *Chicago Catholic Worker*, *Work*, *Initiatives*, and his own recollections. Graciously, he shared stories of Ed in action: networking, intriguing, challenging, and smiling. Bill helped fill in vital details when a piece of the puzzle was missing or recommended someone who could do so. Generously, he read each iteration of the manuscript and offered substantive suggestions as well as editorial corrections. His clarification of Marciniak's concept of *Church*, capital "C" and *church*, lower-case "c" was most helpful dealing with the substance of Chapter Seven.

Bill eventually led me to Greg Pierce, publisher of ACTA Publications and another Marciniak mentee, who agreed to publish this book despite what he called "more footnotes than all the other books published by ACTA Publications in our sixty-five-year history combined!" I thank him for all his good work in bringing this book to print.

AUTHOR'S NOTE

I am indebted to Mel Piehl, Senior Research Professor of Valparaiso University, for organizational assistance with this manuscript and editorial contributions to the first and last chapters. Likewise, I am indebted to Kim Baker for his work on Catholic labor activists and his comments on Chapters Two and Three. Chicago historian Dominic Pacyga, Emeritus Professor of Columbia College, added insights about the city's history and Marciniak, as well as reviewing several chapters and providing steady encouragement. Further I am grateful to Margaret McGuinness, Professor of Religion at La Salle University, for editorial advice on Chapter Three and encouragement to publish the book.

A special thanks is due to very close friends who were my colleagues at Saint Xavier University. First is to Kathleen Waller, the Associate Professor of Religious Studies, who read the entire manuscript and shared insights on structure and content as well as offering editorial suggestions. Equally important, the class Kathleen and I co-taught, "Justice for All," and our numerous discussions sustained the book's momentum at critical junctures in the writing.

August Kolich, Emeritus Professor of English at Saint Xavier University, and Jeffery Tangel, formerly of Saint Xavier University and member of the DePaul Institute of Nature and Culture, also provided comments on first drafts as well as continuous moral support during the publishing process. Also, I am grateful to James Scheuermann, my friend and long-time fishing partner, for sharing his keen editorial skills that were honed writing appellate briefs and articles for philosophy journals. His advice on structure and emphasis on clarity were critical in the Introduction and last iterations of several chapters.

This work also relied upon the comprehensive collection of Marciniak's papers in the Joseph Cardinal Bernardin Archives of the Archdiocese of Chicago. The director, Meg Romero Hall, was ready and knowledgeable with assistance in securing files and copies of documents and photographs. Her welcoming smile and that of the Center's interns made the research a walk in the park rather than an uphill slog. I also profited from the help of the archivists of the Catholic Worker Collection at the Raynor Memorial Libraries of Marquette University and the staff of the Chicago Historical Museum for access to the Daniel Cantwell Papers and, of course, the Loyola University Chicago Archives for its comprehensive photography collection.

Perhaps most deeply, I appreciate Ed Marciniak's daughters for entrusting me with Ed and Virginia's courtship correspondence. While I used very few specifics from their letters, they brought the letter-writers to life for me in ways nothing else did.

I am grateful to many others who knew Ed and his contributions to the city and church personally. They added greatly to my understanding of his work and motivation. Among these were his late sister, Bernice Barta, and the late Rev. John Lynch; his friends from Catholic social action and public service, including the late Raymond and Mary Simon, Lawrence Suffredin, and his assistant at the City of Chicago Department of Planning, the late Thomas Volini; and several of Ed's own assistants or interns at the Institute of Urban Life, including Kathy Hills, Mary Schlitz, and Andy Rodriguez.

AUTHOR'S NOTE

I greatly appreciated my interviews and phone conversations with Ed and Virginia's daughters, Christina Marciniak, MD, and Francesca M. Edwardson, and to Ed's nephew Damian Barta for sharing recollections of Ed's personal and public life. They tracked down information and corrected and clarified many matters regarding family history.

I am grateful for the inspiration of historians at La Salle University, Philadelphia—the late John Lukacs and Joseph P. O'Grady—and the lessons of my mentors in urban and ethnic history at the University of Chicago—Professors Emmet Larkin, Arthur Mann, John Hope Franklin, and Rev. Andrew Greeley. All taught me that recounting the past sets a high barrier. I have likewise been fortunate to remain in contact with two of my fellow graduate students, William Poole and Louis Covotsos, who read chapters and shared advice.

I want to thank my long-time friends James Ruck and Steven Murphy for their listening and encouragement on long walks and in phone calls and the support of my wife's daughters, Breann Farstvedt, Amber Smith, and Ashley Anderson for their support at a critical time. I am humbled and grateful for the affirming kindnesses, support, and patience shown me by my sons, Thomas Bryant Shanabruch and Stephen Bryant Shanabruch, and their families throughout.

Finally, I want to recognize the abiding spirit of my deceased wife, Patricia Jane Bryant, whose work as a civil rights attorney and activist inspired my life's work. Similarly,

I am grateful to my recently deceased wife, Dianne Marie Shanabruch, for her steady encouragement and patience and her example of dedication as a healthcare professional and as a volunteer seeking to remediate the impact of poverty. They were both in the mold of Ed Marciniak: never waiting for directives but seizing every opportunity to secure wellness and justice for all.

Charles Shanabruch
Ph.D. in History, University of Chicago
Emeritus Professor, Saint Xavier University
Founding Director,
Historic Chicago Bungalow Association
May 1, 2023

TITLES ON CITY AND CHURCH

www.actapublications.com, 800-397-2282

ADVANCE PRAISE FOR
ED MARCINIAK'S CITY AND CHURCH

How can we stop making the common good a sometime or weekend-only activity and become an encompassing vocation within all our daily settings? Can we move from abstract concerns about justice to practical policies and initiatives through the habit of cultivating public relationships? What are the tradeoffs and personal costs? Glean practical lessons about these and other tensions from this inspiring biography of Ed Marciniak, a long-haul Christian activist, by Chuck Shanabruch, a student of history with a practical bent that Ed would certainly have appreciated. — Bill Droel, editor, *Initiatives*, National Center for the Laity

Insightfully explores the life of a central figure in twentieth-century Chicago history who fought for worker rights and the poorest Chicagoans, whether the specific issue was regarding race relations, child welfare, public housing, community development, partisan politics, or economic disparity. Ed Marciniak was a nationally influential social justice activist who challenged public policies not only within the context of a city with deep fissures based in class and race but also deeply affected by the involvement in civic affairs of its large Catholic community. — Ann Durkin Keating, co-editor, *Encyclopedia of Chicago*

Ed Marciniak was a model and mentor to me ever since 1959, when I wangled an unpaid summer job between high school and college at *Work*, the monthly journal of labor and social justice causes he founded and edited. Charles Shanabruch's essential biography of Ed tells us more about how Christians must live out Vatican II's "universal call to holiness" in our time than any number of stories of well-known saints and martyrs. — Peter Steinfels, former editor, *Commonweal*, and religion writer, *The New York Times*